THE CHRISTIANS OF KERALA

History, Belief and Ritual
among the Yakoba

THE CHRISTIANS OF KERALA

History, Belief and Ritual among the Yakoba

Susan Visvanathan

MADRAS
OXFORD UNIVERSITY PRESS
DELHI BOMBAY CALCUTTA
1993

Oxford University Press, Walton Street, Oxford OX2 6DP

New York Toronto
Delhi Bombay Calcutta Madras Karachi
Kuala Lumpur Singapore Hong Kong Tokyo
Nairobi Dar es Salaam
Melbourne Auckland

and associates in
Berlin Ibadan

Typeset by Mudra Typesetters, Mohan Nagar, Pondicherry 605 005
and printed by All India Press, Kennedy Nagar, Pondicherry 605 001
and published by Neil O'Brien, Oxford University Press,
219, Anna Salai, Madras 600 006

Acknowledgements

I am very grateful to Veena Das, Kuriakose Mamkoottam, Sally Thomas, the late Rachael Mathews, and the many people of Puthenangadi who contributed so generously to the writing of this book. I would also like to thank Rajan John, Pushpa Thomas, Liza Antony Kurien, Marty Tom, Valsa Pannikkar, Chinnamma Thomas, Susan and Markos Vellappally, Uttara Vellapally, Rajendra Pradhan, J.P.S. Uberoi, Khalid Tyabji, Rekha and Tapan Basu, Punam Zutshi, Deepak Mehta, Ratna Raman, Valsala Kuriakose, Asha Gupta, Leela Dube and Prabhu Mohapatra. The Oxford University Press gave incisive comments, for which I am grateful.

I must record my debt to Fr Gispert (S.J.) Fr George Keeran (S.J.), Fr Volkaert (S.J.), Fr Hambye (S.J.), and Fr T.K. John (S.J.).

I am grateful to the librarian and staff of the Ratan Tata Library, Delhi School of Economics; Vidyajyoti, Delhi; Mar Thoma Seminary, Kottayam Public Library, Kottayam; Connemara State Central Library, Madras, and Jawaharlal Nehru Memorial Library, Delhi.

I owe much to my father, the late Kuruvilla Paul, and to my mother, Mariam.

My husband, Shiv Visvanathan has been teacher and friend in the long years it took writing this book, and I must acknowledge my debt to him for long conversations (which reflected the Hindu–Christian encounter!). This book is for our children.

I also thank Joachim Mathess, Gananath Obeysekere, and M.N. Srinivas.

I am grateful to the institutions with which I have been associated: Miranda House; Jawaharlal Nehru University; Department of Sociology, Delhi University; Hindu College; and the Nehru Memorial Museum and Library.

The map of Travancore-Cochin has been adapted from L.W. Brown, *The Indian Christians of St. Thomas* (Cambridge University Press, 1956).

Preface

This book grew out of two parallel preoccupations: with Emile Durkheim's writings on the collective consciousness of society and its relation to individual representation, and with my own search for a past and a society from which I had drifted away.

As students of sociology we are trained in the teachings of Durkheim. His *Rules of Sociological Method*, in which the methods of objectivity and interpretation of social facts are outlined, had the quality of a sacred text. I was, however, also fascinated by the other dimension of this text which seemed neglected: the question of individual representation. If Durkheimian sociology centred around the idea of collectivities, structures, and the institutional, how could one make sense of individuals and their actions and representations? Durkheim himself was aware of the complexities of studying individual representations as a social fact, so the idea of the relationship between individuals and collectivities was certainly not against the main current of his work.[1] It was with this in mind that I began fieldwork in Kerala in 1981, using speech—individual representation—to understand popular Christianity in a neighbourhood called Puthenangadi, in the town of Kottayam in Kerala, India's southernmost state.[2]

The reason why I wanted to study a Christian community was partly personal. My marriage to a fellow anthropologist within the secular frame of modern Indian urban life in the late seventies did not create any emotional upheavals, even though we belonged to different states, possessed different mother tongues, belonged to different communities, and were bred on different religions. I was content in my secularism;

---

[1] Emile Durkheim, *The Rules of Sociological Method* (Glencoe: Free Press, 1958); *The Elementary Forms of the Religious Life* (New York: Free Press, 1969); *Sociology and Philosophy* (New York: Routledge and Kegan Paul, 1974).

[2] On speech, see, e.g., Roland Barthes, *Elements of Semiology* (London: Cape, 1967); Michael Silverstein, 'Shifters, Linguistic Categories and Cultural Descriptions', in K.M. Basso and H.A. Selby (eds.), *Meaning in Anthropology* (Albuquerque: University of Mexico Press, 1976).

yet my marriage to a Tamil Brahmin raised questions about the society into which I had been born, and from which I had severed myself by breaking the rule of endogamy. My marriage raised questions for me about the dialogue between religions, specifically between the Hindu and the Christian. There were more questions of a sociological kind—about India in general: its unity and its differences, and the question of plural cultures and faiths. My own biography became an individual representation of the theory of similarity and difference by which our complex subcontinental culture is identified.

Being an anthropologist, I also knew I had to find a field for my intellectual and emotional excursions. My father's ancestral village, Niranam, could have been an ideal choice for my study. This was where, according to local myth, St Thomas, the apostle of Jesus, arrived in the first century and made his first brahmin convert.[3] This convert was a young boy returning from the temple, and, according to local accounts, Thomas asked him if the gods heard his prayers. The boy said the gods were carved out of stone, but he worshipped them because his father did, and if he didn't go to the temple his mother wouldn't give him his food. Thomas instructed the boy in the teachings of Jesus, upon which he became an eager disciple. Driven out from his home, the boy carried on the work of the apostle and was later ordained by St Thomas.

In 1980 Niranam still carried a sense of that ancient time. But despite Thomas's continuing presence (even my grandmother Eliyamma had seen Thomas the apostle one moonlit night) fieldwork there was impossible. My father's Marxist past was well remembered; my marriage to a Hindu was still a matter of social discussion. When I went to church I was met with open curiosity and a silence which was frightening in its closure, its excommunication. My secularism was an empty urban word, it had no meaning here. I represented, by birth and a mythologizing collective memory, two thousand years of an unbroken Christian tradition, and by my marriage outside the community I had devalued and desacralized that myth. It was irrelevant that that myth was possibly an illusion. Here, in the village where Thomas had walked, the myth was sacred.

---

[3] E.g. see L. Zaleski, *The Apostle St Thomas in India* (Mangalore: Codiarbail Press, 1912).

The Christians of St Thomas

After the ascension of Jesus Christ, legend has it that the apostles divided the world amongst themselves for the purposes of evangelization.[4] The romantic and apocryphal acts of Thomas say that Thomas was given to India. The possibility that St Thomas visited India is affirmed by the strong commercial links that existed between India and the West. This trade was mostly in the hands of Egyptians and Syrians; the latter played a considerable role in establishing Christianity within ancient India. Besides these frequently traversed sea routes to India, there were caravans that travelled through Mesopotamia, Persia and Afghanistan to the ancient town of Purushapara (Peshawar). By tradition, though, Thomas came by the sea route from the Suez, preaching the gospel on his way at Aden and Sokotra. He is believed to have converted the king of Gudnaphar in the Indus delta, but his church did not long survive here. Within a few years of its foundation the Parthians, who had welcomed Christianity and its apostle, were overthrown by the Kushans. So thorough was the ravage that this dynasty of Christian kings was forgotten until the discovery of their coins and inscriptions in the nineteenth century.[5]

The tradition of the Malabar coast, on the other hand, is a living tradition, represented in the memories and lives of people who identify themselves as the Christians of Thomas. By this oral history, Thomas came to Kodungaloor in AD 52 and founded seven churches in Kerala. Stories and songs describe the many miracles that Thomas wrought, and the conversions to Christianity that followed in their wake.

These myths are important to Syrian Christians because their very identity hinges on the arrival of St Thomas. The centuries, however, have seen much dissension among these people leading to a high degree of ecclesiastical fission. One particular denomination of Thomas Christians are the Yakoba, also known as Jacobites and Orthodox Syrians. For more than a century, their Church has been in a state of chaos, with internal squabbles dividing the people into two factions or *katshi*s. It is the story of this Church that I attempted to chronicle when I lived in Kottayam from September 1981 to November 1982.

---

[4] A.F.J. Klijn (ed.), *Acts of St Thomas* (Leiden: E.J. Brill, 1962).
[5] G.M. Moraes, *A History of Christianity in India* (Cambridge University Press, 1964).

The Locale

Kottayam is the Christian heartland of Kerala. It is a town where I could without difficulty take on the role of participant-observer. I was of the community, and yet I was a stranger.

The town lies between 9.15° and 10.21° N latitudes, and 76.25° and 76.34° E longitudes. The name Kottayam is derived from the Malayalam *kottayakam* which means the interior of a fort, for this was once the seat of royalty. On the banks of the Vembanad lake, Kottayam is twenty five feet above sea level. With fertile soil and rich vegetation, this is a green undulating area where rice, coconut, pepper, ginger and rubber grow. An agriculturally rich hinterland with tea, coffee, cardamom and rubber estates makes this region an important centre of commerce.

It was by sheer chance, perhaps by intuition that I discovered the neighbourhood of Puthenangadi, a small quiet peaceful hamlet, with a stream flowing through it. To come to Puthenangadi from Kottayam town, one must pass the famous Thirunnakkara Temple, climb a small incline and then descend to the village and its churches. In Kottayam, this village is well known for its old Christian families, some tracing their ancestry for thirteen generations.

In Puthenangadi is a 'miracle' church called Kurisu Palli. One of the most well-known churches in Kottayam town, pilgrims flock here in search of cures and blessings; here, the patron saint, Thomas, mediates on behalf of supplicants and answers prayers. The day that I was in Puthenangadi, there was a festival in this church, and I met many people. My link to the people of Puthenangadi was through my father's sister who lived there. Her neighbours were intrigued by my work, and, playing the role of informants, spontaneously came up with information they thought would interest me.

The neighbourhood suddenly became objectivized—I knew I had found my field. A photographer tends to look at the world as if through the frames of a lens; a novelist observes people and listens to them as potential characters in a story. An anthropologist may combine these attitudes and suddenly realize that here are people to be studied. It is difficult to describe how subjective that moment of choice is. For me, the bridge, the river below, the people that I was walking with, the trees, the still landscape and the pinnacle of the church rising above the low wooden houses had the quality of a dream. It was the moment of externalization: the neighbourhood appeared like a social fact—

objective and external to me, although I was actually there, inside it, a part of it. I had become the spectator.

Looking around, I was startled to find at first glimpse five churches within an area of half a kilometre. As I listened to the conversation around me I realized that these people were involved in the life of the church as though it were a legacy they had to safeguard. Here families existed whose ancestors had represented the Church a century ago in litigation; the descendants seemed equally involved in present-day ecclesiastical events. It was plain to me that Puthenangadi, with its access to seminaries and churches, and old Syrian Christian families was the obvious subject for my study.[6]

The Problem

I wanted to understand the practice of Christianity in a small community in Kerala, to explore how and why Christianity took a particular interpretative form among the people of this neighbourhood. Three inter-related questions sprang out of this situation: how does Christianity survive within the dominant culture of regional Hinduism?; how do Syrian Christians perceive the past to which they are inextricably bound by their identity?; and, finally, what does it mean to be a Christian in terms of ritual and belief?

The task presented interesting complications. A synchronic study was impossible, for Syrian Chrisitians have a long and complex history. I could not, on the other hand, treat history an an unproblematic, unquestioned concept. Representations of the past were complicated, subjective, and often tortuous. Several levels and forms of historical consciousness began to emerge: academic histories, official and ecclesiastical records, the versions of various people. These representations of the past were often varied, being biased by differing ecclesiastical loyalties.

Segmentation continues to express the plurality of interpretation that has characterized all religious life in Kerala; this study is an

---

[6] For the purpose of the study I chose 70 households on the basis of shared patterns of life-style, using the parish register of Cherya Palli (the parent church to which Kurisu Palli and other chapels in the vicinity are attached) as the first point of reference, and participant observation to corroborate evidence provided in the register. I also used literary materials pertaining to the law court cases of the church, popular tracts, written genealogies, newspaper reports, church circulars, oral histories and, of course, academic histories.

attempt to record the pathologies arising out of difference. The Yakoba,[7] as they are commonly known, are divided according to ecclesiastical allegiance to either the Patriarch of Antioch, or the indigenous Catholicos (the chief prelate of the Indian Church). Court cases over rights to property and parishes continue till today to create a sense of anomie among the Syrian Christians.

The early chapters of the book elaborate differences by juxtaposing Hindu/Christian, Romo-Syrian/Orthodox Syrian, Mar Thoma/Yakoba, Patriarch followers/Catholicos followers;[8] subsequent chapters focus on the unity of the Yakoba (the Orthodox Syrians and Jacobite Syrians) in terms of their ritual life. Rites of passage reveal the systematic harmony in which Syrian Christians maintain the exclusive character of their ritual life. The possibility of the cultural interventions of Hinduism beyond a point is de-emphasized by canonical rigour, the tendency being towards a puristic and dogmatic interpretation of the Christian ethos, creed and the ceremonies of the Church. In this sense, variance and improvization are in fact minimal, for Syrian Christians are bound by the liturgical texts disseminated through the sacred office of the priest. The Church, therefore, establishes and sustains through the language of the rite the correspondence between the life of Christ and the life of the Christian.

The rituals of the Christian calendar focus on the syntagmatic progression of Jesus's life on earth, so that the year for the Christian begins with the birth of Jesus. It culminates with Resurrection and Pentecost, which are followed by a period marked by ceremonial effervescence of another kind—the ceremonies centring around the festivals of the saints. Ceremonies celebrating the lives of Mary, St Thomas and other Christian saints and holy man often contribute to the emergence of parallel structures and voices within the Church. Canonical rigour is, for the most part, replaced by laxity, with anti-

[7] The term Yakoba unites two rival factions into a homogeneous cultural and religious unit. The ecclesiastical difference between them has given rise to different names. Those who follow the Patriarch of Antioch are called *Bawa Katshi* or Patriarch's Party, or Syrian Jacobites. Those who follow the indigenous Bishop are called Bishop's Party or *Metran Katshi*, or Orthodox Syrians.

[8] Hindu refers to the dominant regional culture, specifically in this case, of Nair Hinduism. The Romo-Syrians are St Thomas Christians following the Roman Catholic ritual form. The Mar Thoma is a Protestant-like denomination with Orthodox Church strains (a mixed case) which broke away from the Jacobite Orthodox Church in the nineteenth century.

structures being potentially generated. The role of women in this process of possible structural transformation is particularly significant, though I will also argue that, in fact, radical forms of rebellion often confirm the strength of established structures.

The effervescence arising out of the celebration of the saints' lives is in direct contrast to that which culminates the long week called *Kashtanubhavikunna nyyayarcha* commemorating Christ's passion; here there is a starkness and solemnity, yet also spiritual catharsis and rejuvenation that are difficult to express in anthropological terms. In the saints' festivals, the mood is that of a carnival, jubilant and life-affirming, and emphasizing corporeality. However, there are differences in the way each of these festivals is celebrated. For instance, the celebrations for Thomas centre to a very great degree on the fact that, by putting his fingers into the wounds of Christ, he put to the test His Resurrection, therefore proving to the world Jesus's ultimate divinity. In this sense, the doubting Thomas, often perceived negatively, is for these Christians a powerful rational figure. In Puthenangadi, the locus of this study, the apostle has a particularly significant place because of the miracle church (Kurisu Palli), of which he is the patron. Belief in him is seen to transcend ecclesiastic and sometimes even religious differences, when Hindus for instance venerate a Christian saint. Conversely, the festivals relating to holy men show that often such commemorative expressions could be symbols of division rather than communitas in the context of the church quarrel.

The book's concluding argument discusses the place of prelates and priests in the context of Christianity in practice. Clearly the role of the ecclesiasts in the *palli vyazhak* or church quarrel, has served to undermine their position in the eyes of the people over a period of almost two centuries. The ambiguous status of the priest is thus a problem arising out of historical circumstance: my attempt is to show that there is a certain kind of flux which arises out of ecclesiastical disorganization. The people are clear that until litigation between and within the parishes ceases there can be no hope for the church. Despite this anomie evident in the people's voice, there is a deep-rooted belief in the teachings of Jesus. The Apocalypse is always imminent, and the moral code in this small Christian hamlet in Kottayam is defined accordingly. Popular views of history and religion are thus statements which need to be recorded by the anthropologist, for they provide glimpses and insights which would otherwise be lost in the objective accounts of historians and theologians.

Contents

Illustrations and Maps

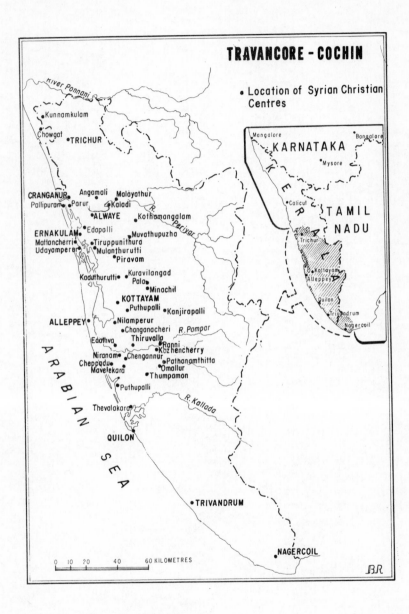

TRAVANCORE - COCHIN

• Location of Syrian Christian
Centres

River Ponnani

Kunnamkulam
Chowgat
•TRICHUR

CRANGANUR Angamali Malayathur
Pallipuram•Parur •Kaladi
•ALWAYE •Kothamangalam
ERNAKULAM •Edapalli
Mattancherri •Muvathupuzha
Udayamperur Tiruppunithura
•Mulanthurutti
•Piravam

Kaduthurutti•
•Kuravilangad
Pala
•Minachil
KOTTAYAM
•Puthupalli
•Kanjirapalli
ALLEPPEY •Nilamperur
•Changanacheri R. Pampar
Edathva Thiruvalla
Niranam •Ranni
Cheppadu Chengannur•Kozhencherry
Mavelekara •Pathanamthitta
•Omallur
•Thumpamon
•Puthupalli

Thevalakara R. Kallada

A
R
A
B
I
A
N

QUILON

S
E
A

•TRIVANDRUM

NAGERCOIL

Mangalore KARNATAKA Bangalore
•Mysore
•Calicut
TAMIL
Trichur NADU
•Kottayam
Alleppey
Quilon
Trivandrum
Nagercoil

0 10 20   40   60 KILOMETRES

BR

1

Introduction

Christianity in Kerala[1] must be understood as a unique configuration arising out of two kinds of situations. The first is its historical dimension: it came to the coast of Kerala in the early centuries of the Christian Era, and was sustained by the Churches of the Middle East (hence the appellation Syrian). Secondly, it has existed within the encompassing framework of a dominant regional culture. It is my contention that the Hindus and Syrian Christians of Kerala shared a 'world' in common. A model of their 'world' is reconstructed here, though it has become subject to severe strain in the modern period.

The features of their social life make Syrian Christians recognizable as a unique cultural group in the comparative analyses of Christian communities in the world. Kerala society, however, was traditionally plural. It allowed for the interpenetration of Hindu, Christian and Syrian codes. Edward Shils has argued that pluralism is a system of many centres of power, many areas of privacy, and a strong internal impulse towards mutual adaptation among various spheres rather than the dominance or submission of any one in relation to the others.[2] Moreover, these areas must be bound by a pluralistic system of values in which the other spheres of activity are accorded their due. The balance between what Shils calls the 'private' (the world which marked community identity) and 'public' (the wider universe) describes the quality of pluralism sustained in Kerala.

The 'private' world of Christianity in Kerala related to its ethic and world-view, its ritual and ecclesiastical life, with the norms of endogamy determining the level of contact and intimacy between individuals. Its 'public' life related to its political affiliation to Hindu kings, its acquiescence to Hindu norms of purity and pollution, its own status and rank consciousness, and its adherence to customs linked with food, language and culture. In these matters Syrian Christians were included in a wider framework of interaction. Respect was accorded to the 'private' and 'exclusive' domains of the Christians and, in turn, they respected the closed and exclusive domain of the Hindus. Communication was possible in the intervening spaces which were common to both communities. The blurring of lines between the two groups was not arbitrary but a reflection of clearly defined codes, and at no point did the dividing lines completely disappear. Each group maintained its individuality, aware of similarities with other groups yet conscious of the points of difference which separated them. In a plural society, interaction and communication do not occur through the loss of identity; the relationship is symbiotic, with the operation of hierarchy lending coherence to the differences. In this sense, caste organization is a good example of the culture of plurality.[3]

THE SYRIAN CHRISTIANS AND THE CASTE SYSTEM

Syrian Christians have been seen as part of the Hindu caste system in many anthropological studies.[4] According to Fuller, Syrian Christian groupings 'form part of the total segmentary caste structure and are ranked to each other and to the Hindu castes'.[5] In fact, this community defines itself as a *jyati* or sub-caste.

When St Thomas converted several Namboodiri brahmin families to Christianity some decades after the death of Christ, this conversion was taken to mean the loss of caste status. Syrian Christians were thus segmented off from their original caste group. However, they took with them certain privileges including their attendant castes. Converts from labourer and artisan castes related to their Syrian patrons in much the same way as they had to the higher Hindu castes.[6] Servants belonging to lower castes were sometimes converted to Christianity but strict endogamy prevailed along with commensal restrictions and, though allowed to worship in Syrian Christian churches, they did not have equal status. 'New' Christians (those converted in the nineteenth century through the efforts of the Church Missionary Society) were discouraged from entering Syrian Christian churches.

In the sense that the Syrian Christians claimed to be apostasied from Namboodiri brahmins, they could, in certain contexts, claim higher status than the Nairs, who were next only to the brahmins. For instance, rich landowning Syrian Christians with political power could claim higher status than Nairs where they were dominant in number.

Syrian Christians were traditionally traders and landowners. Land-owning is a function common to many dominant castes but trading was typically a Syrian Christian profession.[7] The Hindu kings, pleased with the hard-working and prosperous Syrian Christians, gave them privileges and honours that distinguished them as a high caste.[8]

The relationship between Nair and Syrian Christian is marked by ambiguity. While hierarchical relations between Syrian Christians and brahmins are clear cut (as also between them and other, lower, castes), the relation between castes of approximately the same status is problematic.[9] Relations between Nairs and Christians in each locality depend upon the prevalent demographic, political and economic variables. Status-shifts depend upon each situation, the differences often not large enough to warrant that either community is categorically higher or lower. On the other hand, similarities are not so extensive that one could state definitively that both are of the same status.[10] Interestingly, in the traditional system, Syrian Christians had the power of neutralizing 'pollution', and were called upon to purify by touch, for the brahmin and Nair, such substances as had come into contact with lower castes. Distance pollution, typical to traditional Kerala, has been documented in the literature dealing with Syrian Christians.[11] One custom which survives among the Yakoba of Kottayam recalls this. After the Easter service, people cry *poyin poyin* as they walk in procession down the street. *Poyin* means 'go away' and is heraldic in nature, signifying that higher castes are abroad and lower castes must therefore remove themselves from the path.

Syrian Christians are dictated to in the modalities of choice-making with regard to food, occupation, marriage, birth and death and their accompanying rituals by their identity as a caste group. Strict rules regarding the eating and distribution of food existed in the traditional system. Lower castes were not allowed in the kitchen but were fed separately on ritual occasions, being considered capable of 'polluting' Christians. Taboos relating to menstrual pollution were followed strict-ly by women of the generation which is now about sixty years old. Old women insist that in their early youth ('before the changes came') they had to bathe before entering the kitchen.

The Christians, like the Hindus, had faith in horoscopes, the tying of the *thali* or marriage locket, death pollution of ten to fifteen days, vegetarianism during mourning periods, ceremonial bathing to remove death pollution (*pulakuli*), funeral rites followed by feasting (*adyantram*), celebration of *Onam* and *Vishu* (harvest and new year festivals), the celebration of *annaprasanam* (the first feeding of a child with rice) and the non-admission of low castes into the house. Low castes in fact continue to remain at the door in all relations of interaction other than work. They eat separately at floor level, and are served in dishes not used by the higher castes. The concept of pollution may be unstated but the nature of hierarchy is clearly discernible.

A concern with charting genealogies is also typical of these Christians, and signifies their need to keep marriages endogamous and status-bound. Syrian Christians also had councils for corporate action typified in the activities of the *sabha* (the Church as an association). The *sabha* had complete control over its members, and used the traditional rules of caste organization—disgrace, ostracism and excommunication—as its instruments. Modes of dress, etiquette, music, literature, food, ornamentation and styles of education were typically bound by the rules of custom and tradition.[12]

The categories of time, space and the body articulated in social use represent the 'world' held in common by the Christians and Hindus of Kerala. While these elements are not thought of as constitutive of Hinduism, they are acknowledged as having developed in the idiom and language of Hinduism. These categories are seen as belonging to the domain of the natural world with nature itself becoming a cultural category. While nature is seen to be independent of culture at one level ('out there'), at another level it is perceived and socially constructed in such a way so that the 'Christian' sphere, in this sense, becomes subjugated to the Hindu. The Christian strand remains an ethical or normative code from which the cultural grids of cognition (here, the natural world) may be set apart. The sacred categories of these texts of knowledge, being Hindu, are here only of surreptitious significance, denied by the Church and publicly denounced by the self-conscious Christian as superstition.

Time

Ritual time for these Christians has its basis in Jewish as well as Christian traditions. Preparation for the Eucharist begins on the evening of the previous day, as is the custom among other Eastern Churches. Prayer and fasting, which demarcate the days of the week (Sundays, Wednesdays, Fridays and Saturdays), are usually set apart as sacred days relating to events in the Christian calendar. For instance, Sunday breaks the fast, being the day commemorating the Resurrection, Friday and Saturday are days of fasting associated with the crucifixion of Christ and his entombment, Wednesday is associated with the Virgin Mary.

However, time relating to the events of the mundane life is conceived of by the Christians in the same way as the Hindus. The Malayalam Era, which follows the Christian Era by 825 years,[13] is still used in marking the dates of the establishment of churches, houses and gravestones. It is used in everyday speech when referring to the past (particularly the distant past), and for fixing a child's astrological sign at its birth.

The months followed in the reckoning of daily life are the same as those of the Hindu calendar, where each month is associated with certain specific attributes. *Karkadam* (July–August) is considered to be the worst month, a time of rain and hunger. Hunger here is a metaphorical term, conveying the barrenness of imagery provided by torrential rain. Similarly *Kanni* (September–October) is thought to be an inauspicious month. During this period houses are rarely constructed nor do marriages take place. *Dhanu* is the best of months and seasons yet twenty-five days of Lent or *noimba* must be carefully observed before Christmas. There are no marriages during Lent or the monsoon. Agricultural cycles also follow this calendar, and one of the most significant determinants of activity is the *vavu* or lunar eclipse, connected with death, childbirth and harvesting.

The calendar also has its accompanying astrological signs; these have always been considered important though parish priests try hard to convince the laity that such beliefs are against the tenets of Christianity. According to one informant, astrology is neither Christian nor Hindu, being based on calculation and the belief that all things are signs. Syrian Christians often point out that even the discovery of Christ's birth was made possible to the Magi through their astronomical calculations.

It is in the building of houses that time in its astrological dimension is given the greatest weight. Astrology is not employed in the finding of a suitable marriage partner though at the birth of a child the *naal* or astral sign is recorded. The *naal* of each person is known to his or her family who are also familiar with its associated characteristics, considered identifiable in the person's disposition and behaviour.

The calculation of the passage of moments is still sometimes reckoned by the *narhika*. The day is divided into 60 *narhikas* (each *narhika* is 24 minutes), and each *narhika* consists of 60 *vinarhikas* (24 seconds). One *vinarhika* equals 2/5ths of a second times sixty.[14] This mode of calculation is used only by very old people and usually in the calculations of time required for the making of Ayurvedic preparations, which follow traditional recipes with traditional weights and measures.

Days have special significance in terms of their auspiciousness. Wednesday is considered so dangerously inauspicious that there is a saying that even a leopard cub will not emerge from its mother's womb on this day. Fridays and Tuesdays are inauspicious and generally no baptisms, marriage proposals or marriages take place on these days. However, these two days are considered auspicious by both Hindus and Christians for oil baths and 'washing the head' in an elaborate, ritualistic fashion. On these days men traditionally avoided transactions and travel as these were thought to create work on a day which belonged to women.

The Body

Some common ideas about the body and the maintenance of health are held by both the Hindus and the Christians of Kerala. Bathing is very much a part of the institution of general medicine as known and practised. The bath is considered to be important in maintaining and regulating the health of the body, particularly in situations following disease or childbirth, when the body has to be returned to a state of normalcy. In this context, elaborate preparations involving diet and medicines (both for anointing and ingestion) were undertaken.

The making of *ayurvedic* oils and medicines, an elaborate ritual conducted in silence and near secrecy, continues today in many houses. Prescriptions are often very old, having been given to the family several generations ago by the *vaidyan* or physician who was usually a Namboodiri brahmin. Some Christian families have been given the gift of *ayurvedic* knowledge by *vaidyan*s, and this knowledge is passed on from father to son and used for the benefit of those who are in need.

Space

It is in the building of houses that the dialogue between Hindu and Christian customs is most evident. The Hindu *asari* (master builder) who builds for the Christian keeps to the customs and rules that he would follow for a Hindu client. Astrology, naturally, plays a major role. The house, for instance, is compared to a bridegroom and the building site to the bride, about to be united in holy wedlock, with the perimeter of the structure used in the calculation of its horoscope. Every house must be located within its own seat of strength, and if this is not so, then misfortune may fall upon its inhabitants. Sickness, failure or melancholy which continue without cause are ascribed to such unfortunate placement of houses.[15]

The Christian places whole-hearted trust in the *thaccan* or carpenter who follows the rules laid down by the *Thaccu Shastra*, containing rules of measurement, location and construction. The Christian house is in architectural style essentially like any Hindu house of similar status. A traditional *thacan* said: 'In this matter, the Christians have full faith in the Hindu *shastras*; they know that if we don't do as the books say then some misfortune will befall the house or its occupants.'

Thus the site of the land has to be most carefully chosen. Those sites which are three, five or six-cornered in shape are considered inauspicious as also those shaped like a trident or the square reed sieve. A site which resembles an elephant's back is considered inauspicious; so also sites in which are found bones, ash, coral, hair or worms, because these are definitely polluted spaces. To build a house facing the church is inauspicious for the church emanates *shakti* or power.

The planting and placement of trees is also significant. *Elanji* (Mimosopo elangi) and *peral* (Ficus indica) are grown on the eastern side of the house, *atti* (ficus racemosa) and *puli* (Tarmarindus indicus) on the southern side, *aryal* (Ficus religiosa) and *pala* (Asclepias annalaris) on the west, the *naga* tree (Trico Santhus Angina) and *itti* (Ficus venosa) to the north, to bring prosperity to the occupants. Jack fruit, mango, coconut, and areca palms may surround the house. This classification of space and the planting of trees has its own logic, related to a particular mode of thought, with its associations of peace, prosperity, sickness, health, melancholy or strife.[16]

In the building of houses, the months of the year, being part of the astral framework, are divided according to their auspiciousness by the *asari*. Thus *Medham* (April–May) is associated with disease, *Edayam* (May–June) with money and jewels, *Mithunam* (June–July) with death, and so on. All days of the week are auspicious for construction except Sundays and Tuesdays.

There are various rituals that accompany the building of a house. These include prayers by the craftsmen to the Hindu deity Ganapathy at the time of laying the foundation stone. Offerings to the god include fried rice, beaten rice, molasses, plantains, fruit and offerings of flowers and money. *Manas puja* or worship through contemplation is performed by the *asari*. The Christian clients, while not active participants in these rituals, are nevertheless interested onlookers. They keenly observe the activities of the *asari* and can describe some of the events that take place, although with no real understanding of their significance. They accept the auspicious nature of the powerful sacred materials—gold, silver, copper, bronze and iron, and of things such as sugar crystals, grapes, pounded rice, and puffed rice. When the *panchaloham* (five sacred metals) is buried, the foundation is laid. The parish priest is then called and prayers are said.

The Christian accepts that the decision about the direction of the house rests with the *asari*. This is based on his interpretation of the movement of a *tulsi* (basil) leaf in a coconut shell filled with water. The Christians also accept that in the event of some untoward movement, the *asari*s will refuse to continue. Sometimes they may laugh about it, but they accept the existence of contradiction in their lives, and while they do not actively participate as believers, they provide whatever materials are required by the *asari*s and feast them as custom requires.

The other rituals which the *asari*s perform express the animistic nature of life where all objects have sacred properties. These rituals are manifestations of an attitude to the physical and social world where every thing belongs and participates in a cosmic order, and permission for its use must be sought. The data on architecture expresses the animistic conception of the natural world that the Christians vicariously have—it is legitimate for the Hindu *thaccan* to say prayers to the spirit of the woods and the earth; the Christian, while not participating actively, allows the Hindu to make use of materials and property that have been procured by him. He is the proprietor, but the property is still only potentially his. The land still belongs to nature, and the craftsman asks permission for the use of this property. Here, ecologically speaking, arises the distinction between personal property and private property. Nature gives to man articles which may be used but which do not belong to him. Thus the permission sought for the use of natural things is accompanied by propitiation and requests. Man is submissive to the will of Nature and controls the natural world with its permission. Man sees Nature as being both good and evil, and while striving to incorporate the good, he does not externalize the evil by destroying it; he redirects it elsewhere. The Christian rituals, in fact, focus upon the purification of the house through prayers of exorcism.

Before the carpenters and workers are sent away they are given the gift of a feast by the owners of the house, the link between craftsmen and proprietors being severed by this farewell meal.[17] Once the house has been built, the property belongs to the Christian. Nature gives way to culture—the forest, earth, sea and mountain and other natural resources are bound down and accommodated to become a home. The liminal period of construction must give way to the completed moment of possession. Nature in an animistic world-view must consent to its own subjugation. Quite clearly, then, the Christian sees Nature as that over which he has control. The very act of naming implies man's mastery: 'and whatsoever Adam called every living creature that was the name thereof.'[18]

The *veedu kudasa* or ritual for making the Christian house ready for occupation takes place to exorcise the Hindu influence. The *bhavanam shuthikaranam* (purification ritual) begins with prayers for peace and grace for the house and for all those who will live there. It includes prayers for the dead, for comfort to the living, for the quality of remembrance, as well as prayers for the soul and safety from danger and evil. The priest and the deacon go through every room with a censer, holy water, and strips of palm leaf, and mark each door with the sign of the cross. After this ceremony, the house is ready for habitation.

Like domestic architecture, church architecture also borrows from the Hindu perception of the natural world. But unlike domestic architecture, it simultaneously draws from the Jewish tradition. The Christian church resembles in its internal structure the Jewish synagogue. However, the construction of the church takes place in the manner prescribed by the *Thaccu Shastra*, and the rules followed are those adapted from the building principles for temples. In the facade of the church, the cultural elements of Hinduism, Christianity and the Syrian tradition are clearly in juxtaposition.

The complex relationship between the Hindu, Syrian and Christian can be understood through the metaphor of a tapestry. It is not a simple plait but, in the warp and the woof, a pattern emerges which is ethnographically unique. The nature of this reality must be seen in terms of consonance and dissonance, where moments of conflict are balanced by attempts to maintain a harmony born of the union of nature and culture. Here one must take into account the fact that nature and culture are not mere opposites, each excluding the other, but are dichotomies in relation. Thus culture, from whose aspect man conceives the world, both natural and social, is the idiom in which all codes are expressed.

Notes

1. Syrian Christianity has been of intense academic interest to theologians. However, the problems raised have been restricted to the problems of history, culminating in the Portuguese ritual colonization of the sixteenth century; see e.g. A M Mundadan, *The Arrival of the Portuguese in India and the Thomas Christians under Mar Jacob 1498–1522* (Bangalore: Dharmaraj Press, 1967); P J Podipara, *The St Thomas Christians*, (Bombay: Darton, Longman and Todd, 1970); H C Perumallil and E R Hambye, *Christianity in India* (Alleppey: Prakashan, 1972). The documented literature for the period following Portuguese intervention and consequent schisms (also arising from British colonial influence) is relatively sparse. See e.g. L W Brown, *The Indian Christians of St Thomas*; P Cheriyan, *The Malabar Christians and the Church Missionary Society* (Madras: CMS Press, 1935); Stephen Neill, *A History of Christianity in India* (Cambridge: Cambridge University Press, 1984). In this sense, the Dutch and Anglican periods of Syrian Christian history lack systematic published treatment by scholars. The early twentieth century presents a face of absolute discord. Here the materials for analyses are provided not by historians but by representatives of the Church, by ecclesiasts with subjective and vested interests, and by journalists who may also be partisan in the quarrels besetting the Church. There has been no reliable history of this contemporary period in English; in the vernacular, Z M Paret's works are widely read. The most objective formulations are sometimes provided by judgements of the law courts, see e.g. T Chandrasekhar Menon, *Copy of Judgement in Original Suits 1, 2, 3, 4, 5, 6, 7 & 8/79 dated 6.6.1980* (Ernakulam: High Court of Kerala, 1980).
2. Edward Shils, *The Torment of Secrecy* (London: Heinemann, 1956), p. 154.
3. M N Srinivas, *Social Change in Modern India* (Delhi: Orient Longman, 1972).
4. L K Anantha Krishna Ayyar, *Anthropology of the Syrian Christians* (Ernakulam: Cochin Government Press, 1926); Brown, op. cit.; C J Fuller, 'Kerala Christians and the Caste System', *Man* (n.s.) vol. II 57–70, 1976; J M Hutton, *Caste in India* (Bombay: Oxford University Press, 1976).
5. Fuller, op. cit., p. 58.
6. Brown, op. cit.
7. The Christians of Kerala were traditionally masters of the pepper trade. The vaisyas or trading castes were missing as a category, their place being taken by the Syrian Christians in the caste system of Kerala.
8. Hocart writes that 'there are vacancies to be filled' and 'numerous instances of kings fixing the privileges of caste in South India'. A M Hocart, *Life-giving Myth and Other Essays* (London: Methuen, 1952), p. 49. Narratives relating to the origins of residence in Puthenangadi attribute gifts of land and patronage to the king who had courts and palaces in the neighbouring quarter or *kara* called Pazheangadi.
9. Louis Dumont, *Homo Hierarchicus* (Chicago: University of Chicago Press, 1980); Srinivas, op. cit.

10. Here my position differs from that taken by Fuller, who argues that Syrian Christians were lower in the caste hierarchy *vis-à-vis* the Nairs. (op. cit.)

11. Anantha Krishna Ayyar, op. cit.; Brown, op. cit.

12. Anantha Krishna Ayyar, op. cit.

13. The Malayalam Era begins with the reign of a heroic king, Udaya Marthanda Varma of Quilon. 'In the Kali year 3926 (AD 825) when King Marthanda Varma was residing in Kollam (Quilon), he convened a council of all the learned men of Kerala with the object of introducing a new Era, and after making some astronomical researches and calculating the solar movements throughout the twelve signs of the Zodiac, and counting scientifically the number of days occupied in this revolution in every month, it was resolved to adopt the new Era from the 1st of Chingam of that year, 15th August 825 as Kollam year one and to call it the solar year. This arrangement was approved by all the wise men of the time, and every neighbouring country began to adopt the same. And this system of reckoning continues upto the present day throughout Keralam.' K P Padmanabha Menon, *History of Kerala*, vol. IV, p. 265 (New Delhi: Asian Educational Services edition, 1986).

14. See e.g. K P Padmanabha Menon, *History of Kerala*, vol. I. (Ernakulam: Cochin Government Press, 1924).

15. See e.g. Valentine Daniel, *Fluid Signs* (Berkeley: University of California Press, 1984).

16. Claude Lévi-Strauss, *The Savage Mind* (London: Weidenfeld and Nicholson, 1976), p. 9.

17. Marcel Mauss, *The Gift* (London: Routledge and Kegan Paul, 1972).

18. Robin Attfield, 'Christian Attitudes to Nature', *Journal of the History of Ideas*, vol. XLIV; Genesis, 2: 19.

The Converts of St Thomas (AD 52)

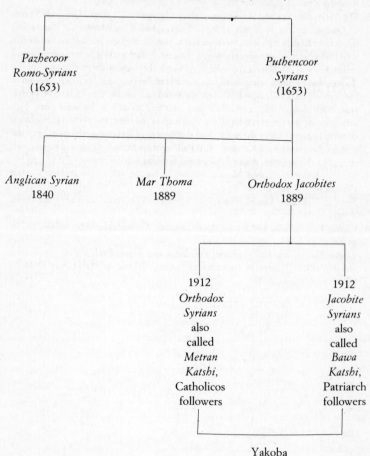

Pazhecoor
Romo-Syrians
(1653)

Puthencoor
Syrians
(1653)

Anglican Syrian
1840

Mar Thoma
1889

Orthodox Jacobites
1889

1912
Orthodox
Syrians
also
called
Metran
Katshi,
Catholicos
followers

1912
Jacobite
Syrians
also
called
Bawa
Katshi,
Patriarch
followers

Yakoba

2

Reconstructions of the Past:
Forms of Historical Consciousness

Syrian Christians popularly believe that they are the descendants of high caste (brahmin) converts of Thomas, the Apostle of Christ, thought to have arrived in Malabar on his apostolic mission in AD 52. Discussions of the oral and written traditions relating to this visit are to be found in the corpus of writing on Syrian Christian history.[1]

The Persian Period

A dispersion of the early Christians seems to have taken place following the departure of St Thomas. There was no organized Church not only because of internal dissension but also because of the appearance of a sorcerer, Manivakkachar, whose origins are still under historical dispute.[2] Consequently, there developed a crystallization of the relationship between India and the Church of Persia. A Christian, Thomas of Cana, set out in AD 345 with the permission of the Catholicos of the East, taking with him a number of Christians, both lay and ecclesiastical, from Jerusalem, Baghdad and Nineveh, to provide succour to the spiritually impoverished Thomas Christians of Kerala. The immigrant Syrians merged with the indigenous Christians both commercially and spiritually. But, by tradition, they remained separate and endogamous groups called the Southists (*Thekumbhagar* or the Canaanites) and the Northists (*Vadakumbhagar* or indigenous Christians) respectively, jealously conscious of their different racial identities.[3] However, this link, reinforced by the arrival of Syrian prelates through the centuries, had a variety of ecclesiastical consequences. The Indian

Church was drawn by this association into a number of controversies not of its own making which were to affect its existence and identity, especially in the sixteenth century when the Portuguese came to India. Every schism affecting the Persian Church was to have its effect upon the Syrian Christian Church. As the Church of Persia also claimed to have been founded by Thomas the Apostle, this led to an allegiance between the Indian and the Persian Churches.[4] The Church of Persia actually consisted of two churches in a hierarchical relation—the Persian Church proper, and Seleucia, though for many centuries the Indian Church had direct links with the former and only indirect, mediated contacts with the latter.[5]

By the ninth century, however, India was under the control of the See of Seleucia Ctesiphon, and from the thirteenth century on, prelates came to India solely from Seleucia.[6] The most important of these prelates were the saintly Mar Sapor and Mar Prodh of the eighth or ninth centuries.[7] Tradition also states that the Christian community in Kerala was reinforced by immigrants from Persia at this time.[8]

In the last decade of the sixteenth century, the ritual control of the Seleucian See over the Syrian Christians slipped (a reflection of dissensions in the line of prelatial succession), and they came under the domination of the Portuguese Latin jurisdiction.

The Portuguese Period

The 'discovery' of a sea route to India by Vasco da Gama in 1498 marks the beginning of the Portuguese period in Syrian Christian history, and this seafarer's arrival with his two ships at the port of Calicut signalled an end to India's political isolation from the West.[9] Portugal was quite the most efficient tool in the expansion of the Church in all the newly discovered countries.[10] Trade was not the only concern of the Portuguese, whose ecclesiastical and civil administration were closely linked.

Thomas Lopes, a chronicler who accompanied Vasco da Gama, describing the first meeting of the Syrian Christians with the Portuguese states that the 30,000 strong Syrian Christian community gave da Gama a rod of justice, thus gifting him with a position of authority over it. From the narrative of Empoli, another chronicler of this period, it appears that the Christians asked to meet Latin priests more out of curiosity than from any need for spiritual sustenance. The Portuguese priests were shown the local churches, and allowed to preach there.[11]

Over time the relationship underwent a change. The Portuguese expressed dissatisfaction with the Syrian Christians' interpretation of Christianity. Ecclesiasts who followed the first Portuguese travellers and discoverers began to establish what was eventually the Portuguese ritual colonization of the Malabar, and were adamant about the use of a unified Latin mode of worship. Penteado, a Portuguese priest working among the Syrian Christians wrote in 1516/18:

> The Christians of St Thomas do not care for communication with the Portuguese, not because they are not happy that they are Christians as we are, but because we are among them as the English and the Germans are among us.[12]

Stephen Neill's work has documented the cultural cannibalism of the Portuguese in India, particularly in Goa.[13] The Syrian Christians in Malabar were to resist this, wanting instead to retain their identity, to incorporate without assimilation; the Portuguese, on the other hand, wanted absorption and subjugation not only of ritual and doctrine but also of culture.[14]

The Syrian Christians had no desire to transfer their allegiance from the Patriarch of the Eastern Church and receive patronage from Rome. Since commercial and trading interests were at stake (the Christians holding monopoly over pepper, of which they were producers and merchants), total or direct repudiation of Portuguese ecclesiastical demands was not possible. Consequently, for almost a century, they were non-commital in their response. However, by 1523, the Portuguese openly attacked the Syrian Christians for being Nestorean heretics.[15] The culmination of Portuguese ecclesiastical domination came in 1599 when the Synod of Diamper (or Udeyemperoor) began its proceedings. The decrees of the Synod of Diamper are interesting because they give the reader an idea of the nature of the imposition of the new, organized doctrines, and also an idea of the existing social system, the ritual practices and 'abuses'. There was a clear elaboration of Christian dogma—for instance, on the nature of the Holy Trinity, the place of Mary, ideas regarding sin, heaven, hell and purgatory, the Last Judgement and so on. Two kinds of errors were carefully weeded out—those connected with Nestoreanism and those relating to practices influenced by the Hindu code of rituals such as transmigration, the determination of men's lives by fate or fortune, and the belief that everyone had to follow his own *dharma* or way of life, all of which would lead to salvation.[16] Books which did not meet the prescription of the Portuguese ecclesiasts were burnt. The traditional archives of the Thomas Christians suffered great losses.

In 1653, following certain events which were to act as catalysts, centred around the alleged murder of an Eastern prelate by the Portuguese, the Christians broke free from Portuguese ecclesiastical domination with the *Koonen Kurisu* Revolt. The Christians gathered at Mattancherry and, tying a rope to the cross, each touched the rope (and hence indirectly the cross), swearing to break free from Portuguese ecclesiastical oppression. Not all the Christians, however, repudiated the Portuguese ecclesiasts; there were many who preferred the rites and celebrations of Rome. Those who revolted against the Portuguese came to be known as the *Puthencoor* (the new group). In 1664, with the arrival of the Jacobite bishop Mar Gregorious, the West Syrian Church became established in Kerala, and the relationship between the two churches continues tempestuously till today.

The *Koonen Kurisu* Revolt of 1653 signalled the first of the schisms in the community that had been united under the name of Thomas the Apostle. By this time the Portuguese had lost control of the sea; the coming of the Dutch was welcomed by the Syrians, heralding the end of Portuguese control. The Dutch, though sympathetic to Syrian Christian interests, left no lasting impact on the historical consciousness of the Thomas Christians.

THE BRITISH PERIOD

In 1800 a British Resident was appointed to the court of Travancore. Ecclesiastical interest on the part of the British began as early as 1806, with efforts being made to bring to the Syrian Christians a vernacular Bible. The institution of a trust fund for the welfare of the Syrian Church by Colonel Macaulay in 1808 was another significant step as was the establishment of a Syrian seminary in Kottayam in 1813.

The narratives of the Church Missionary Society (CMS) describe the state of Syrian Christianity in the nineteenth century as viewed through missionary eyes. From their first expressions of concern for an ancient but 'degenerate' Church, we see in these accounts a growing desire for reform in the Syrian Christian Church. Following Anglican ecclesiastical intervention, the Syrians were to enter a period of internal dissension which would continue for more than a century and a half, remaining unsettled even today. The *Puthencoor* Syrian Christians are severally divided, and have different denominational identities.

To describe this period in Syrian Christian history, I have used narrative accounts of three different but related kinds in the syntagmatic reconstruction of the past. These are: a) Church Missionary Society Records (1816–56), b) Judgement Reports including Witness Depositions in the Royal Court of Final Appeal (1879–89), and c) Ethnographic Accounts of 1981–2. The three sources of narrative material are separated in time by as much as hundred years. These sets of material and the narrators presenting the accounts must be seen in the same way as scene-shifts in a play. A break in the context of time or setting does not constitute a break in the story. Moreover, the argument implicitly presented here is that the anthropologist needs to look at three modes of historical consciousness—academic and official records as well as peoples' versions of history—in order to have a fuller understanding of the relationship between the past and the present. Each level explicates some aspect of reality which may be suppressed by the other.[17]

The first set of narratives consists of letters and reports of the CMS missionaries, these being personal statements made public, and published in the CMS records and proceedings from 1816 to 1856. This marks the period of direct Anglican influence in the affairs of the Syrian Christians, the consequences of which are to be felt even today. The perspectives of the narrators are often subjective, the movement from thought to writing not necessarily mediated by speech, as is exemplified in letters and extracts from journals. Only at a second level are the narratives exposed to a reader or listener. Many of these accounts are first-person reports and, though presented in the guise of official statements for record to the Church Missionary Society Committee, they do not lose their biographical flavour. Through the records of the CMS, an attempt is made to reconstruct the etic and official world-view of the nineteenth century Syrian Christians in Kerala as presented through the writing of these missionaries.

Two modes of representation are linked in a chronological chain. First, the official but 'subjective' records of the Anglicans; secondly, the official but 'objective' records of the Syrian Christians. Together they produce a syntagm of the ecclesiastical society of these Christians in the nineteenth century, offering us a backdrop against which the present is to be viewed.

The second level of discourse consists of the oral depositions of witnesses (recorded by scribes) in the court cases of 1879 and 1886. The Syrian Christians took their quarrels born out of Syrian confrontation with Anglican theological influence to the courts. These narratives are less personal than official; biases are representative of the faction for whom the witnesses stand; their statements, though oral, are to be fixed in writing at the moment of speech. Truth and falsehood are the moral dimensions of the narratives and in fixing them all variability is denied. Speech itself must take on the objective rigour of the written, it may not be flexible: once spoken it takes on a concrete character which inscription further imposes. These narratives offer an account of how nineteenth century Syrian Christians perceived themselves; more interestingly, how they perceived each other for by now they were a divided family seeking to demarcate their differences and trying to articulate their identities in opposition to one another.

The third set offers narrative material from an ethnographic present. These are oral accounts recorded by me in the field between October 1981 and November 1982. They serve as mirrors which reflect the other two levels of discourse, creating images which both partake of the other levels as well as establish and possess an identity of their own. The analogy with mirrors is apt because it takes into account the problem of distortion. Informants' accounts are important in establishing the relation between past and present; yet what is remembered is very often structured by present events, leading to both reflections *and* distortions born of ecclesiastical bias. Variations in narrative thus exist, and are in themselves collective expressions of a society and Church divided, where the very nature of truth is constantly changing.

Church Missionary Society Records

The First Ecclesiastical Contacts   When the English missionaries encountered the Syrian Christians in the early years of the nineteenth century, the latter were in a poor state, having neither political nor economic power.[18] In 1806 Lord Wellesley sent the Rev Dr Claudius Buchanan to investigate into the life and conditions of these Christians. This was to be the first important British ecclesiastical contact with the Syrian Christians.

To demonstrate the concern which the British Resident had for the condition of the Syrian Christians, Buchanan offered to send them translations of the Bible in Malayalam, an offer to which they responded gratefully. But in spite of their keen desire to receive the text, there was doubt about its veracity.

'But how,' said one old priest, 'shall we know that your standard copy is a true translation of our Bible? We cannot depart from our Bible. It is the true book of God, without corruption, the book which was first used by the Christians of Antioch. What translations you have got in the West we know not, but the true Bible of Antioch, we have had in the mountains of Malabar for fourteen hundred years or longer.'[19]

Their doubts would not be put at rest and were constantly articulated, until Buchanan offered them an English Bible for comparison with a Syrian one.

They turned over the leaves of my Bible with surprise, having never seen a printed Syrian Bible before. After some consultation, they proposed that the 3rd chapter of Mathew's gospel should be critically compared word for word, in the Eastern Syrian, Western Syrian and English... It was an interesting scene to me to behold the ancient English Bible brought before the tribunal of these simple Christians in the hills of Malabar. They sat down to the investigation with great solemnity, and the people around seemed to think that something important depended on the issue...[20]

The Translation and Printing of a Bible in the Vernacular and Other Measures of Help The chief impetus for the translation of the Bible into the vernacular came from the British Resident in Travancore and Cochin, Colonel Munro, who had been assigned to that position in 1810. He offered to pay for the expenses from his own pocket '...although I am not very well able to afford it', rather than allow any delay in the work of translation.[21] He further appointed the missionary Reverend Bailey at Kottayam to be in charge of the work of translation. Besides the efforts at procuring for the Syrian Christians a vernacular version of the Bible, the British were responsible for the institution of a trust fund to benefit the community. In October 1808, 3000 star pagodas were banked at eight per cent interest which was to be paid to the Metropolitan of the Syrian Church. This was perhaps an amalgamation of money from several sources.[22] This trust fund was in later years the cause of great strife and litigation since it became the symbol of the legitimate church once the quarrels and divisions had set in.

The third important act of ecclesiastical significance was the establishment in 1813 of a Syrian College or seminary. The Missions'
Report of 1816 stated that

> The principal object of the establishment of a college in Travan-
> core was to instruct the Cattanars and officiating priests among
> the Syrians in a competent knowledge of the Syrian language in
> which they are at present too generally deficient.[23]

The original intention of the missionaries was to sustain and support
a unique and ancient Church rather than to bring about change.[24] In
the early years of this interaction with the Syrian Christians, the
missionaries were cautious in their relations with them. Whatever
changes were desired were to enter this Church as if spontaneously. At
this time, the Syrians themselves were undoubtedly receptive to
Anglican influence.

By 1821 Bailey had a 'Malayalam Moonshee' working with him on
the translation of the Bible. The Report for 1819–20 mentions that he
was helped by 'a learned respectable Jew belonging to Cochin, [and]
some Brahmins and Nairs as well, skilled in the language of the
country, were also entertained as Munshis'.[25] At this time too, the
necessity for a printing press manifested itself. Meanwhile, the missionaries asked

> For an allowance of three or four writers at the salary of four or
> five rupees per month, to multiply copies of selected portions of
> scripture and of other tracts till a press can be resorted to.[26]

The urgent need for a printing press was resolved by Bailey himself
who with local materials and craftsmen had one made for the express
purpose of printing a Malayalam Bible. The report of 1824–25 said:

> Mr Bailey, without ever having seen a Type Foundry or its
> apparatus of any kind, eager to get some portion of the scriptures
> and some other works respectively printed as soon as possible,
> set himself to endeavour to form his own types with such aid as
> he could find from books alone and from common workmen.
> He had recourse chiefly to the Encyclopaedia Brittanica.[27]

The missionaries wished to see the Syrian Christian Church freed from what were considered to be superstitions such as the use of prayers for the dead, to the saints, the veneration of Mary and other similar 'excesses'. In the discreetest manner possible, they attempted to maintain the channels of communication between the Syrians and themselves so that some day a reformation in the Church could be effected.

Educating (and so theologically influencing) the priests or *kattanar*s was one way by which reform could be achieved, and that, in fact, was the express function of the Syrian College. The missionary Fenn wrote in 1825 to the CMS:

If a small portion of the ideas of Locke and Bacon, and similar writers gets entrance among them, many of their errors and of the errors of their Heathen Neighbours also must fall to the ground.

The free circulation of the Bible among the Syrian Christians could be the only ray of hope for the missionaries. Decades after he had begun the work, Bailey wrote on the problems of translation:

I am not so apprehensive as some valued friends of mine are, respecting the imperfections found in some translations of the scripture. No doubt, I should wish that every translation were as perfect as I believe. It is the want of the Bible and not the imperfections of the translation that this society has to deplore and cure.[28]

This much desired 'Reformation' did come about in 1843 but it affected only one part of the Syrian Christian community. The translation of the Bible into the vernacular and its easier dissemination through printing brought about several changes among those who called themselves Reformists. Under the leadership of Abraham Malpan, a scholar priest at the Syrian College, the Reformists attempted to change and vernacularize the liturgy and prayers, and repudiated the mediatory powers of the saints and Mary. Sermons and hymns began to assume great importance as did personal perusals of the Bible. A great revivalist movement occurred during this period with some degree of emphasis on devotional music. The Eucharist (*Qurbana*) was changed from a 'Mystery' into a 'service', and was celebrated only on Sundays when there were communicants, unlike on earlier occasions when the priest performed the ceremony regardless of partakers. An attempt at organizing the clergy was made, including the payment of salaries so that they were freed from their dependence on their parishioners. Simony was frowned upon, as was the burning of candles before images and the sounding of gongs and cymbals during euchar- istic ceremonies.

On the other hand, the Reformists did not accept entirely the form and content of Anglican theology from the CMS. They kept much of the style of their traditional worship including ceremonial vestments, church architecture and prelatial celibacy, as well as the Liturgy of St James with certain amendments. It was, in fact, a middle path between the old *Puthencoor* ecclesiastical rites and the newly available Protestant rites of the CMS. The Reform Movement divided the *Puthencoor* Syrians into two groups who would drag each other through the mire of the law courts, from which situation one section of them was not to be freed even a century later. The attempt to make these 'interesting Christians' conform to Anglican theological doctrine was not very different (though less emphatic) from the earlier Portuguese attempts at unification under the Latin rite. What is important is that both ecclesiastical interventions led to cleavages in the parent body of the Church.

Changes in Relations between the Syrian Christians and the CMS   With the entry into the Syrian Christians' life in 1833 and 1834 of the missionaries, the Reverends Peet and Woodcock, the careful handling of ecclesiastical affairs characteristic of the early missionaries was to disappear.

The reaction of the Syrian Christians to the changed attitude of the representatives of the CMS was clearly antagonistic. The missionary Peet wrote in his report in 1836: '...in the prosecution of my duty I have met with every kind of opposition (short of personal violence) from some of the leading men'.[29]

Peet was to write of these 'superstitious' Christians in 1841 that

> They are very interesting people ... possessing one great and redeeming quality, one which ought to enlist the sympathies and best feeling ... and one which, in spite of the devil and their priests, will certainly rescue them from misery, and invest them with attributes which none but dreamers imagine they now possess. That one good thing in them is they reverence the Bible

as the word of God, not in the Popish sense of the word, but as held by the reformed churches in Christendom.[30]

With this, the Syrian Christians and the CMS had officially parted. Describing the difficult and unfulfilling years with the Syrian Christians, the report in the CMS Intelligence of 1856 was severely honest.

Thus at its commencement, the aspect of the work was most encouraging; but, as time advanced, it stood out more clearly in its true character, as one of no ordinary difficulty. Promising appearances faded away. The Syrians as a body, exhibited a growing distaste for the efforts made for their improvement.[31]

In 1836 the Syrian *metran* imposed on the clergy a solemn oath to have no dealings whatever with the church missionaries, and thus the acts of separation were concluded.

The Cochin Award: Severing of Ties between CMS and the Syrians   Following this separation of the Syrian Christians from the CMS, there were some disputes with regard to property which was submitted to a committee for arbitration. An award was passed in April 1840. The 3000 star pagodas (*vatti pannam*) and the interest on it (which had been invested in 1808 by Colonel Macaulay for the Syrians), the college at Kottayam and the land, granary, and other property attached to it, were awarded to the Syrian Metropolitan (chief prelate), to be held in trust by him and two others, an ecclesiast and a member of the Syrian Christian laity, who were to be chosen by the people as caretakers of their Church's property. The impact of the missionaries' work, however, was to be felt long afterwards among the Syrian Christians.

It was under Abraham Malpan that the changes among the Syrians began to manifest themselves. The *malpan* (scholar) had been closely associated with the missionaries at the Syrian College, where he taught Syriac. The close relations which he maintained with the missionaries aroused in him a desire to reform the Syrian Christian Church of its 'corruptions'. He was persecuted by those Syrians whom he antagonized, and excommunicated by the Metropolitan. Some of the clergy, however, approved of his practices and followed Malpan, becoming the Reformists.

His nephew, Mathews, a deacon and student in a CMS institution in Madras, went to the Patriarch of Antioch and lived there for two years, returning to Travancore with documents ascribing to him the status of Metropolitan of Malankara. Mathews Athanasius, being related to Abraham Malpan, was considered by many to be a heretic. In 1846, in response to protests by the Syrian Christians against his conduct, the Patriarch sent a Syrian prelate, Mar Kurilos. The latter brought with him the Staticon or document which stated his title and powers-to-be as those of the Metropolitan of Malabar. A royal proclamation, however, was made in favour of Mar Athanasius by the Travancore Government, doubting the authenticity of Mar Kurilos's credentials.

The conflict in the Syrian Christian Church continued; the people remained divided in their loyalties. Finally, in 1863, the government stated that those who wished to follow the Syrian Mar Kurilos might do so but must build churches for themselves, leaving the existing churches and properties in the possession of Mar Athanasius. In 1865, a young priest of the conservative party was sent to the Patriarch and returned in 1866 as Mar Joseph Dionysius, armed with a Staticon appointing him Metropolitan. Then began a long struggle for ecclesiastical authority between him and Mar Athanasius, one the head of the conservative party and the other of the reformist party in the Church. It is this confrontation which was pursued in the Royal Court of Final Appeal, Case No. III of 1061 (1886).

Witness Depositions: Royal Court of Final Appeal 1879–89

The Law Courts Cases   The move the Syrian Christians made to take their ecclesiastical differences to the law courts is one that established the movement of a community from one based on resemblances to one based on differences.[32] The Syrians resorted to the secular court with the advent of a major dispute over ecclesiastical power and temporal rights. Earlier incidences of differences are recorded in the available literature but these were settled by local councils and finally by the Synod.[33] Representatives of churches were called, and decisions taken on all matters which affected the parishioners or *pallikar*. With the reform movement of the 1830s and the problems of power it posed, the balance of authority was constantly shifting. Legitimacy depended at one level on the one who had the support of the Travancore raja and the British Resident. At another level, the shifting locus of power centred on the number of parishes (and parishioners) the *metran* had in support of his claim. (One of the questions asked by the court was 'Do you consent to the decree being passed in favour of majority?')

While the Reformists had the support of the institutions of authority (the raja and the Resident), the number of churches on the side of the Bishop of the Conservatives was greater. The necessity to go to the law courts lay in the breakdown of traditional bonds and the inability of custom to regulate conflict. Many of the tensions were those generated by a society in change; the gap between Reformists and Conservatives was almost definitely brought about by the instruments of change that had come with the British—education and the printing press—leading to changes in the concept of the eucharistic worship, and hence to the place and function of the priest.

The court was to decide several matters for the Conservatives and the Reformists: the legitimacy of the indigenous throne of Thomas the Apostle *vis-à-vis* the See of Peter in Antioch; consequently, the place of the Metropolitan of Malankara versus the Patriarch of Antioch; and, finally, the rights to church property depending upon the staking of legitimacy.

Legitimacy could no longer be conferred by sacred law alone. All kinds of irregularities were posed. One of these was the error in the consecration of the Reformist Metropolitan, which he himself denied, saying that he held his position in terms of sacred office which could not be taken away as if he were a 'mere employee'. The appeal to the courts would emphasize a society that was veering toward the secular, toward the institutional specialization of roles, the differentiation of function and the use of restitutive law.[34]

It is important to examine the issues that came up before the court since they endlessly and inconclusively resurfaced in the generations that followed.[35] Many of the Christians of Puthenangadi today recall this turbulent period as being the genesis of their present troubles. The followers of Athanasius, the Reformists, lost the court case but the problems that had presented themselves through this first confrontation were to remain with the *Puthencoor* Syrian Christians and remain unresolved.

The Symbols of Legitimacy: Law Court Depositions 1879   In 1879, the Conservatives and the Reformists went to court about rights over certain properties. These holdings were important not merely in terms of their material worth but also as symbols of legitimacy. While the immovables included land, a seminary, a church with its attendant kitchen, granary and boat house, the movable property included the famous 3000 *poovarahan* (star pagodas) which were to haunt the litigants for generations after. This was the chief symbol of legitimacy, the mark of the true heir to the throne of ecclesiastic power over the Syrian Christians of Kerala. Besides these, the list included boats, a printing press, cauldrons, lamps, spitoons, a palanquin, jugs and a blackwood bed. There were items of personal property such as gold crosses set with rubies and emeralds, a mitre of red velvet with designs made of gold, a silver staff with a serpent hood.[36] Each of these objects marked the special status of the Metropolitan and were quite clearly necessary adjuncts to winning the title and rights of the Metropolitan of the Malabar Syrian Christians.

The problem of disputes over the control of the Syrian Christians was not new. In court the rival bishops faced each other with accusations that were highly personal and derogatory. Thomas Athanasius, the leader of the Reformists, declared his rival Mar Dionysius to be involved in debt and unfit to be accorded the dignity of Metropolitan, 'his conduct being contrary to the ordinance of religion and custom and being also one physically defective'.[37] Athanasius claimed that the Kerala Christians, of whom he was the legitimate head, were independent of the control of the Patriarch of Antioch. According to him, Thomas the Apostle founded the See of Malankara (Kerala), while the Apostle St Peter established that of the Patriarch, the See of Antioch. 'Both of them had equal authority and were respectively independent'.[38] Athanasius said in court:

Foreigners and others have at different times come forward and carried on intrigues with a view to obtaining these rights to possession and management, etc. but the successive Metropolitans have from time to time withstood and baffled these intrigues.[39]

He defended his rights as Metropolitan of the Syrian Christians saying,

The sacraments of the church are performed with certain specially sanctioned prayers, and a position thus vested, and the right of possession derived by virtue of a religious office cannot be divested or reinvested as that of a mere employee.[40]

The weakness of Thomas Athanasius's position lay in the fact that his predecessor Mathews Athanasius had been ordained by the Patriarch of Antioch, and had used this as his seal of legitimacy to gain control over the *Puthencoor* Syrian Christians. Thomas Athanasius was forced to explain this anomaly to the court, and did so by expressing the relationship with Antioch as accidental and unpremeditated:

> The late Athanasius was consecrated as *metran* (bishop) by a Patriarch of Mesopotamia. I am not sure whether the Patriarch of Antioch and the Patriarch of Mesopotamia are one and the same person. The late Athanasius was studying at Madras as deacon. On the completion of his studies he travelled with a view to see Jerusalem and other places. On his way, he visited Besanagiri and saw the Patriarch. The Patriarch was very pleased. He detained him there and asked him to receive consecration as *metran*.[41]

This narrative version expresses a vagueness of detail, a confusion as to whether the Patriarch of Antioch and Mesopotamia were one and the same, leading the listener to believe that it was a fortuitous set of circumstances which led to the ordainment of Mar Athanasius as Metropolitan of the Syrian Christians of Malabar. Answers to the same kinds of questions elicit different responses; the version offered by the witnesses of the rival conservative party is more definitive:

> It is from Antioch that Mar Athanasius received consecration. At that time Mar Athanasius was a deacon. He went to the Patriarch and informed him that he was a *kattanar* (priest), that he was sent by the people and that he should be made a *metran*. The Patriarch, thinking that a foreigner would not deceive him by telling a lie, consecrated and sent him...It was while Athanasius was studying at Madras in the school of the Church Mission Society that he went. He was sent away because of his wicked deeds. It was in 1028 [1843] that he came back and was consecrated. He was not able to rule the *sabha* between 1018 and 1028 [1843–53] because the Syrians of Malabar complained to the Patriarch of Antioch as to how it was possible that one who was turned out of the *sabha* while a deacon and who, therefore, joining the Anglican Church was dismissed from there also for bad conduct, managed to return as consecrated at Antioch; and that even if he was consecrated such a heretic cannot be acknowledged.[42]

In response to complaints by the Syrian Christians of Malabar, the Patriarch, refusing to acknowledge the returned prelate Athanasius, sent one of his own prelates, Joachim Kurilos, in 1846. One of the witnesses belonging to the conservative party described this difficult period.

> I think it was from 1022 [1847] that Kurilos began to govern the church. Kurilos ruled without doing anything repugnant to the faith, while Athanasius ruled as he liked. Athanasius exercised his authority wherever he could without obeying the Patriarch's bill of excommunication, on the strength of the Royal Proclamation, issued by the Travancore Sirkar in 1028 [1853] and on account of the support of the officials . . . I was not under Athanasius to any extent. Myself and some others like me, of the Parish of Cherya Palli, Kottayam, were under another *metran*. There were also some in that parish who were under Athanasius. Kurilos and Athanasius were ruling separately.[43]

Chakko Chandapilla Cattanar, a leading Reformist, was a priest at the Kottayam Cherya Palli. His review of the incidents that occurred during this period was a representation of the official view of the Reformists:

> Before 1030 [1855] the Patriarch had sent a *metran* called Kurilos to Malankara. That *metran* joining some who had been excommunicated as defaulters from the Syrian Church of Malankara, entered our Syrian churches and caused disturbances. The Metropolitan and the people of Malankara complained to the Travancore Government about it. Thereupon, a circular order was issued in 1038 [1863] that who those were not willing to be under the *metran* of Malankara should build separate churches for themselves and that if they have any claim to any of the churches, under the *metran*, they should settle the matter by a Civil Suit.[44]

The Relation between Antioch and the Syrian Christians   Since the central issue in the courts concerned the relation between Antioch and Malankara, Athanasius's party underplayed this connection, expressing confusion about the geographical location of Antioch, or even as to who had consecrated Mathews Athanasius. Moreover, while the

Conservatives asked Antioch to settle their differences, the Reformists turned to the Travancore Government. Most interesting, however, are the differences in the depositions about the geographical and ecclesiastical position of Antioch.

The successor of Mathews Athanasius, Mar Thomas Athanasius said in court:

> The late Athanasius was consecrated as *metran* by a Patriarch of Mesopotamia. I am not sure whether the Patriarch of Antioch and the Patriarch of Mesopotamia are one and the same person.[45]

Chandapilla Kattanar the Reformist priest expressed the same vagueness of detail:

> What he has told me is that he (Athanasius) was consecrated at Besanaharim by the Patriarch of that place. But he has not told me whether the place called Besanaharim is near or far from Antioch.[46]

The deposition of Thommi Kurien of the Thekkaethallakal family in Puthenangadi, on behalf of the Conservatives, was more definite, articulating the privileges and duties held by the Patriarch of Antioch in relation to the Syrian Christians:

> It was at Antioch itself that the Patriarch of Antioch lived before. As that place was ruined, it is at a place called Merdeen that he resides now. It was approximately about some five hundred years ago that the See of Merdeen was founded. The powers of the Patriarch over the church of Malankara are—to appoint *metran*s, to dismiss them if they are found guilty, and to give instructions to the Syrians on spiritual affairs through letters. Besides these, the Patriarch has a right over the properties of the church. The Patriarch has the power to deal with the churches and the seminary and the properties belonging thereto.[47]

The Reformists denied this ecclesiastical authority over them by the Patriarch of Antioch. Chandapilla Kattanar flatly stated:

> The *metran*s of Malankara have never acknowledged the supremacy of the *metran*s sent by the Patriarch of Antioch or of the Patriarchs themselves.[48]

The court called upon the brother of Kurilos, the Antiochene
Prelate sent by the Patriarch for clarification. Malki Makkuthisa
Gabriel said:

> I was born in the country called Turabdien. It was in 1022
> [1847] that I came to Malabar. It was with my elder brother,
> Mar Kurilos Metropolitan, that I came here.

> It was at the place called Kurkmadayara, where the throne of
> Antioch is now established, that Kurilos Bawa was staying before
> coming to Malabar. The Patriarch of Antioch is the chief resid-
> ent of Kurkmadayara. Whoever be the Patriarch that resides
> there, he is the Syrian Patriarch of Antioch. If we start now from
> here we can reach Merdeen in two to two-and-a-half months.
> Besanagari is a place between the two rivers Deelertue and
> Euphrates. What is called Kurkmadayara is in the country be-
> tween the two rivers.[49]

Kurilos's brother further described the close relations as he perceived them between the Patriarch of Antioch and the Syrian Christians
of Malankara:

> I have seen letters and complaints come from Malabar while I
> was staying at Kurkmadayara. I have read the books in which
> the Patriarchs have noted down the events of the day. They
> contain entries as to several *metran*s having been sent to
> Malabar.[50]

Kurilos brought with him the sacred anointing oil called *muron*
made by the Patriarch, for which ritual service the Syrian Christians
were dependent, repaying him with *rassisa*, a kind of tax. Ritual
prestations from the Patriarch to the Syrian Christians, according to
the conservative party, included not merely *muron*,

> For when Athanasius was sent out consecrated book, staff, cross
> and the dress called *kappa* (cope) were given to him.[51]

Kurilos died in 1874. In 1875, as matters grew out of hand, the
Patriarch Peter, at the request of Mar Dionysius, came to Malankara.[52]
Koratha Kewarithu, a farmer, said in court:

It was from the time of the arrival of the Patriarch that the congregation divided into two parties.[53]

The Synod of 1876   The Patriarch Peter convened a synod at Mulanthuruthy where he formalized the relationship of Malankara with the Patriarchal See. This act was an attempt to make concrete a hitherto unclear relationship. The Malankara See was to have the same relation to the Patriarch as a diocese in Syria, and each parish was to execute a registered deed of complete submission to him. The Mulanthuruthy Synod was to set a seal on the relation of Malankara Christians to Antioch, the effect of which is to be seen in their society more than a hundred years later. A witness was to describe that momentous event in court:

> I had gone to Mulanthuruthy about 1051 [1876]. It was according to an order from the Patriarch. It required that all the *pallikar* (church people or parishioners) of Malankara should in obedience to the order assemble at Mulanthuruthy. Members of about one hundred churches had come there. It was said in that order that it was with a view to settling the disputes and quarrels that were prevalent in all churches and to set matters right that the meeting was called. The *pallikar* met and passed resolutions as to future conduct. It was resolved that a committee should be appointed, that schools should be opened, that funds should be collected to take civil action for recovering the seminary and property, and that an account should be kept of the receipts in churches in connection with burials, marriages, etc. The next day after I went there, such a committee was appointed.[54]

Besides the 'heretical' practices of the Reformists (alteration of prayers—particularly, omission of those addressed to Mary and the saints, and for the dead; the marriage of priests), there was also the matter of faulty ordainment resulting in ecclesiastical authority which was illegitimate. It was on these grounds that the conservative party led by Mar Dionysius took the Reformists to court.

The reformist party lost the case, the judgement of the Royal Court of Final Appeal of 1889 being that the Patriarch of Antioch was head of the Church in Malabar and that consecration by him was essential for the Metropolitan.[55] The conservative party under Mar Dionysius was in full control of the temporal properties of the church, and was recognized as the victorious and legitimate church.

Continuing Conflicts: The Bifurcation of the Conservatives   However, the relationship of the Kerala Syrian Christians to Antioch continued to be problematic. The history of this period is difficult and unfixed, and only brief lines are offered here. Official histories, divided about the truth, are unacceptable, and academic historians have been wary of handling this period.

In 1909 a Patriarch, Abdallah, visited Malankara and demanded complete obedience from the Metropolitan of the Syrian Christians. The church was again divided into two, those following the indigenous Malankara or Kerala *metran*, and those loyal to the Patriarch of Antioch, Mar Abdallah.

At that time there was also living a 'deposed' Patriarch, Mar Abdel-Messih, who, according to informants, had been removed from office by the Turkish Government of Damascus either for political intrigue or because of his alleged lunacy.

The Malankara *metran*, Dionysius VI, invited this ex-Patriarch, who established a Catholicate or semi-autonomous See in Malabar in 1912. Abdel-Messih also annulled the excommunication of the *metran* that had been laid down by the Patriarch of Antioch. With the establishment of a Catholicate in Malabar the autonomy of the Indian Church was established. The Kerala Syrian Christians had now been given the right to consecrate their own Holy Chrism (*muron*) and their own Catholicos, the Patriarch having only purely ritual powers. However, disputes were to arise. Was an 'ex-Patriarch' capable of establishing a Catholicate or removing the stigma of excommunication?

The Kerala Jacobite Orthodox Christians were now clearly and vociferously divided into two factions: the Syrian Jacobites (also called the *Bawa Katshi*) loyal to the Patriarch of Antioch, and the Syrian Orthodox (*Metran Katshi*) who followed the *metran* or, in his place, the Indian Catholicos. For many decades after, they were in the law courts, constantly in conflict with each other, like brothers in a house divided.

Oral Accounts: 1981–2

Popular Versions of History   While the analysis of the relation between past and present may have been difficult in societies without written records of the past, it becomes crucial in societies which have a long and literate historical tradition. This is very evident in the oral narratives of contemporary Christians, who have learnt almost by rote entire sections of church history in their attempt to keep abreast with the conflicts in the church. Folk or popular forms of historical consciousness constantly expose and threaten the reifing structures of official ideology and official history as presented by ecclesiasts. The people's narratives are parallel formations to the versions offered by the ecclesiasts and the church. The term *Attagsgeschichte*—the history of everyday life—has been used to explain what 'people's history' stands for.[56]

Silences, contradictions and hesitations in the narrative material are important because they express the complexities of human experience and consciousness.[57] I have argued here that memory cannot constitute pure reality but is a refraction of event and personal experience, of the effects of dominant ideology and the dialectic between the conscious and the unconscious.[58] The advantage of people's history lies in the fact that we are provided with a different kind of knowledge which affords us a much more immediate sense of the past. We escape some of the deficiencies of documentary record, we receive evidence which is open-ended, which is available nowhere else but in the memory of our informant.[59]

It is true that the narratives express the play between the questioner and the informant and are articulated in terms of this relationship. But this is one of the peculiarities of both *verstehen* generally and the oral history method in particular. The 'omniscient narrator' of traditional historiography is here replaced by an active narrative style in which an entirely 'new narrative attitude' emerges, where the telling of the story is now part of the story being told.[60]

The dialectic between past and present has been expressed most vividly by Marc Bloch. According to him, the present can only be understood with reference to the past, for the continuity of civilization depends upon those transfers of thought made possible by the function of the written word or the relation between alternate generations.[61] This collaboration between the oral traditions of a society, handed down from generation to generation, and the written histories and records form the substance of my data. Together they serve to produce a certain historical consciousness which is articulated in accounts to the ethnographer.

What I am dealing with in the present section is clearly not History in Collingwood's sense of the term, but those accounts which perceive themselves to be 'as if' History.[62] It is also what Bloch called historical evidence, since anything that men do may constitute the basis of data.[63]

The data expresses the relationship between past and present as crucial to informants. Witnesses to the present, they rely heavily on the written word to corroborate not only what they see but also what they have been told. Distortions are an accepted part of this testimony, but then as we well know, 'there is no reliable witness in the absolute sense'.[64]

What I attempt to construct is not so much a chronology as the state of a society in the present, and as perceived by those who constitute it. This perception involves the capturing of a society's past in oral narratives—chronological, seemingly objective, and undeniably subjective. Memory is externalized as a social fact and expressed in writing and in speech. Biography, autobiography, genealogy and some types of locodescription may not be History; but they take the form and function of History. Memory articulated in the oral accounts reviewing the past reflects the play of time, space, persons and events as perceived by the informant. It is this matrix of variables which offers differing accounts. Historical consciousness is not merely .expressive of chronology but of the relations that emerge out of these varying and substantial combinations.

Time   Time expresses both continuity and change.[65] For the Syrian Christian, collective memory goes back to the birth of Christ and, hence, to the coming of the apostle Thomas in AD 52 to the coasts of Malabar. These are historically 'true' events. Dating 'true' events brings them closer to the paradigms of history. The oral traditions (*Margam Kalli Pattu, Thomas Ramban Pattu*) attempt such a historicization.[66] The academic historian would say that there is no conclusive proof that Thomas came to Malabar but Syrian Christians have preferred to rely on the traditions handed down from generation to generation, and crystallized into the collective memory of a community. The time continuum for the Syrian Christian in a historical (not a theological) perspective is marked off from the coming of St Thomas to the town of Muziris in the first century AD.[67]

However, with the most recent cleavage in the Malankara Church, what was once perceived as 'true' in the sense of historical usage by all Syrian Christians is now viewed self-consciously as 'myth' by one section of them. Those who wish to express affiliation to the Patriarch of Antioch and to the 'Throne of Peter' oppose themselves to the Catholicos of India and the indigenous 'Throne of Thomas'. For the Catholicos's followers (the *Metran Katshi*), the coming of Thomas to

Malabar must take on more than ever the colour of history, for the purpose of establishing ecclesiastical legitimacy. For the Patriarch's people (the *Bawa Katshi*), what was once accepted as 'true', for it was what one's forefathers had said, must now be put to the test of objective academic history. As one informant said, 'There is no proof that Thomas came to Malabar, while everyone knows that Peter was given the keys, and is the head of the Church'.

Proof then becomes the central concern and the marker dividing history from myth and legend. Yet the same Christian who asks for proof of the Thomas tale while talking of the ecclesiastical authority of Peter will say proudly of himself that he belongs to those who are descendants of the brahmin converts of St Thomas. What is 'not history' of any kind in one context, is sacred history in another context. The same tale is 'true' at one level and 'not true' at another, for the same person. For another, it is true both at the ecclesiastical and biographical level. The tale's historical character is further underlined by the charting out of the sea route that Thomas could have taken, and the statement of historical facticity that travellers from the West knew of favourable winds to India in AD 47. Such an informant would make the historicity of Thomas more credible by adding that Thomas preached in China too. The possibility that the tale of Thomas's arrival in Malabar has no truth to it does not decrease its function as a marker. It is still the source and the beginning of Syrian Christian identity. At no point will any Christian say that Thomas did not come. Those who suspect this tradition for ecclesiastical reasons say, 'Our traditions say that Thomas converted our ancestors who were brahmins but this is not adequate for establishing an ecclesiastical throne in his name here'.

The perception of the past reflects homogeneity till the sixteenth century after which the effects of Portuguese ritual colonization can be seen. Needless to say, a shared historical consciousness is also expressed in the idea of community identity. Often one hears statements like 'Till the Portuguese came, we were one community'.

Cleavages create differing interpretations of events; fission creates its own genealogies. Differing histories are expressed from the point of cleavage and always from the viewpoint of the subject. Discrepancies, therefore, must also be viewed from this perspective.

With Portuguese ritual superordination (which achieved its full crystallization in 1599 and ended in 1653), there came, as we saw, the first split of the Syrian Christians into those who threw off the Roman cloak, reverting to the Syrian liturgical rite, and those who preferred to remain within its shelter. With the split came the formation of a new historical consciousness, growing out of their differing historical ecclesiastical experiences. The level of historical consciousness is extremely high in this community as compared to other Christian denominations, perhaps as a consequence of their continuing to be in a state of crises. From now on, the two denominations would have different trajectories, rarely meeting in ecclesiastical terms, culturally similar but separated by endogamy.

A second cleavage occurred in the nineteenth century, dividing the *Puthencoor* Syrians into the Anglican Syrians, Mar Thoma or the Reformist Church, and the Conservative Jacobites. The Jacobites split once more in the early twentieth century into the Orthodox Syrians and the Jacobite Syrians. (*See diagram on p. 12.*)

Yet again, the Syrian Christians are capable of fusion once a common antagonist has been identified.[68] So Orthodox Syrians and Jacobite Syrians will unite as one unit (Yakoba) when confronted with the Mar Thoma, and, at another level, all *Puthencoor* Syrians may submerge their differences in opposition to the Romo-Syrians.

While time is historically perceived in this context and is therefore linear and irreversible, it constantly confronts the complexities of sacred time. For the Syrian Christian, Adam and Eve may be an origin myth of the birth of the cosmos, of which men are a part. But sacred histories are of varying orders. Adam and Eve and the birth of the universe are read symbolically by the people. The life of Christ is, however, of a different order altogether. Here, sacred time and historical time shade into each other, resulting in a particular kind of temporal perception. Again, the Apocalypse projects such a dual nature. Historical time is seen to be a continuum, but the continuum has an end, and towards that end all mankind must move.

This idea of the Apocalypse as the 'end of time' causes the Syrian Christian to pause and survey his actions in the light of what is to be. Events occur not merely in a particular temporal situation but have within them the potency of retrospection in another time—the time of the Christian Judgement. Each act then is accountable. Therefore, the perception of history and the events that constitute history constantly take on a moral tone.

Space   Time, as history concretized in event, occurs in some fixed place. Places on the neighbourhood map act as mnemonics to the

Syrian Christian and articulate indirectly the fact that certain events once took place.

The neighbourhood churches represent the existence of conflict because each is a symbol of specific ecclesiastical affiliation. Puthenangadi, in an area of half a square kilometre, has three churches, while two churches lie across the main road in Pazheangadi. Cherya Palli belongs to the Catholicos's party, as do Kurisu Palli and Puthan Palli, which are chapels. Simhasana Palli belongs to the Patriarch's party, and Pazhanthe Palli belongs to the Mar Thoma. A sixth church, Valiya Palli, lies a kilometre away from Puthenangadi, and belongs to the Canaanites.[69]

According to one old woman, 'the churches are spawned of quarrels'. The narratives of the people express the manner in which the churches came into existence, and every account is a description of ecclesiastical conflict. Each church, then, calls to the informant's mind a particular episode in the long history of the ecclesiastical feud.

The house or *taravat* similarly serves as a sign in the deciphering of 'tracks'. A *taravat* is associated with a house-name, the very pronouncement of which calls forth certain historical associations. Thus a particular *taravat* is said to have hosted the famous Konat Malpan (a key figure in the early twentieth century phase of the feud), and out of this hospitality came- the marriage of one of his daughters into a Puthenangadi household. Biography and history are woven closely together in these narratives, especially when a place is of both private and public significance. Genealogies play an important role here, for a house is a concrete symbol, embodying a particular genealogical moment. Houses are associated with specific families, and express the relation between past and present.

The neighbourhood, consisting of houses and churches, must itself be read off as a place of historical interest.[70] Perhaps the most important feature of topography articulating a history is the idea that local history is important and must be written. Puthenangadi has its own local historian, Kurisumootil Lukose, who has published in Malayalam a history of Puthenangadi, based on oral accounts and family genealogies.[71]

A place is a mnemonic, expressing the continuity and linearity of historical time. It is an episode to which architectural forms have given a permanence. It offers itself as a testimony that must be encoded in narrative, where the gap between present and past is bridged, and 'where past thought is allowed to reawaken itself in the present'.[72] It has the ability to generate or to house innumerable events and historical associations. Houses and churches thus carry within them a variety of historically significant symbols, each expressing different moments of its past.

Architectural styles, graveyards, portraits of saints and bishops, hanging lamps and carvings, everything expresses a period peculiar to it, and accretions are as noticeable as exclusions. For example, the wall paintings in the nave in both Cherya Palli and Kurisu Palli are unusual and unique, signifying their age. However, Simhasana Palli, built in this century, is bare of these and is merely lime washed. It has neither wooden carvings nor stone embossed figures as Cherya Palli does. All these details and many others, are landmarks whose meanings are known to the people, expressed in their narratives to the ethnographer, and also passed on to their children and grandchildren.

Similarly, specific festivals commemorate historical incidents, reliving events of the past in the places where they occurred. The celebration of certain festivals relive historical events in the context of a sacred idiom. Feast days of certain *metranmar* (bishops) bring into prominence the part that they played in the history of the church. Eucharist is celebrated in their honour, and such days are called *Orma divasam* or commemoration days. Processions are taken out in their names, pilgrims gather to pay homage, and food is served to all those who have gathered in the church.

Characteristically, the feasts celebrating the commemoration day of the *metranmar* are occasions of importance to one party or the other, depending on which side the *metran* belonged. On these occasions the neighbourhood is divided according to its ecclesiastical affiliation. While one side will celebrate Eucharist, carry out its processions, host visiting pilgrims, organize the food for the feast, the other side remains aloof, dissociating itself from all ceremonial activities, seemingly amnesiacal about the person and event commemorated. It is, after all, an episode re-enacted from the history of the 'other' side. While from one point of view the person remembered is a saint, from the other he is a betrayer and a traitor.

Character   The concept of historical character is important in analysis as it locates events in terms of a particular actor. Local versions of history are always a complex blend of autobiography, biography and the general history of the community. Every person playing an important role in the ecclesiastical domain is viewed not merely

objectively in his role as ecclesiast, but also subjectively, as an individual related by blood or marriage either to oneself or to some
acquaintance or friend whose life history expresses certain vulnerabilities
of character, and certain strengths. Role and person, therefore, are
closely inter-related in these narratives.

The *metranmar* are usually the most important figures in the public
eye. In the past, as today, they acted as representatives of the Syrian
Christian, and appeared frequently on public platforms. They represent the official viewpoint of the *sabha* which all faithful laymen must
accept as the truth. The *metran* represents the unity of the believers,
and is treated as a symbol by the people; their attitude is one usually
marked by veneration and awe, because the *metranmar*, as lords of the
church, are not only holders of sacerdotal but also of temporal (secular)
power. Consequently, they are seen to be men of knowledge, not only
theological, but also, of necessity, historical and litigational. By their
dress and ornament, they are marked apart from the laity and other
ecclesiasts.

The law court cases which the divided *Puthencoor* Jacobite Church
has been plunged into for several generations are a battle over sacerdotal
and temporal properties of the Syrian Christians. In so much as it is a
dispute over ecclesiastical supremacy, one may say that the issues relate to
the sacred ideas of Syrian Christians, since what is being questioned is the
place and authority of the apostles and their successors. These are
necessarily theological questions. But when these issues lead to disputes
over the land and properties of the church, the problem is temporal, as
the law court depositions clearly express. The list indicating the
property in dispute in the earliest of the law court proceedings contains
many personal items and, clearly, as symbols, these objects were as
important to the prelates as holders of power as was the title of
ecclesiastical head. The symbols supported their claim and were essential as the marks of legitimacy by which they were recognized by the
laity. The control over churches (and church property) has been of
central significance in the law court cases because these embody the
parish and its constituents, over which the *metranmar* exercised
power. The problem of legitimacy is central here. The *metranmar* are
legitimate according to the dictates of secular or sacred criteria, and
the people may choose either or both to support the claims to power
of the bishops.

The church quarrel dividing the Jacobite–Orthodox Syrians into the
Jacobite Syrians and Orthodox Syrians expresses two opposing views

of history. Each of these views is seen to be the truth by its defendants, and the versions offered by the other group are thought to be lies (*nonna*). The *metranmar*, as key players in the ecclesiastical drama, are the chief 'tellers of the truth'; they are also the official chroniclers of the people. The players are thus simultaneously witnesses and narrators, and in the multi-dimensionality of their role lies their importance. They are the historians of their own movement. What is interesting perhaps is that the histories are written as if by academic historians but the biases evident are offered as the only possible rendering of the truth. Here, sources are important in claiming legitimacy but they are not treated as evidence in the manner an academic historian would.[73]

The official historian's main function is to create legitimacy for a particular group. He must offer in the form of history what to him and his followers is the truth. Where dogma loses strength, history must fill its place. The official historian, usually an ecclesiast (priest or *metran*) or someone close to ecclesiasts, is thus given the responsibility of creating a particular historical consciousness. For the Syrian Christian, increasingly exposed to secular ideas, history and law are important organs of legitimacy, and to these the official historians take recourse in expounding what were once primarily theological issues. The acceptability of 'scissors and paste' history, written to convince the laity of a particular ecclesiastical position, lies in its posing as objective history. Sources culled to substantiate claims lend it an academic air, and many of these essays begin with a scholastic question such as 'What is meant by the term Patriarch?' To the people, these are written by 'learned men' and when the historian is a monk, the credibility of the history is far greater than if he were lay. While official histories serve to articulate the claims of the prelates, they derive their own legitimacy from having been written by the sacred heads of the church, and thus the relation between the two is a dialectical one. The newspaper is the most important medium for the transmission of such official accounts, and it too reflects the idiom of the division in the church. Each party has its own mouthpiece, and the followers of each subscribe only to its own newspaper, treating the writings of the other faction as pure fiction.

The *metranmar*, then, are the most important characters in the drama of the ecclesiastical feud. While being the active agents of history, they also double as its narrators, both of the past and the immediate present. Constantly in the public eye, they are like collective representations. They are the repositories of sacred tradition, they provide the definitions of what is true and what is false, they lay down the codes of conduct for the Syrian Christians.

But every Syrian Christian, even if comparatively passive, sees himself as an agent of history; he must take sides, must belong to either the Catholicos or the Patriarch. Every individual is part of the historical process even though his actions and perceptions may not be incorporated into the written histories of academics or ecclesiasts.[74]

Syrian Christians are well aware of this. A circular brought out at the time of the Patriarch of Antioch's visit in February 1982 said: 'What will Christ say to us on Judgement Day about our quarrels?' Yet the unity of the truth must be affirmed, and the legitimacy of the one truth is established by the ecclesiasts. The Christians themselves are puzzled by the nature of the true. An informant said:

You may say there are different sides to it and that you want to look at both. There can be no two truths, that much is my belief, but I shall tell you the truth as I know it.

Through the hegemonic influence of the written and the spoken word, the ecclesiasts affirm on each side the 'unity of the truth' as affirmed by them. In moments forgetful of their role as representatives of one ecclesiastical position against another, Syrian Christians are critical of the ecclesiasts. But the necessity to support a clerical position lies in the nature of denominational identity. The Christians of the neighbourhood are thus caught in the double bind of being both part of the historical process as well as being its objective viewers, capable of exegesis.

The categories of time, space and character are encapsulated in the perception of events as articulated in the narratives to the ethnographer. Further, people's history, in my analysis, must be a reconstruction, borrowing elements from the 'academic' and 'official' versions of the general history of the community, and weaving into it elements which are local, genealogical and biographical. It is a narrative which embodies within it those levels of social structure that are part of its daily life—the Church (both at the level of association and the local church or *sabha* and *palli*), the neighbourhood with its complex kinship and friendship network, and the house (*taravat*) which includes associations at the wider kinship level.

The relation between units of social structure and forms of historical consciousness coincide in some ways. General history refers to the narratives about the Syrian Christian community, its past, its ecclesiastical developments, and so on. It tends to consist of, for the most part, narratives about the church (*sabha* or association). Local history, while incorporating elements of general history, tends to describe neighbourhood life and its concerns. Genealogy is a form of historical consciousness that makes the link between family histories and church history. Biography, in turn, articulates most vividly the relation between individual Christians and the ways in which church quarrels affect their lives.

Moreover, in the context of the neighbourhood, the physical, spatial and symbolic geography of house and church remain constant units at the level of particular description. This is because narration and narrators are to be seen here more in the context of dramatic enactment than of narrative as merely a story told in the folktale sense of the word. Necessarily, then, neighbourhood, church and house, in their physical and architectural dimensions, are like stage props which the narrators and actors live with and in, and take for granted as essential accessories of those parts which they narrate or play, but which have in themselves an essential symbolic significance.

The importance of informants' accounts lies in the relations they establish between past and present; while remembering the past, it is the nature of present events that structures what they remember and what they suppress. The category of remembrance is, therefore, a problematic one—what needs to be emphasized here is that remembrance too is a social fact, constrained by official ideologies and diversities of interpretations born of uncertain situations.

Therefore, variations in narrative are themselves collective expressions of a divided society and church, where the very nature of truth is constantly shifting. I offer here some variations in narrative that express the nature of neighbourhood relations in terms of the ecclesiastical feud.

Ecclesiastical Feuds and Neighbourhood Relations Predominantly Yakoba (a generic term), the Syrian Christians of Puthenangadi are divided according to their ecclesiastical differences into two factions: those who are loyal to the patriarch of Antioch or the Syrian Jacobites (they are called the *Bawa Katshi* or Patriarch's party), and those who owe allegiance to the Indian Catholicos, the Syrian Orthodox (*Metran Katshi*). The relationship between members of the two different groups when neighbours is tinctured by some embarassment and disagreement. However, they constantly say, 'There is no difference in culture or belief. We are one. The difference between us is the allegiance we owe to separate heads'. Quarrels in Puthenangadi over the 'rightness' of one's affiliation take place frequently over neighbours' walls, taking predictable directions.

Though many people cover up the issue of the differing allegiances by saying that there is no ritual or cultural difference between the two, others say:

> You cannot use the overall term Yakoba to describe us any longer. We are either Syrian Orthodox or Syrian Jacobites.

The question of identity is problematic, and the more marked the sense of dermarction, the more definite the informant's loyalty and views. There is no way one can tell the difference between the two groups by looking at them. In their manner of dress and ornament they are identical, as in their customs and way of life.

Before Abraham Malpan and the CMS missionaries brought the Reform Movement with its Protestant overtones into the Syrian Church, the Syrian Christians, as we saw, were divided into the Romo-Catholic Syrians (or the *Pazhecoor*, consisting of those following the Latin liturgy) and those called the Jacobites (the *Puthencoor*), following the Antiochene rite. The Reform Movement which gathered strength in the first part of the nineteenth century was an attempt to shed all ritual elements which seemed 'superstitious' such as prayers mediated through saints and the Virgin, ostentatious feast days and prayers for the dead. Concerted effort was made to promote an interpretation that allowed for a more personal and direct approach to God, through Christ as the sole mediator.

The differences between the two groups resulted in conflict so severe that the matter was taken to the law courts, where the separation of the Reformists from the Jacobite Church was legally confirmed, church property partitioned, and the Mar Thoma group formally opted out of the church in 1889. But the issues raised by this earlier segmentation nevertheless remained unsettled, and soon the Jacobites were confronted with internal dissension, dividing the remaining members of the original Jacobite Church of the pre-reform period.

The Mar Thoma, followers of Abraham Malpan, had moved away over time so significantly from the practices of the Jacobite Church that the family resemblances with the mother church decreased. But the remaining Jacobites (who were to be divided in the twentieth century and renamed Orthodox Syrians and Jacobite Syrians), are culturally very alike. Their differences are born not so much out of religious differences (or differences in the principles of faith) but out of matters relating to ecclesiastical allegiance.

The nature of rifts and peace-making between the two halves of this church is extremely complicated. Informants, though able to keep up with general trends, important personages and certain specific events, tend, at times, to give chronologically irregular descriptions of the events. Most accounts of the quarrels are prefaced with the phrase *Kurrae varsangal numbil* (some years ago).

These quarrels and the divisions in loyalty are deeply regretted, particularly by the women of both parties. An old woman said:

It is we who feel the impact of these quarrels and divisions. It is for us that the quarrels between churches are difficult to accept. For every quarrel a new church is spawned: churches grow out of quarrels, not out of faith. At every corner we have a new church, and each of these is a living memory of bitterness.

Informants, however, constantly reiterate that the quarrel between the two parties, which can at times take pathological expressions, has little to do with the question of faith. The differences in loyalty and allegiance to the 'true' head of the church, the divisions of property and wealth, are the central issues.

Narratives often show a concern for detail, for names, dates, and a subjective identity with the characters and events of this chronicled past, which is asserted in statements like 'Then in 1653, we came together and revolted against Portuguese rule'.

Three narratives are presented here, describing the general history of the community. Their differences depend upon the social position of the narrator. The first narrative is one offered by a representative of the *metran*'s party, a man closely associated with ecclesiasts, and who, as a supporter, accompanied them to the courts. The second is presented by an ecclesiast whose household once belonged to the Catholicos's party but shifted away for the sake of certain ideals to the Syro-Malankara denomination. An interest in church history is typical of all those who are in any way connected with the quarrelling parties of the church. The third narrator is of the Patriarch's party. By the first narrator's account:

> The problem for our people began with the coming of the Portuguese. In 1599 the rulings of the Synod of Udeyemperoor were imposed on us. One hundred and eight churches in Malabar were summoned and forced to sign an agreement in which the most distressing clauses were, firstly, the introduction of the Latin Rite, and, secondly, the allegiance to the Pope. For 165 years the Papists ruled us, but we were allowed to keep the liturgical language as Chaldean Syriac. In 1656, the Koonen Kurisu episode occurred where, at Mattancheri, the Thomas Christians gathered and vowed not to be oppressed by the Romans. From Antioch came Gregorious, and Pakalomattam Thoma was ordained as Mar Thoma I. The old genealogy of the priestly lines was remembered which the *Latinkar* [literally, those who use the Latin liturgy] sought to destroy. However, Gregorious of Antioch insisted on changing the liturgical language from Chaldean Syriac to Maronite saying that this was the language in which Christ spoke. Out of the 108 churches, thirty-six under the leadership of Itti Thomas Kattanar complied with Gregorious in the change of ritual language. Seventy-two churches objected to the change and retained Chaldean. The thirty-six churches which came to Mar Gregorious were called the *Puthencoor* [new people] by local people and the seventy-two who remained with the Chaldean languages, into which the Roman liturgy had been translated, were called the *Pazhecoor* and are what we call the Romo-Syrian denomination.

In this narrative one notices a command over numerical data, which is possible only through frequent exposure to the source materials of either oral or literary history. It expresses the need to be 'objective' in the presentation of facts, and to present the formal narrative style of academic history. The one error in dates (the Koonen Kurisu episode occurs in this narrative in 1656 instead of 1653) suggests to me that it may be a slip rather than an actual error, arising from the earlier use of the number 165. Further, it is interesting to note that the informant provides information as to why the Romo-Syrians are called *Pazhecoor* (because they retained the older liturgical language), for this was a question which had puzzled me since, from the reading of academic history, it would seem that those who returned to the Eastern Church would be called the older. To continue:

> During the time of the sixth Mar Thoma, a Bishop from Antioch ordained a *metran* who was called Dionysius I. The Portuguese period had by now given way to the peaceful time of the Dutch and the constructive toleration of the British. Later, during the time of Cheppat Mar Dionysius, altercations occurred between the English CMS and the Syrians. The rift became acute, the majority joined with the Bishop Cheppat Mar Dionysius, a small group of Syrians went with the CMS.

The narrative offered here, in the formal language of academic history, now suddenly breaks into the subjective voice of the narrator.

> It so happened that the educated among the priests and the people of the Jacobites received the faith of the CMS. Abraham Malpan, the strongest among them, manipulated a scheme for getting ordination from Antioch. He sent his nephew at the age of twenty-one (a deacon ordained by Cheppat Mar Dionysius) to the Patriarch. At twenty-two, he was ordained a bishop. The person who sends a young boy to the bishop, and the person who ordains him are both rogues. Everything is based on a politics of power. From there it all begins.

In the following portion of the narrative one sees a familiarity with the events of the nineteenth century and, in fact, the voice of the twentieth century narrator resonates with that of the witnesses in the Royal Court of Final Appeal in the previous century.

> The young bishop, Mathews Mar Athanasius returned and said, 'I am the *Tirumeni* (Lord) who should rule the Malankara Church'. His rival, Cheppat Mar Dionysius, was an old man, less educated, but had the *firman*—the *rajagiya vellambaran*, and the application of Athanasius was rejected. Mar Kurilos was brought from Antioch to depose Cheppat Dionysius but ultimately Mathews Athanasius and Kurilos became rivals. Cheppat Dionysius became very old, and resigned. The Maharajah decided that no foreigner could be ordained a bishop, and so

Mathews Mar Athanasius became the only claimant. He told the court: 'I am ordained by the Patriarch of Antioch', and thus a precedent was created. But Mathews Athanasius himself violated this precedence by ordaining his uncle Abraham Malpan's son, Thomas, who was thus *not* ordained by Antioch. Kurilos meanwhile died, and Poolikootil Kattanar was sent to Antioch by the conservative party and returned as Joseph Mar Dionysius. He filed a suit against Thomas Mar Athanasius which the latter lost. The Jacobite–Reformed Party split came about during this time.

Then followed the time of the *vatti pannam* case, and he who got the *vatti pannam* was the rightful leader of the Syrians. Some way for the Orthodox Syrians to win had to be found. The result was the *Kalla* canon (false canons). Our forefathers came together and produced a document which was a forgery. In order to win the case they gave great weight to the Patriarchate and added a line which was attributed to the Nicene creed:[75] that Malankara did not have the right to ordain its own bishops and must depend on Antioch. This clause was later scraped off the palm leaf manuscript with a kitchen knife. After the case was won, one party wanted the right canon to be reinstated. This was the party which came to be called the Catholicos's party. It made a confession of its wrongdoings.

Interestingly enough, the subject closes a critical section of Syrian Christian history with the comment that 'It made a confession of its wrongdoings'. It would seem that, with repentance, there should automatically follow absolution.

In 1912, this party gained legitimacy for itself by bringing to India one Abdul-Messih, who had been deposed from the Patriarch of Antioch for political reasons. The reason for his overthrow had been given as insanity. The Catholicos's group believed that, even if deposed, the bishop once ordained still carried the blessings of his ordainment. He was brought to Malankara and he ordained Moorimattam Mar Ivanios in 1912 as the Catholicos of the East. Since then, the two parties have not left the law courts.

Narratives chronicling this period are significantly different in detail, expressing in each case the concerns of the narrator and the personalization of history. According to the second narrator:

When Mathews Athanasius returned from Merdeen his claim to
the headship of the Malankara Christians lay in that he had been
ordained by the Patriarch. This is an important fact because it is
this ecclesiastical supremacy attributed to the Patriarch that was
partly the cause for the tribulations that followed.

The next bit of the narrative shows that much of the material that
goes into the making of popular history is a blend of the recorded and
explicit dimensions of church history, and the stories that circulate
about what ecclesiastical authorities do—that, in fact, priests too may
be venal:

The other side (the conservative party) then sent their delegate
to the Patriarch. They won the case through what they now
concede are mischievous means. There was the *Kalla* (false)
canon for instance. Centuries ago, Mar Hebraeus compiled a
canon from all the sources existing. Of the four Christian centres,
Rome was to be head over Constantinople, Alexandria and
Antioch. Antioch being an important Christian centre with an
undeniably good geographical location, its Patriarch had the title
Patriarch of Antioch and all the East—this pertained to pro-
vinces east of the Euphrates. In order to convince the courts, the
Jacobites copied out the canon and added 'of all the East and
India'. They copied the entire canon and dropped the manuscript in tea to make it look old.
So they won the case. But look at all the troubles they are
having now. Nothing can come of falsehood. The *vatti pannam*
case is an example. Its worth is almost nothing now—I think it
was 3000 *fanam*s that was gifted by the English Resident—the
money keeps shifting between the two groups depending on
who last won the case. Most of the time it remains sealed behind
a stay order. It is a spiritually impoverished church and the
quarrels only prove it. Do not be fooled by external piety. If
there was true religious feeling, there would be more understanding on each side, more ability to come to terms. This
quarrel is only a symptom of the lack of true faith in Christ. After
all, what are they quarrelling about but money? Litigation,
enmity, anger—these are not the things that a church can survive
on spiritually.

The narrator then introduces an element of biography to explain a development in the history of the church. The central character in the drama is a 'friend of my father's'.

There was a man, Ivanios, a *metran*. In fact, he was called 'M.A.' *achen* when he was a priest because he was one of those rare men who had attained a degree in higher education and knew English. There was no one as knowledgeable as he. When these quarrels had reached a point when there seemed to be no return, he told Dionysius, who was on the verge of losing the battle, 'Let us go to the Roman Catholic Church, for if we continue in this way we shall only lose spiritual merit and energy'. Dionysius gave his permission and expressed agreement. So Mar Ivanios wrote to the Pope who accepted the community on their own terms—that they could keep their liturgy and their Oriental Rite. When Ivanios told Mar Dionysius that the way was cleared for their acceptance of Roman jurisdiction while keeping their oriental faith, the latter said, 'We have won the case, there is no need to go over to Rome'. Ivanios replied: 'I have made a commitment to the Pope so I must go'. He was such an honourable man, and so greatly loved, that many of his parishioners went with him. He was a friend of my father's: that is why we went. These are the kinds of stories that go into the making of the Jacobite/Orthodox Syrian Churches and explain the kind of trouble they are in.

While the first narrative came from an informant belonging to the Catholicos's party who had followed the twists and turns of the quarrel since his youth, the second narrator is someone who, while being denominationally outside the quarrel, has a keen interest in it. The two preceding narratives describe a period of history focusing on the development of ecclesiastical events up to the early twentieth century. In the following narrative the subject articulates the trauma of the years following the schism in the conservative party of the Orthodox Jacobite Church, splitting them into two groups. It is offered by follower of the Patriarch, whose loyalty to the Patriarch is undisputed.

Whatever I tell you, the Orthodox, if they hear it, will say, 'All lies, nothing but lies'. In fact, if you mention my name they will say 'Liar' at once. But I stick by my story, for it is the truth. You may say there are different sides to it, and that you want to look at both. There can be no two truths, that much is my belief, but I shall tell you the truth as I know it.

The quarrels began because Geverghese Dionysius tampered with a democratic constitution as it existed, and manipulated things so that all power came to himself. Till that time trust properties were under the care of a *metran* (bishop) trustee, a *kattanar* (priest) trustee and an *ayamennam* (layman) trustee respectively. These three were elected from the highest body of elected representatives of the church. The *metran*, without consulting the other two trustees, called people of his side sufficient to form a quorum, and had the constitution amended so that he was now credited with full powers. In fact, the land where Alleppey Zilla Court now stands was sold by the *metran* without consulting the other two trustees. It was church property gifted by our family. My grandfather was extremely angry and said that he would resign (he was the lay trustee) and that the *metran* should choose whom he willed. At that time, the Patriarch was on his way (perhaps it was 1085 [1910]) and the *vatti pannam* case was in progress. The Patriarch excommunicated the *metran*.

This narrative expresses the close interconnection between biography and general history. However, biographical details are presented because they are in a sense undeniable, and grandfather and uncle are *dramatis personae*. Events are also described which are not of importance to 'official' historians or to 'academic' historians, but which are very much a part of local history; where chroniclers may ignore certain events and details, relatives and neighbours may remember. The informant continues:

To make sure that the records at the Old Seminary would not be lost, both parties posted guards. The other party had a man called Anna Papi in their pay, a known drunk. One day, Anna Papi went to the toddy shop near the Seminary and was stabbed. The Orthodox say that my family was involved in the stabbing. My grandfather thus got involved in two court cases at the same time. One, the Anna Papi case, and, secondly, the case against the *metran* demanding his excommunication and denying him entry to our churches.

In this narrative too, one finds an ability to correlate dates and events. Here I am concerned not so much with facticity as with the message of the narrative: it is important to remember events and their chronological sequence.

My grandfather lost in the Zilla Court but in 1099 [1924], he was victorious in the High Court. The Orthodox sent a review petition but had it withdrawn since they believed that the Chief Justice was not favourable to them. After three years they sent the Review Petition again and that was accepted. The Court believed that the excommunication was against the principle of natural justice, and that the *metran* had been excommunicated without proper enquiry or a chance to vindicate himself. The court revoked the *modak* (excommunication). As a result, Gevarghese Dionysius became the Malankara *metran.*

There were certain clauses to be fulfilled to become the Malankara *metran*—that the priest must be from Malabar, and should be selected by the people, and approved and ordained by the Patriarch. Before the excommunication the *metran* had all these attributes and so the Court gave him right over the Malankara *sabha*. But the people were divided, and hence some churches remained with the Patriarch's party and some went to the *metran*. Neither of them would allow ecclesiastical representatives of the other into their churches.

After the Orthodox won the review petition in 1118 [1943], the Jacobite Syrians filed a case which they lost in the Zilla Court but won in the High Court. The Orthodox filed a review petition which was rejected by the Supreme Court. The matter was turned to the High Court for a second hearing and the decision was favourable to the Jacobite Syrians. The Orthodox appealed to the Supreme Court and won on a technical point.

The following narrative is from an elderly woman who took active interest in the litigation and the quarrels since her husband was a devoted follower of the *metran*. It is interesting to note that, being a follower of the Catholicos, she should underplay the causes of the dispute. The narrative begins by expressing the very trivial nature of the origin of the dispute. It also speaks of the apostasy of a particular family closely associated with the Patriarch's party, by which group they are, on the other hand, labelled as heroes and martyrs.

There was some quarrel about the felling of some coconut trees and their disposal—something to do with the income (*varumanam*) of the church. The *metran* was isolated in the matter while the priest trustee and the lay trustee stood together. Church affairs, as you know, are always managed by a representative layman, a priest and a bishop. A man who was employed to guard the *metran* was murdered. They say that there was an attempt on the *metran*'s life too. He was coming out of the *madabaha* (sanctuary) after saying *Qurbana* when he was attacked. P T Mani's family was suspected and everyone says that there is a curse (*shabam*) on the Mani family, and it is true, from being an extremely well placed and honoured family they have become ordinary; no one makes any progress among them now.

The rest of the narrative describes how Konat Achen, one of the most famous Syrian Christian figures, was disillusioned with the progress of the quarrel. This is an Orthodox Syrian view:

Konat Achen, who was involved with church affairs (on the Patriarch's party side) was so unhappy with the events of that time and their repercussions that before he died he told his son that he should stand for the truth. The son went over to the *Metran Katshi*—a matter of deep regret to the rest of his family who remained strongly with the Patriarch. They refused to believe that he was doing what his father had wished. They said, 'How is it that only to you our father has spoken of the matter in this way?' Perhaps it was because his son was a priest that the father spoke but the rest of the family would not accept this.

Konat Achen (or Malpan) is legendary among the Yakoba Christians, remembered particularly for the loyalty with which he stood for the Patriarch of Antioch's cause in Malankara. During the early years of the church quarrel, he would come to Puthenangadi which was in its own way a central battlefield since three of the most important churches in dispute stand here: Cherya Palli, Puthen Palli and Kurisu Palli. He stayed with C J Kurien (the lay representative, who had joined Konat Achen against the *metran*) at the famous *nal kettu* house, which even now is the pride of Puthenangadi for the craftsmanship that went into its making and the beauty of its traditional design. Konat Achen used to stay in this house because C J Kurien too was deeply engrossed in the affairs of the church. After the latter's death, however, it was not convenient for him to stay there on his visits.

At that time, there were around him a group of young men who supported the *bawa*'s party, the *bhehlakar* (loud angry young men looking for fights and causes to support). Of these, one belonged to the house of Ancheril, and had parents who also supported the Patriarch very actively and so Konat Achen came to live with them. The lady of the house was very keen that one of the daughters of the Achen should be given in marriage to them, and so Sara, the fifteen-year-old daughter of the Malpan came to Ancheril House sixty years ago.

Konat Achen's daughter narrates the reason why, in a family that has been associated with the Patriarch's party for decades, the son of the Malpan should be with the *metran*:

My father had sent my brother to Alwaye to study English and so he had not been able to see to his education in Syriac. This he entrusted to his student who was later to become Ougen *metran*. So my brother grew close to Ougen in the relationship of *guru–sisya* [teacher–student] and when Ougen joined the *metran*'s party so did my brother. We were all very unhappy because for so many generations our family has been loyal to the *bawa* and it was not that he had to go, but went out of loyalty to his teacher. [See the previous narrative to gauge the disbelief of the people regarding the fact that the Konat's son shifted party allegiance.]

While narratives that describe the general history of the community for the last hundred years have a staccato quality about them, formal and constrained, borrowing from the language of the courts and circulars, the subjectivization of this general history through the events of personal history (biography) brings about a change, expressing the emotional context of narration.

The language used in these formal expositions of general history was frequently English, or a terminologically equivalent Malayalam. Most narratives of this type were offered by male informants, who uniformly have an interest in church affairs and are, for the most part, well-versed in the major movements of church history. The women, when asked about even the most dominant details of such a community history will say, '*Kettitundu, Achayenodu choyichel parinutharrum*' (I have heard of this. If you ask Father [the head of the household] he will tell you). But when general history becomes subjectively oriented, when it becomes part of an informant's biography, then narratives are offered both extensively and in depth by the women. We see that even general history has a strong core of the personal and the subjective, as when family members are involved in its making. Here, the narratives still exhibit a formal structure because the uncle or the grandfather who played a dominant part in the court cases was an actor on an official stage, a representative of one party or another, playing a part that was demarcated not as kinsman but as lawyer or unswerving follower. The fact that the behaviour of such an actor resulted in the impoverishment of the family or its increasing fame or notoriety is incidental to the narrative. These personal details are brought in incidentally and parenthetically. The main focus of the narrative is the telling of a story about the church and its problems and the historical format of that story, referred to by informants as *sabha charithram*.

Biography, Neighbourhood Life and the Church Quarrel Reconstructions of the past often include narratives which emphasize the biographical. Such accounts weave together three strands—community, neighbourhood and the individual—which together form the tapestry of an event recollected. Beyond the biographical dimension, the events also reflect a moment in the general history of the Syrian Christian community, and the particular history of life in a certain neighbourhood. This juxtaposition of the two levels, community and neighbourhood, has its effect on the life of individuals and families.

The present narratives, to a great extent, express the pathologies of neighbourhood life. They are accounts of events which express the deviation from the ethic of 'neighbourliness', undisputed in times of harmony. The Syrian Christians of Puthenangadi though divided in their allegiance to an ecclesiastical head are otherwise bound together by the common denominator of a cultural ethos. They share the same world-view, expressed most vividly by the manner in which they celebrate rites of passage at both individual and calendrical levels. What we shall examine now are the differences, articulated at the time of societal crises, exaggerated by the tension born of the ecclesiastical divide.

Events recollected here either took place in Puthenangadi or in the life of a Puthenangadi resident (narrators often being actively involved in the events); thirdly, there are events born of the intrusion of certain

characters into Puthenangadi life who are public personages. Two kinds
of situations are described by these narratives. One set is primarily
biographical, and includes accounts of marriage or death in the neighbourhood which were affected by the *palli vyazhak* or church quarrel,
so that neighbourhood or household life was disrupted for a time.
Then, there are narratives which are about events in the neighbourhood affecting the people in general, such as the visit of the Patriarch
of Antioch, the anniversary celebration of the establishment of the
Catholicate in Malankara, and the commemoration of the death anniversaries of those holy men not shared by both parties. These are
occasions ostentatiously celebrated by one church faction, and equally
ostentatiously ignored by the other.

First, let us examine those narratives which emphasize the biographical but incorporate in their text the dimensions of the collective
and general, as all personal statements must.

People often make the statement that the church quarrel is the affair
of priests and bishops.

> Outside the church we are good friends, attend each other's
> marriages, even give our children to each other. It's all very well
> for our *metrans* to say that we should not, but when a good
> proposal comes differing affiliations cannot stand in the way.

Yet, when the *palli vyazhak*, during its cycles of development,
reaches periods of great tension, it is bound to affect the relations
between otherwise friendly neighbours and normally compatible
conjugal partners. Women, profoundly regretting the division of loyalty,
sound most melancholy:

> It is we who feel the impact of these quarrels and divisions. It is
> for us that the quarrels between churches are difficult to accept.
> For every quarrel a new church is spawned; churches grow out
> of quarrels, not out of faith. At every corner we have a new
> church, and each of these is a living memory of bitterness.

The women bear the consequences of divided loyalties most because,
at the time of marriage, they must accept the loyalties of their husbands' affiliation, and abide by them. They must teach their children
to stand by the ecclesiastical affiliation of the patriline. The women
must suppress their own sympathies, and it is often painful to betray

childhood loyalties. When they fail to do this, it is embarassing for the household. With the license of old age and widowhood, a woman sometimes reverts to the ecclesiastical loyalties of her natal family. One old woman in Puthenangadi, for instance, publicly affirmed her loyalty to the Patriarch of Antioch, much to the consternation of her children and grandchildren, who, following the patriline, are staunch followers of the Indian Catholicos. She frequently reviled the Catholicos's party, and vocally supported the Patriarch, even though her children always said, 'You married our father and you must respect his church'.

For the most part, however, women stand quietly in the church into which they have been married, and are unable to defend their mother church when their affines make damaging statements about it. The most evocative pleas for union between the estranged groups come from such women.

> The quarrel is like that between the Pandavas and the Kauravas;[76] what need is there for it? But it exists and we live with it. Is the issue one that will lead us to salvation? Because I am married into an Orthodox family, I do not have the fortune to see the Patriarch when he comes to visit his people. Why must we deny him? It is true that St Thomas brought Christianity to us, and taught us to say prayers and worship God, but it is well known that after he died, darkness fell on the Christians of this land. There was no one to ordain priests, no one to teach the people the way in which God is worshipped. Whatever we have regarding the customs of our faith we have got from Antioch, we did not make them up ourselves. Why should we not then give honour to the Patriarch, and the Patriarchs before him, who since the time of the Apostles have made and blessed the laws of the church?

When two women in a family loyal to the Patriarch are by birth followers of the Catholicos, they are able to say things more easily and openly in defence of the latter than if there was one alone. In one such case, however, the head of the household, a staunch Patriarch follower, said to a neighbour, 'Two Catholicos's party women in my house and I am ruined'. The tension between the loyalties of the natal and conjugal home, expressed through differing affiliations, is thus most apparent in the women. Constant intermarriage between members of the two parties has however tended to blur the issues at the everyday level.

*Events in the Neighbourhood Affecting Biography: A Prelate's Visit;
A Death Followed by Disputes* Many narratives express the nature of
ecclesiastical crises that occur from time to time, and reflect through
language the assertion of party identity at the individual level, and the
tensions of conflicting loyalties. Wives of staunch Patriarch loyalists
who grew up in households which were affiliated to the *metran* find
themselves unable to continue hearing insults being heaped upon the
Catholicos, since they are supposed to have accepted completely the
allegiance of their husband's family. Their sole recourse is to return to
their father's home for a span. This is the only possible act of catharsis
available to them. An eighty-three-year-old woman said: 'The Patriarch is
coming as close as Simhasana Palli, just two streets away, but my sons
will not let me go'.

After decades of living in the staunchest of Catholicos families, with
a son who has inherited his father's steadfast loyalty to the *metran*, she
still yearns to see the Patriarch. Her children have told her that she
must remember that she now belongs to the *metran*. A wife is supposed to voice her husband's opinion at all times, and it is a sure sign
of the strength of the conjugal bond when a woman argues to defend
her husband's sentiments when they are under dispute.

The quarrel in its dialogic manifestations at the neighbourhood level
is usually the sport of men. If women happen to be there, they join in
by commenting usually on the moral aspect—the spiritual poverty in
the church that leads to litigation and quarrels over property, where
one party curses the other and closes to them the doors and cemet-
eries of the local church. The men talk about it in terms of strategies, of money spent, of promises and lies, of floors crossings and
manipulations. Syrian Christians, however, constantly reiterate that
the quarrel between the two sides has nothing to do with differences
in faith.

While conjugal relationships may express the tensions of differing
affiliations, these are usually not conspicuous since the woman is
always expected to submerge her views and articulate openly only
such opinions as will coincide with her husband and his household.
Certainly the affines of a man cannot impose their views upon him or
he upon them, although there are heated discussions should they be
neighbours who meet frequently. These arguments are most common
at the time of crucial local events such as the visit of some important
but controversial ecclesiast to the neighbourhood or the celebration of
a saint's day not shared by both parties.

At the time of death, however, pathological situations can arise which are not limited to the contained vehemence of neighbours' verbal insults but can break into physical fights and abuse. The focus of difference here lies in the question of property—that is, which party has jurisdiction over the cemetery. Some years ago an incident occurred which upset the equilibrium of Puthenangadi life by its very severe violence, and which the Christians even now remember with regret. A man named Cheryan died and was to be interred in the tomb of his fathers—the *kudumba kallara*—at Puthen Palli. It was customary for the body to be taken to the small cemetery chapel where prayers are said by priests, incense burnt, and the family allowed its last farewells. But members of the Catholicos's party locked up Puthen Palli, which was under Catholicos's jurisdiction, and the deceased was thus refused the right to be buried with his forefathers.

Since they were denied permission to use the cemetery church, the Patriarch's people constructed a *pantalam* (canopy) outside Cheryan's house, and it was here that priests prayed and people gathered for the last rites. The body was allowed burial in the cemetery but priests of the Patriarch were not allowed to officiate. The negotiations took very long, and the burial was severely delayed, rendering the whole situation extremely disturbing for the mourners who had to wait long hours before the body could be interred. Such an event is not unique to Puthenangadi, and is reported in several places where Catholicos and Patriarch party hostilities reach a climax. A woman spoke of a similar incident in her natal village:

When my father died we wished access to our *taravat* church so that he could be laid to rest in the family tomb. But we, as Patriarch's people, were not allowed to use the church since our priests were not given permission to enter churches controlled by the Catholicos's party. We said the last prayers in the house and only when these were completed could we take the body to the cemetery. When we got there, they would not let us in and, finally, after much argument, they allowed a few people to enter the cemetery with the body, but not the priests, and the body was lowered without ceremony into the grave.

The same was to happen when my father's mother died. When we took her body to the cemetery, again we had to fight for entry. They would not allow her only daughter's husband (a priest) to officiate saying that they would not allow priests of the other side to enter. Finally he gained entry as a *marimakkan* [daughter's husband] and not as a priest, so my father's mother could be interred with the dignity befitting her age and status. But how terrible a moment it was to watch all this happening, our mourning put aside by anger.

The following day we wanted a priest to come with us to the cemetery to say prayers for the soul, as is the custom, and to burn incense over the grave. We knew that their priests would not do it for us (nor would we wish them to) nor would they allow our priests to enter with us. My brother who was already upset by the events of the preceding day, and not willing to take things in a subdued manner, took hold of the *kappiar* (sexton) and brought him to the grave where we all gathered and prayed. The *kappiar* said a few words of prayers in place of the priest and burnt the incense over the tomb. When he returned to the church, the priest was ready to give *him* a beating saying, 'Who said you could take the censer to them?'

Worse was to come with the *adyantaram* (commemorative feast) which we held on the sixteenth day following the date of grandmother's death. All our relatives including our *bendhakar* (affines) were to come and the traditional vegetarian meal was to be served at noon. But as it happened, when we woke to the day, we found that there were van loads of policemen stationed at every corner, even at the door of the church. How embarrassing it was for us, just as if our people were criminals and it was with shame that we welcomed our relatives. The presence of the police said that our neighbours felt that our relatives could not be trusted to behave themselves.

Just as death in its dual dimension of the biographical and collective can mark off the nature of neighbourhood relations, so also events dominantly collective (such as ceremonial visits of ecclesiastical dignitaries to the neighbourhood and celebrations of certain saints' days) express and demarcate such relations. Narratives describing these occasions are to be seen as the representations mediating collective and individual experience.

The oral reflections on events occurring in the very recent past do not have the same quality as narratives which describe events occurring a century or so ago. The narrator infuses into his account a subjectivity that can be born only of direct participation, and the semi-objective format of oral accounts is replaced by highly coloured emotional statements. The subjects of the narrative are not merely characters or personages on a public stage but are persons for whom the narrator has certain strongly defined and clearly articulated feelings. So when the Patriarch or one of the Syrian Metropolitans visits Puthenangadi, or when the Catholicos chooses to celebrate his birthday in Puthenangadi's parish church (Cherya Palli), the Christians are here relating to a person rather than to a personage.

The earlier narratives (*sabha charitram*) showed how the Syrian Christians remembered their past, and expressed the fact that their conception of the chief actors was based on hearsay or on what they had read. These were men out of the passages of history, distilled in narrators' accounts as tales told by an older generation, and produced as a kind of bricoleurian history by each narrator.[77] On the other hand, accounts of the recent past, accounts of events that occurred a year or month or week ago lack any claim to objectivity, being dominantly and vividly biographical and personal. In such instances, the attitude of the narrator to the subject of his account is not merely to a character outlined in the clear sharp lines of brief newspaper articles and official histories of the church but to a person whose actuality lies in his vulnerabilities constantly exposed to a watching people.

All Puthenangadi Christians were consciously aware of the Patriarch's ceremonial visit to their town and neighbourhood in February 1982. The Catholicos's followers constantly expressed their antagonism to the Patriarch's visit, and repeatedly stated that they would not give him permission to enter their churches (Kurisu Palli and Cherya Palli). They said that they would ask for a 'stay order' from the government, since the Patriarch's proposed visit was bound to cause trouble among the Christians in the neighbourhood.

The Patriarch's people, on the other hand, were eagerly looking forward to the day that the *bawa* was to arrive at Puthenangadi. It was fifty years since a Patriarch had visited the neighbourhood. The earlier prelate had died while visiting his people in their local churches, and every year, in February, the Patriarch's people commemorate his death anniversary. This event divides Puthenangadi into two groups, the followers of the holy man and the sceptics. In February 1982, the Christians of the neighbourhood were emotionally divided not just because of the fiftieth anniversary of the death of Patriarch Moran Mar Elias but also because of the imminent arrival of the present Patriarch, Moran Mar Ignatius Zakka.

As the days passed the sense of distance between ordinarily friendly neighbours began to grow and was often barely concealed. When acquaintances belonging to the 'other side' came to the house, discussion ceased if it had centred around the matter of the split in the church. With close friends of differing affiliations with whom one was at liberty to express anger, loud discussions took place. Even in jokes, this matter of conflict was expressed, and loyalties reaffirmed or challenged. A follower of the Catholicos said:

I went to Jacob Mani's house yesterday just to find out what Patriarch's party people thought of the statements that the Catholicos's people were making regarding the independence of the Catholicos. As soon as they saw me they started discussing the affair. They mimicked and mocked our Catholicos. Their tone of voice and speech were calculated to offend, but we are good friends on all matters other than the developments in the church. I said nothing, not wanting to make their mood any worse, and the Catholicos has always told us that whatever is said, we should not respond, at any event we must never let the situation for a quarrel arise. So I kept quiet, even though they provoked me. Finally, I said, 'You know me, I know nothing about these matters. I stand on the Orthodox side because I am married into such a family, they give me rice'. They laughed at that and said, 'Are you not tutored by your husband?'

Although no physical violence reflecting the latent anger between the two groups occurred in Puthenangadi during the Patriarch's visit, the tension between them was evident. A follower of the Catholicos said:

We went to Devalokam where the Catholicos lives and we asked him, 'How shall we behave, what attitude must we take?'. Of course it is embarrassing for us to be the only ones who are not greeting the Bawa; but now we are justifiably angry for the Bawa has called us 'prodigal'. He says now that he did not do so but we have heard that he did. If he were the true shepherd, we would have recognized his voice; the lost sheep understand when their master calls, but this Patriarch has no command over us.

The Orthodox Syrians in the neighbourhood constantly asserted that Thomas the Apostle was the Head of the Church, the *eddayan* (shepherd) who holds the shepherd's crook, and the people are his flock. The legend of the division of the world by lot, each apostle thus allocated his domain of evangelical activity, is recalled.[78] Peter was sent to Rome and Thomas to India. 'We do not say that in Rome Thomas should be *eddayan*.' Interestingly, the myth that Thomas came to Malabar has taken on the dimension of history (that is, an objectively true fact) to the Catholicos's party, while for Patriarch's followers it has been relegated to the status of a folk-tale. The latter now say, 'Perhaps he (St Thomas) came. But it is all *ooham* (anybody's guess)'. For the Patriarch's people, it is important to assert that 'the Patriarch is like our Father, he is head of all of us. He stands in the place of the Apostle Peter. It was Peter who was always with Christ, who loved him, even though in fear he denied Christ'.

One of the key points of debate in Puthenangadi, thus divided at the time of the Patriarch's visit, was the question of Thomas the Apostle's legitimacy. An earlier Patriarch, Ignatius Yakub III, in a letter which informants refer to as the 203 Kalpana of June 1970, had said that St Thomas was not even a priest, that he did not have *pattatham* (ordination), and so no ecclesiastical line could be drawn from him. This, more than a decade later, continues to draw the wrath of the Catholicos's people.

A Patriarch's follower said:

> To explain what was meant, let me remind you that in the Gospel of John it is written that Jesus breathed on them [the apostles] and gave them the Holy Ghost. 'But Thomas, one of the twelve, called Didymus was not with them when Jesus came.' (John 20:24). That is all that was meant, that even though the Apostles were equal, and Peter their leader by the choice of Christ, Thomas was not present at the crucial moment, and did not receive the Holy Ghost through the breath of Christ. So he cannot have a throne as Peter did.

The Visit of the Five Patriarchal Delegations   In September of the same year that the Patriarch paid a visit to the Jacobite Syrians, the Orthodox Syrians celebrated the seventieth anniversary of the establishment of the Catholicate in India. This, Orthodox Syrian informants stated, was an anniversary celebrating the aspirations of freedom and autonomy from the Syrian Church. The establishment of the Catholicate is expressed as a gift from the Syrian Patriarch, Mar Abdel -Messih. That he was deposed when he made the gift is a different matter. His dethronement is considered by *metran* followers to be the consequence of ecclesiastical intrigue. The Orthodox Syrian believes that he had the *pattatham*—the holy seal of ordainment which was something no dismissal from office could remove.

The newspapers were again full of articles by leading spokesmen of the Church, both clerical and lay, each of which led to much acrimonious discussion in Puthenangadi. A newspaper war raged in the neighbourhood. While the Patriarch's people only bought newspapers like *Kerala Bhushanam* and *Deepika* (which are biased in their favour), they stopped borrowing or subscribing to the *Malayala Manorama*, which has traditionally been associated with a family belonging to the Catholicos's party. Articles in the newspapers attempt to clear misconceptions regarding various issues in the matter of the split in the church. The background facts are easily comprehensible to the layman though the references may be theological or historical. However, each side denounces the other's version as being rubbish and a tissue of lies (*nonna*). When the Catholicos's people read out triumphantly *lekhna*s or essays favourable to them, their friends who are affiliated to the Patriarch refuse to listen. The theologian–intellectuals who play the role of the official chroniclers of the two respective parties were represented by colourful personalities on each side—Paulose Mar Gregorious for the Orthodox Syrians, and Cor Episcopa Kaniamparambil for the Jacobites.

The Patriarch's people viewed the seventieth anniversary celebrations as merely spectacle creating; they saw it as a rival show, produced to counteract the event of February, when the Patriarch of Antioch came to Kerala. The Patriarch's people have their own version of how the rival celebrations 'happened' and describe the scenario, providing appropriate dialogue.

The Catholicos was extremely worried about the response the Patriarch was getting on his visit to Kerala in February this year. It meant loss of face for his own followers. So as he was sitting, worrying, his bishops came to him and the cleverest said, 'We must have a similar show; a show of strength. We must call other Patriarchs; they shall be our guests for a few days and chant *Qurbana* (Eucharist) for the people. We will make it a celebration of the seventieth anniversary of the establishment of the Catholicate'. To this, the Catholicos said, 'Who celebrates seventieth anniversaries on any large scale? Fiftieth, seventy-fifth, hundredth—these may be celebrated, but how can we suddenly celebrate the seventieth?' But that was strategy and that was how it was done.

Crisis situations such as these always serve to demarcate the neighbourhood population strictly along the lines of differing affiliation. At these times, too, while one group is subdued, the other is jubilant; while one is triumphant and exults in the festivities of commemoration or celebration, the other is silent, disillusioned and unhappy.

One of the clearest dimensions of this anomie is the disillusionment among the people regarding their ecclesiasts.

A Patriarch's supporter said:

These quarrels within the church have in some ways affected the priests. Even in our neighbourhood they are unable to view the situation honestly or to make decisions which they can stand by. One of the priests belonging to the Catholicos's party has switched sides three or four times, but now it seems he is with the Orthodox for good. Another we know is sympathetic to us but he does not want to lose his rights or his income in the Cherya Palli *edavaga* (parish) so he stands with the Orthodox too. Everyone knows he is really with us, so the Orthodox in Puthenangadi are always angry with him, because he is officially their priest.

It is the *purohit*s (priests) who are responsible for the quarrel—for beginning it and continuing with it. In the old days a priest was chosen by the people when he was a child and showed a true disposition toward such a calling. Today no one has the same sense of dedication or vocation, there are no loyalties—they change sides according to Supreme Court decisions.

Speaking of their high priests in general, the people of Puthenangadi express discontentment though individually, bishops are treated with utmost deference, and it is the greatest honour for the average Syrian Christian to be connected by blood or marriage to a bishop, or to be socially recognized by him. In this context, the life of the saint, Parimala Tirumeni, is often stated to be the symbol of peace and

Christian unity. Most houses in the neighbourhood can be identified as belonging to the Patriarch's or Catholicos's party by the pictures on the wall of the respective ecclesiastical leaders. But all houses, regardless of affiliation, tend to have a portrait of *Kochu Tirumeni* (little lord), as this indigenous saint is affectionately called. In Puthenangadi, he is revered as a holy man who lived beyond quarrels and differences and it is universally wished that present-day ecclesiasts were more like him.

Notes

1. T K Joseph, 'St Thomas in South India', *Indian Antiquary*, Dec. 1926; 'Was St Thomas in South India?', *Young Men of India*, July 1927; H Hosten, S J, *Antiquities from San Thome and Mylapore*, (Calcutta: Baptist Mission Press, 1936); H C Perumallil and E R Hambye (eds.) *Christianity in India*; G M Moraes, *A History of Christianity in India* (Bombay: Manaktalas, 1964); Mundadan, *Sixteenth Century Traditions of the Christians*.

2. See G M Moraes, op. cit; Neill, *A History of Christianity in India* (Cambridge: Cambridge University Press, 1984).

3. Brown, *The Indian Christians*; Perumallil and Hambye, op. cit.

4. Moraes, op. cit.

5. See Xavier Koodapuzha, 'The History of the Church in Kerala' in G Menacherry (ed), *St Thomas Christian Encyclopaedia*, vol. 2. (Trichur: B N K Press, 1973), p. 31.

6. Podipara, *The St Thomas Christians*.

7. See Moraes, op. cit., p. 77.

8. Brown, op. cit.

9. K M Panikkar, *Asia and Western Dominance* (Bombay: Asia Publishing House, 1959), p. 30.

10. A M Mundadan, *The Arrival of the Portuguese in India and the Thomas Christians under Mar Jacob 1498–1522* (Bangalore: Dharmaraj Press, 1967), p. 30.

11. See Mundadan, *The Arrival of the Portuguese in India*, p. 66.

12. Ibid., p. 83.

13. Neill, op. cit., pp. 94, 129–31.

14. Mundadan, op. cit., p. 83.

15. Nestorius, Bishop of Constantinople, AD 428–431. Nestorius objected to the use of the term *theotokos* (God-bearer) to describe Mary, preferring instead the word *theodoxos* (one who receives God). He used the word *upostasis* (substance)—that is, two *hypostases* and the Lord's two natures. The Council of Chaldea (AD 451) fixed the terminology by affirming that in Jesus there was one *upostasis*, one person (*prosopon*), two natures, without confusion, without change, without rending, without separation.

   Nestorianism emphasized the reality of Jesus's humanness by arguing that there was a unity of two persons—the *logos* and the man—and that these two persons were so inseparably united that they might in a sense be deemed a single entity. This does not allow for the idea of incarnation and leaves out the presence of the Holy Ghost. See James Hasting, ed., *Encyclopaedia of Religion and Ethics*, vol IV (Edinburgh: T & T Clark, 1953), p. 328.

16. Brown, op. cit., p. 36.
17. See e.g. Ranajit Guha, 'The Prose of Counter-Insurgency' in Ranajit Guha (ed.), *Subaltern Studies II* (Delhi: Oxford University Press, 1983).
18. Proceedings of the CMS, 1822–3, p. 236.
19. C M Agur, *Church History of Travancore* (Madras: SPS Press, 1901), p. 82.
20. Ibid., pp. 82–3.
21. P Cheriyan, *The Malabar Christians and the Church Missionary Society, 1816–40*. (Madras: CMS Press, 1935), p. 353.
22. W S Hunt, *The Anglican Church in Travancore and Cochin 1816–1916*, vol. II (Kottayam: CMS Press, 1916).
23. *Missionary Register* (London, 1816), p. 453.
24. *CMS Register* (London, 1819), p. 427.
25. Cited in P. Cheriyan, op. cit., p. 178.
26. *CMS Register* (London, 1821), p. 518.
27. *Proceedings of the CMS* (London, 1824), p. 133.
28. Ibid., p. 526.
29. *Madras Church Missionary Record* (London, 1836), p. 34.
30. Ibid., p. 167.
31. *Church Missionary Intelligence* (London, 1856), p. 221.
32. Emile Durkheim, *The Division of Labour in Society* (New York: Free Press, 1964).
33. Brown, op. cit.
34. Durkheim, op. cit.
35. See e.g. T Chandra Shekhar Menon, *Copy of Judgement in original suits 1, 2, 3, 4, 5, 6, 7 and 8/79*.
36. *Royal Court of Final Appeal-I* (Trivandrum: Keralodayam Press, 1890), p. 12.
37. Ibid., p. 13; M N Srinivas (personal communication) suggests that according to Hindu belief one who is not 'whole' may not be a king and this had been extended by the Syrian Christians to the person of the Metropolitan.
38. *RCFA-I*, p. 15.
39. Ibid., p. 13.
40. Ibid., p. 14.
41. Ibid., p. 15.
42. Ibid., p. 132.
43. Ibid., p. 132.
44. Ibid., p. 153.
45. Ibid., p. 40.
46. Ibid., p. 144.
47. Ibid., p. 183.
48. Ibid., p. 144.
49. Ibid., p. 267.
50. Ibid., p. 276.
51. Ibid., p. 271.
52. Brown, op. cit., p. 145.
53. *Royal Court of Final Appeal-II* (Trivandrum: Keralodayam Press, 1890), p. 75.
54. Ibid., p. 93.

55. Brown, op. cit., p. 148.

56. Roderick Floud, 'Quantitative History and People's History', *History Workshop*, Issue 17, Spring 1984, pp. 114–24.

57. See e.g. *History Workshop*, Editorial, 1978, p. ii.

58. See Luisa Passerini, 'Work Ideology and Consensus under Italian Fascism', *History Workshop*, Issue 8, Autumn 1979, pp. 82–108.

59. Raphael Samuel, 'Local History and Oral History', *History Workshop*, Issue 1, Spring 1976, p. 199.

60. See e.g. Allessandro Portelli, 'The Peculiarities of Oral History', *History Workshop*, Issue 12, Autumn 1981, p. 108.

61. Marc Bloch, *The Historian's Craft* (Manchester: Manchester University Press, 1954), p. 71.

62. R G Collingwood, *The Idea of History* (Oxford: Oxford University Press, 1980).

63. Bloch, op. cit., p. 66.

64. Ibid., p. 101.

65. Ibid., p. 28.

66. The sources of the local Thomas legends include many written and unwritten songs and other types of oral and literary material such as legends connected specifically with certain families and churches. The most famous of these are the ceremonial songs in use at the time of church festivals such as the *Margam Kalli* typifying 'The Way' and *The Thomas Ramban Pattu* which is claimed to have been originally composed by the first disciple of the apostle in Kerala. See for detailed analyses, Mundadan, op. cit.

67. Brown, op. cit., Moraes op. cit.; Zaleski, *The Apostle St Thomas in India*.

68. Syrian Christian identity is homologous in practice to that of the Nuer of Sudan described by E E Evans-Pritchard, and we may describe them, then, as belonging to a segmentary society. Evans-Pritchard showed that Nuer self-identity shifted according to the circumstances of feuding. Similarly, the Christians shift levels according to context: they may be Syrian Christians as opposed to Latin Christians who are converts of Portuguese ritual endeavour, or they may be Orthodox as opposed to Romo-Syrian and in the final analysis they may be *Bawa Katshi* (Patriach's Party) as opposed to *Metran Katshi*. E E Evans-Pritchard, *The Nuer* (New York: Oxford University Press, 1979).

69. The Canaanites are those descendants of the Christians who accompanied Thomas of Cana in AD 345 from the Middle East, and settled as an endogamous community in Kerala. See Brown, op. cit.; Hosten, S J, op. cit.

70. See e.g. Samuel, 'Local History and Oral History'; Natalie Zemon Davis, *Society and Culture in Early Modern France* (London: Duckworth, 1975).

71. K L Lukose, *Kurisupalliyum Puthenangadiyum* (Kottayam: Ancheril Printers, 1983).

72. Collingwood, op. cit., p. 294.

73. Ibid.

74. See e.g. Paul Ricoeur, *History and Truth* (Evanston: North-Western University Press, 1965), p. 100: 'There is another history, a history of acts, events, personal compassions, woven into the history of structures, advents and institutions.'

75. The Council of Nicaea was held in AD 325 and dealt with such matters as the doctrine, organization and discipline of the church. Its major contribution was to the theology of the Incarnation by the acceptance of the Nicene Creed (*see below*) and, in particular, the phrase that Jesus was the same essence as the Father.

Encyclopaedia of Religion and Ethics, vol. IX, p. 191.

The Nicene Creed
We believe
In one God, the Father Almighty, maker of all
things visible and invisible.
And in one Lord Jesus Christ, the son of God, begotten of
the Father, only-begotten that is of the substance of the Father,
God of God, Light of Light, very God of God, begotten, not made,
of one substance with the Father, by whom all things were made,
both those in heaven and those on earth.
Who for us men and for our salvation came down and was made
flesh, and lived as Man among men,
Suffered
And rose the third day
Ascended into heaven
Is coming to judge the quick and dead

And in the Holy Ghost.
76. In Hindu myth, the cousins whose quarrels led to a mighty war, described in the epic, *Mahabharata*.
77. I use the term 'bricoleur' in the sense given it by Lévi-Strauss. He argues that the myth-maker, unlike the engineer, is able to put his tools to a diverse number of uses. The patterns and combinations that he can achieve are therefore various, because every element is utilized in relation to another, and can function in some other context just as well, though perhaps differently. Claude Lévi-Strauss, *The Savage Mind*, p. 17.
78. Zaleski, op. cit.

3

Puthenangadi: Morphology and Legends of Origin

Puthenangadi is a predominantly Syrian Christian neighbourhood in the town of Kottayam in Kerala. *Angadi* (or *annadi*) means 'bazaar', conveying the fact that Syrian Christians were often merchants by profession. There are many other such Syrian Christian settlements in Kerala which go by this name surrounding Puthenangadi: Pazheangadi (Old Bazaar), which is said to be the older settlement since Puthen (new) is seen in opposition to it, Valyangadi (Big Bazaar) and Thazha-tangadi (Lower Bazaar), which are all situated close by. All these have a marked Christian population, and most inhabitants are related through kinship or friendship, or are acquaintances.

Puthenangadi lies on one of the main arteries which in just a few moments brings one to the heart of Kottayam town. However, as one goes deeper into the neighbourhood through its by-lanes, it becomes more and more rural in character.[1] The relation of the town to agriculture is clearly evident in that Kottayam can be described as a market town. It provides an outlet for the agricultural produce of the outlying district of the same name while supplying its consumer needs.

Like the 'urbanites of antiquity' described by Max Weber, the residents of Puthenangadi were, till a generation ago, semi-peasants.[2] According to local narrative, the neighbourhood as a residential form had its origins in the sixteenth century. Puthenangadi emerged out of a rural world-view; dwellings were built close to each other for reasons of safety, the rice fields being situated some distance away. Today, the *kandam* or rice fields continue to lie to the west of the neighbourhood.

The structure of the locality can be understood in terms of three topographical categories with associated relationships and symbolic expressions: these are the neighbourhood, its houses, and its churches.

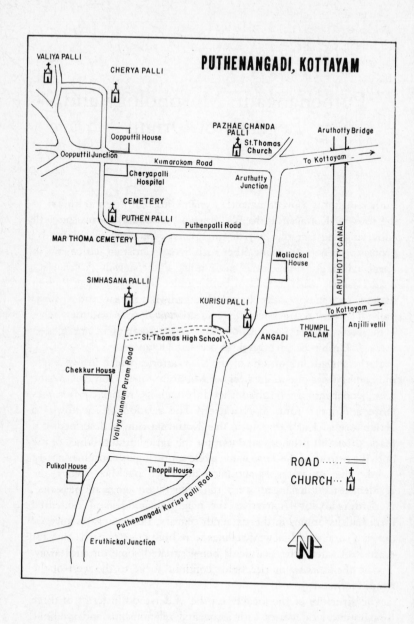

The neighbourhood must be seen as a marked off territory or an area delimited by a particular boundary. It expresses not merely the notion of a delimited territory or locale, but also a web of relations arising out of close residence, the sharing of collective events, and the existence of an implicit structure of norms and expectations relating to those who are particularly 'close' neighbours. However, the definition of a 'good' neighbour becomes problematic in the context of Puthenangadi and the ecclesiastical feud. Neighbourly relations fluctuate according to the phases of the feud. A neighbour, then, has to be distinguished from friends and kin, although in Puthenangadi these categories may coincide.

NEIGHBOURHOOD AS LOCALE

Most *taravat*s (houses) in Puthenangadi are ancestral property. The people who live in these houses have often no idea how many generations ago their ancestors came to live here. The majority of the houses are of traditional design, surrounded by large gardens in which grow mango, jackfruit, pepper, coconut and plantain trees. Certain dominant lineages (*pradhana kudumbam*) have houses located in the street called *Angadi*. This is the earliest known part of the neighbourhood, the nucleus around which Puthenangadi as it is now exists has grown.

The popular notion about the origin of Puthenangadi goes back to the sixteenth century migrations of Christians into Kottayam from places such as Nillekal, Tiruvalla, Athirampuzha, Pallam, Chenganoor, Kothamangalam, Thodupuzha and Poonathra. Informants say that some of these movements occurred as a consequence of Portuguese ritual domination in the sixteenth century, whereby Syrian Christians were coerced into an interpretation of Christianity alien to their forefathers.

Other possible reasons for these early migrations into Kottayam include moves prompted by the destruction in other areas of crops by locusts and the consequent poverty, and the fear of a tribe of dacoits of Tamil origin called *Pandammar*. Not surprisingly, the *angadi* or nucleus of the neighbourhood where the earliest of the migrants are thought to have settled, consists of a street of houses which are built very close to each other to ward off the attack of thieves.

The land that the immigrant Christians bought is thought to have once been in the possession of artisan and servicing castes. Even today, there are Christians in Puthenangadi who have house-names like *Asariparambil* (in the carpenter's field) and *Chakkallaparambil*. *Chakkala* (owners of bulls which were used to rotate crushing and pressing instruments), *asari* (carpenter), *kollan* (iron smith), *vellan* (white washer), *pannen* (tailor), *kosavan* (potter), and *vanniyan* (oil presser) are some of the castes from whom the migrants bought land. Informants say that their ancestors were clever and had the patronage of the Hindu kings, and so the land came easily into Christian hands.

Through Puthenangadi runs a tributary of the river Meenachil. The river was once a bathing place for the Christians. Two generations ago, this waterway had much greater significance, when boats were an important mode of transport. Today, boats still pass by, the *parathi* (washer-woman) washes clothes there, and children sit on the steps leading towards the river.

Much of the *angadi* is believed to have been under water, with the land reclaimed little by little and made habitable (*nella negechu*). Surrounded by dense forests (*kaadu*), these Christians developed their own legends of protection, one of which survived and had credence even a generation ago. According to this legend, Thomas, the apostle of Christ, was the personal caretaker of the *angadi*; he rode on a white horse at night to keep the *angadi* safe from thieves and evil. Thomas is described as a man of very small stature, whose presence is confirmed by the smell of incense which lingers after he has gone. On the occasion of *Puthiya Nyyayarcha* (the Sunday following Easter), the celebratory procession that is taken out from the church follows the route that Thomas is believed to take when he rides to protect his people at night.

The House: Physical and Symbolic Uses[1]

The house is a symbolic system, and the ordering of space in buildings is really about the ordering of relations between people. Most *taravat*s in Puthenangadi are built on a piece of land between 30 to 50 cents (about half an acre), and this space is successfully used for growing vegetables, tapioca, yams, coconuts and, occasionally, cocoa. Jackfruit and mango are popularly grown fruit trees, around which tamarind, chillies, drumstick (*Moringa oleifera*) and curry leaves are cultivated. Many houses had cows till a decade ago, several existing cattle sheds being evidence of this fact. These days owning a cow is associated with wealth, and only hens are found in almost every courtyard.

In Puthenangadi, all the *taravat*s present similar, almost uniform, facades and interiors to the observer. Three or four stone steps lead up from the road to the gate which is usually of modern design, made of wrought iron for purposes of security. The stone walls, however, are fairly low, mossy green with age, and with flat rounded surfaces. In one particular street in Puthenangadi, the wall of each house merges with the next in a continuous line. In the original *angádi* itself, however, there are no walls around or in front of the houses. Verandahs look out on to porches, yards, and private gardens, and these are used as thoroughfares by visitors, workers and vendors. Families here see no reason for walls; privacy is not a major concern, and safety and security are at a maximum. This original *angadi* consists of two rows of six houses facing each other with front yards which overlap. The sense of closeness that exists among *angadi* families in this original hamlet is very strong: it is as if they share one great courtyard, the physical intimacy reaffirming social intimacy. They refer to themselves as *angadikar* (of the *angadi*) which marks them as a kind of core group. They are the 'first families' because it was from the *angadi* that the rest of the neighbourhood grew.

Many traditional houses still have a *patippuram* (house at the steps) which precedes the courtyard and threshold. This is a kind of gate house with a tiled or thatched roof. Sometimes it may have a bench. This area serves as a place where conversation is initiated or terminated. Here the visitor stands and calls out to enquire if people are at home, particularly in the evenings when doors are left open even if no one is to be seen in the front rooms. Houses are often built at some height from the road and the ordinary wayfarer cannot look into the house, thus ensuring privacy. The *mittam* or courtyard, which lies in front of the house between the threshold and the gate, is always kept scrupulously clean. In fact, one of the first duties of the day is to sweep the courtyard (*mittam addikuga*). The broom, made of the ribs of coconut leaves, is splayed while sweeping, and attractive fan-shaped designs appear on the red river sand.

Boundaries simultaneously create a category of inner space (or spaces) and outer, and represent a domain of control. The house must be seen as habitation which defines the inhabitant as opposed to two categories: the stranger, and the visitor. The places where persons may enter into an 'encounter' are various, depending upon their status and function. Strangers (beggars, wayfarers, unknown vendors) can have no access beyond the *patippuram*. At this very outer entrance is determined the right of any individual to enter the private domestic space. The steps, *patippuram*, gate, courtyard and verandah are to be seen as enclosing zones, the crossing of each being a symbol of social passage and acceptability. These boundaries must be interpreted in terms of the relation between inhabitants and outsiders. The stranger is one who must pass through such transitional phases before he is incorporated by rites of greeting and acceptance. Territorial passage from the outside to the inside is hierarchically marked by what Van Gennep termed 'neutral zones'.[4]

In Puthenangadi every house has a well even though 'municipal water' is available. Wells are usually on the eastern or northern side of the house, the southern side being considered inauspicious. According to tradition, when a well is dug the land that is credited to *Meenam*, *Medam* and *Magaram* (three astrological divisions of land) are considered auspicious sites. For this reason the well is not necessarily near the kitchen or outhouse but may be situated in the front. The Christian house is in architectural style essentially like any Hindu house of similar status. Puthenangadi's *taccan* (traditional house-builder/carpenter) said that the Christians have full faith in the Hindu *shastra*s in so far as building a house is concerned.

A house in Puthenangadi is thought to be located within its own seat of strength, and if this is not so, then there may be tendencies towards misfortune. Sickness, failure or melancholy which continue without cause are ascribed to such wrong placements of houses.

Most of Puthenangadi's houses are *pazhe taravat* (ancestral houses) whose walls and ceilings are completely built of teak or jackwood (*anjili*). The woodwork is often elaborately carved and decorated with brass knobs. Those who have the money have had the walls raised on granite. Some roofs are still low, and at the entrance one has to bend one's head. Most people are proud of the old houses in which they live, and point out its distinctive features, the intricate woodwork, panelling, the cross carved into the door and the lattice work which decorates the entrance of the house in overhanging filigree patterns.

Traditional houses had one important function, storing grain, and in their spatial geography, these houses draw a picture of another way of life. The houses express architecturally the fact that the *ara* (granary or strong room) was very often the heart of the house, with the other rooms built around it. The main rooms in a Syrian Christian house thus centred around the *ara* which served to keep safe the harvested grain, money and valuables of the house. Some houses had two *aras*. In the old days it was the custom to build the *thallam* or *kedaka muri* (bedroom) next to this domestic granary. Houses consisted basically of the *ara* (granary), the *thallam* (bedroom), the *porravarram* (a kind of passage), the *adukala* (kitchen) and the *thinna* (a long enclosed or open verandah, and a public and male space). Frequently, there was a cattle shed (*kannukali kood*) and the outhouse or *ara purra* where the grain was boiled and dehusked. The fact that the *ara* was traditionally the most significant part of the house is explicit in the term *arayum-purrayum ondu* which literally means to have a granary and house, but implies that a person has shelter, comfort, and is prosperous.

Given this central place of the *ara* in the symbolic ideas constituent in the arrangement of domestic space, many people are superstitiously hesitant about dismantling or removing the *ara* though in most houses it is in disuse, being used only to store cooking utensils of an older time—the giant bronze vessels, heavy wooden chests and urns which are no longer used, now that celebrations of a collective nature are minimal. The rooms around the *ara* are thought to be the most comfortable since the temperature here is believed to be moderate, never too cold even during the severest monsoon or too hot during the summer months. People with rheumatism, a common ailment, and old people generally live in the rooms around the *ara*.

A Christian house can be recognized by the 'holy' pictures on the walls. Among the people of Puthenangadi, the most popular picture is one of Christ praying at Gethsemane. Pictures of Mary with the infant Christ are also frequently displayed, as also those of the saints Gevarghese and Thomas. Geverghese (St George) is shown in combat with a dragon, referred to as *pambu* or snake by the Christians, while Thomas is often represented as standing with his feet placed on Malabar, on a globe in the centre of a starlit universe. These pictures express the continuing interest the Christians have in mythological motifs and the literature of the colportege.[5]

Family photographs also cover the walls and these—the holy pictures and the family photographs—are what one first sees, stepping across the threshold of the house. Beyond the threshold one enters the *thinna*, which is a long hall partially open since there are many windows opening on to the courtyard. Here, items of furniture usually include an easy chair, a couch and a few other simple pieces of furniture such as a table and a few straightback chairs. In upper middle class houses, the modern 'sofa-set' and dining table are found but rarely carpets or rugs other than the *paaye* (reed mat). There are few items of decoration besides old sepia-tinted family pictures which line the walls.

A few houses do have a 'show case' often full of neglected things like shells, wooden dolls, elephants or palm trees carved out of wood. Some traditional furniture to be found in the average *thinna* is of specially fine craftsmanship, particularly old wardrobes, rocking chairs, the ubiquitous *chaar kasera*, (vast lean-back armchairs which are extendable so that one's legs may be stretched out on them), and intricately carved couches made of rosewood. Calendars are rarely pictorial; for the most part they state only the date, the day and the 'star' or zodiac sign, along with detailed information about Christian feast days and ritual occasions. Natalie Zemon Davis has illustrated the difference between Protestant and Catholic calendars in Lyons in the sixteenth century;[6] Protestant calendars were bare of information regarding saints' days or astronomical features, and expressed the impact of the printed Bible and Protestantism upon calendar art. The Jacobite and Orthodox Christians display calendars which fall midway between the pictorial extravagance of the Romo-Syrians and the bareness and austerity representative of the Reformed Syrian churches.

Bedrooms have very few items of furniture—ordinarily only beds, which in some houses may be four-poster, carved and of rosewood. These are rooms which are used only for resting, and are essentially private spaces, accessible only to those who are intimately connected with the family.

While the *ara* is the physical centre of the house, the kitchen belongs to the women and is the social core of the house. In traditional houses, the kitchen is as big as the main room. It is like a hall, with grills on the high walls to let in light and let out smoke from the hearth. The kitchen and the hall are in many ways similar, though they define female and male spaces respectively. Women hardly use the living room except at times of family prayer or on ceremonial or formal occasions. It is a place where men gather, where the head of the household reads the newspapers, keep his accounts or listens to the radio. During the day when men are at work, a visitor will find the front part of the house absolutely unoccupied, and no amount of knocking will elicit any response. People usually go around to the back of the house where the kitchen with its washing and grinding spaces lies. The women are found here almost right through the day—

washing, cleaning, pounding, grinding, cooking, polishing, sweeping and talking.

In most houses, the kitchen has a rough concrete unpolished floor; sometimes, in poorer houses, it is made of beaten earth which has hardened to a cement-like consistency, and can be easily swept and kept clean by brooms made from the dry leaves of coconut palms. Almost all preparatory kitchen work—the sorting of vegetables, the cleaning and cutting of meat and fish, the peeling of potatoes and onions—is done sitting on the floor on extremely low flat wooden seats.

Hearth fires are still used to a great extent; good food is associated with slow wood fires and earthenware pots. Food when cooked on the hearth is also prepared in the traditional *ottupathram* (large bronze vessels) in which water is heated and rice cooked. Fish, meat, pulses and vegetables are cooked in the earthen pots (*chatti*), often black with use. The women, particularly on occasions of family reunions, sit together and work. It is in the kitchen that moral codes become most vividly expressed, where the world-view of the women is constructed and reaffirmed. Here family histories are recounted, and kinship relationships remarked upon.

GENEALOGIES AND RECONSTRUCTIONS OF FAMILY HISTORY

Narratives relating to the personal lives of the householders of Puthenangadi express the subjective character of personal reconstructions, showing once more the relation between language and the world. Gabrielle Spiegel suggests that genealogies are expressions of social memory, and thus have affinity with historical thought. Genealogy as history is mimetic, is perceptual rather than cognitive, and is controlled by dynastic rather than annalistic or calendar time. So also, genealogy serves to make time secular by grounding it in biology, transforming the connection between past and present into a real one 'seminally imparted from generation to generation'.[7] I shall now turn to popular reconstructions of family history among the people who live in Puthenangadi.

People who live in these traditional households consider themselves to be of 'old stock' (*pazhe taravat*). If today some of them are not very wealthy, they have memories of an earlier, grander, time. Some of these memories are not their own but are vicarious, handed down by parents or grandparents. The older people of Puthenangadi are given to reminiscences expressive of nostalgia and pride. Accounts of events in the family are frequently prefaced with the statement, 'Our family was one of the best, but it is exhausted now' (*sheenam vanu*—'exhaustion came'). In many such houses, the memory of past grandeur is articulate and vivid, and corroborated by neighbours who will say, 'Now they may have nothing, once they were lords'. While material prosperity is being underlined, we are also made aware of a claim towards rare privilege:

> We were once a fine family, one of the most important (*pra-dhanapettathu*). All we have now are memories, and a few things that I will show you which belonged to our fathers, and even these we could not take care of. See this *veeravalli pattu* (a kind of silk). It was worn by the men of our family at marriage. It was silk which was given to the *deva*s (gods) in the temple to wear, priceless even in the old days, but our privilege to wear during weddings. And gold, there was so much worn by our women at their marriages. Jewellery was a woman's right and a gift from her parents, part of her *stridhanam*, which was for her own use.

Some objects remain which reflect the family's past: the house itself, certain pieces of furniture (for both house and furniture, the kind of wood used and the extent of ornamentation are significant indices of status), utensils, particularly those made of bronze, and family portraits. Ownership of various kinds of bronze lamps is a status symbol even today, since the ritual use of lamps (*villaku*) is predominant.[8] As times grow hard, these lamps are being sold one by one, particularly since traditional items fetch a good price as *objets d'art*. Today, candles or oil lamps borrowed from wealthier relatives or neighbours are used for ceremonial purposes.

Family histories (*kudumba charitram*) are commonly known though subjective considerations colour narratives of this kind. Expressions of such bias are extremely interesting. Narratives of this kind reveal what people highlight about themselves, what they forget, what they choose to remember about others or about themselves. Each narrative, then, is to be seen as a symbolic system which represents the self or the other in a particular mode, and must not be judged according to the categories of truth and falsity as commonly understood.

Everyone knows everyone else in Puthenangadi. Kinship connections are seen to be of ultimate importance. The emphasis on these is clear from the fact that where connections through blood or marriage however distant are not recognized, there virtually stands the stranger. Since households are related to each other through some specific bond, knowledge of each family's past necessarily follows because the history of each is part of the history of the other. Where *kudumbams* (families) are distinguished enough to warrant the construction of *kudumba charitram* or genealogies, the relations between families are articulated more concretely, and thus provide a mutual reinforcement of status positions.

Genealogies are therefore cognitive maps which people have recourse to when new alliances are to be forged (as at the time of marriage), for claiming prestige or asserting status. Oral genealogies have basically utilitarian purposes, and memory serves with clarity and distinctness up to three generations, beyond which individuals are classified together as fathers (*appannmar*); however, when a family wishes to stake its claim as an 'old family', as one that can trace its genealogy back to eight generations or more, the situation is different. Then, written genealogy is not merely a history of the descent of a family, it is a pedigree. In one case, the construction of a written genealogy was stated to exist because of the ordainment of a member of the clan as bishop. Clearly the family wanted it to be acknowledged that the *metran* came from an 'old line'.

Other reasons why such pedigrees are drawn may be because of the individual interest of a member of the *kudumbam* ('Our grandfather liked doing these things'). The knowledge of family history is often a hobby, characteristic particularly of old men in their last years of life. The perusal of such documents by informants is accompanied by exclamations of surprise for the detailed information that it offers, and for the novelty of knowing about the past objectively so that it can help to answer the subjective question 'Who am I?'

The Thekkaethallakal family is one of the oldest and most dominant of Puthenangadi families, having lived in the *angadi* for twelve generations. This family is thought to have originally come from Chayal (one of the seven places where the apostle had established churches) but the oppression of the *Pandanmar* (a tribe of thieves) made them migrate to Chengannur where they were involved in various occupations. In the seventeenth century, a member of this family called Kurian came to Kottayam to engage in *veluchanna kachavadam* (coconut oil trade). At that time the palaces of the king were in the neighbouring Thazhathangadi, where even now one may see traces of royal courts, trenches and wells. By 700 ME (AD 1525) a prosperous community of Christians had settled in the area at the invitation of the king. A certain event occurred in this settlement around this time which was to affect indirectly the story of the Thekkaethallakal family.

An old woman of the Poonathra family died, and her body was buried inside the church, as was the custom, but in the most sanctified of places, under the *hayakala* (chancel). There were tremendous objections from many Syrian Christians when this was done; one night, the men of the Veloor family dug up the corpse, attached a rope to it, dragged it out, and tied the body to a tree. The Poonathra family went to the king and demanded redress for the insult. The king issued an order that all members of the Veloor family should be captured and brought to him but they, having heard of this command, escaped to the domains of the king of the north, the *vadakkankur rajav*. The king's men found only a woman who was pregnant, who had been unable to make her escape. The king, realizing that he had lost valuable men to the *vadakkankur rajav*, gave to the woman who remained land, money and a house. The present Thekkaethallakal house stands on this site.

The woman gave birth to a daughter, and when she grew up, she was given in marriage to Thommi, the son of Kurian Thekkaethallakal, who had come to Kottayam from Chengannur to do business in oil. Thommi lived in the house with his wife and mother-in-law (*amaiamma*), and so began, according to the family history, the Thekkaethallakal line in Kottayam, separated from the parent line in Chengannur from where Kurian and Thommi the oil merchants had come. Here is a cogent account of several social processes: the migration of groups from a distant region because of the oppression of other groups, whether Portuguese or *Pandammaar* (thieves); people living in close-knit residential groups engaged in traditional occupations (trade) under the patronage of the Hindu king. Internal dissensions lead to their dispersion, mediated through the royal office of justice and the consequent punishment. Migration occurs since the survival of the lineage group depends on this. A chance of circumstance leads to the marriage of the daughter of the one remaining member of the emigrant lineage with a stranger. A new lineage thereby emerges.

Another *kudumbam* which traces its ancestry coherently is the Kurisumootil family. These people trace their origins in Puthenangadi to the migrations of the sixteenth and seventeenth century, when Portuguese pressure in the northern parts of Kerala pushed Orthodox families desiring to keep the ritual traditions of their forefathers to other places. The *koodiyeta kalam* (immigration), according to the written narrative, is said to have occurred in the seventeenth century. These people believe that they stem from either a family in Palai or Kaduthuruthi. Their original name, the one in use before 825 ME (AD 1650), is unknown to them. This is the year in which the legendary cross which became the basis for building the most important church in the neighbourhood—Kurisu Palli—was found by an ancestress of the family (*Nungle de oru velliamma*—'an old mother of ours'). The earliest 'version' of Kurisu Palli, which is now an important pilgrim centre, was established near this *taravat* so that their name became *Kurisumootil* (under the cross).

Kurisumootil's first named ancestor was a man called Chandy who was head of his household in 1755. They were not a very prosperous family but his sons were known to be very fair and handsome, and three of them were 'adopted' (*deth keri*) by their wives' families. For 105 years before the lifetime of this Chandy, Kurisumootil had been a family identified with the discovery of the legendary cross which had been established near their *taravat*. The cross discovered by the ancestress had been placed outside in a small enclosure, and the Kurisumootil family took upon themselves the duty of filling the oil lamps around the cross and lighting them every day, a privilege that they still hold in the present Kurisu Palli. The grandson of Chandy, Oomakanda, was the richest man in Puthenangadi.

Oomakanda's son, Uthup Cheryan, was a tobacco merchant who settled in Veloor (a *kara* or quarter very near Puthenangadi). Ulhannan, the youngest son of Oomakanda, inherited according to custom the house and the duties and privileges connected with the Kurisu Palli. These were passed on to Lukose, Ulhannan's son, since the youngest son Andhreyos was 'adopted' (*deth keri*) by his wife's family. In the following generation, the second son of Lukose named Eipe took on the obligation, for his youngest brother Cheryan had died. Eipe had only three daughters, so the privilege now stands with Lukose's eldest son's son, Lukose, who will pass it on to his own son. The privileges associated with Kurisu Palli are important ones and the Kurisumootil family remains dominant because of these, though in actual number of households they are very few. These privileges include the keeping of the keys to Kurisu Palli. The manner in which privileges are passed down show that the rules of inheritance tend to alter according to circumstance. Thus, privileges of property tend to pass to the youngest son; the others must be established elsewhere or be adopted into wives' families. Death of the younger son allows the older to inherit, the absence of sons causes privileges to pass down the elder male line of the ascendant generation. Further, the local chapel in this sense is almost assimilated in the category of personal property, not in terms of the value that is associated with money or profit, but in terms of the privileges that accrue from taking care of sacred objects.

Some accounts of episodes in a family's past may explain certain features of that particular family which are peculiar to it while not being directly concerned with establishing genealogy as pedigree. The following oral narrative explains the manner by which priesthood may become established in a family, the curious circumstances out of which such a hereditary occupation may grow.

We have a bond that we must have at least one person in the church and so far we have been able to keep the tradition. Eight generations ago a *melpattakaran* (prelate) came to Malabar from Chaldea. He came walking, for he had vowed that he would do so; and when, after a long time, he reached Malabar he was a strange sight in his unfamiliar robes, communicating through sign language. At one hamlet when people saw him they shut their doors and it is said of that particular place that though there was once an *angadi* (settlement) such as there is here, it was destroyed (*nashichu*) because of the curse of a holy man to whom hospitality was denied.

One of our forefathers (*oru nunglde appen*) had emerged from the river where he was bathing when he saw this bishop from *Seemai* (Syria or foreign place), and he took him home and gave him food and shelter for as many days as he required. At that time the Christians used to worship snakes. Near the house was a crevice in which snakes would appear and were fed. The Chaldean bishop, on seeing this, chased away the snakes which then climbed up and hung from the rafters of the house. At this, the woman of the house said, 'Look, what comes when you harbour strangers', at which the foreign bishop motioned with his hands signifying that everything would be all right, and the snakes all disappeared and were never seen at the crevice again.

Our ancestor was ordained a priest by the bishop. Since then, there have always been priests in this *kudumbam*, and it is believed that if ever there is a generation without priests, the *kudumbam* will be doomed to decline. Members of the family have commemorated for generations the day of death of this bishop. The *Orma divasam* (commemoration) is celebrated with a *Qurbana* (eucharist) celebrated in his honour, and then the poor are fed *nei appam* (fried cakes) along with the family. This is done every year. Two generations ago, the *kudumbam* was told by the *sabha* (church assembly) members that there was no need to celebrate the *Orma divasam* of this bishop since he was Chaldean and not Antiochean. The year that they stopped the rite was one in which fever struck the family and some members died. It was felt then that this had happened because they had forgotten the *Bawa* (Holy Father), and since then they have commemorated the anniversary scrupulously.

This narrative reintroduces into popular discourse the three strands of the Hindu, the Syrian, and the Christian. While explaining the origin of priesthood in a particular family, it also explicitly establishes the link between the Mesopotamian (Chaldean) Church and the Indian Church in its most unique form—the sporadic appearance of an itinerant monk. It also establishes the power attributed to the curses of holy men. Here, it results in the annihilation of an entire hamlet of uncharitable Christians. Moreover, the narrative expresses the auspiciousness of bathing in the river and of encountering and sheltering a holy man. Along with this is presented the symbol of the continuation of Hindu customs among the Christians as seen in the worship of snakes.

The function of visiting prelates has often been stated to be that of returning apostasied Christians to the true path. Also represented here is the traditional problem of establishing what or who a saint is, especially when the category of the stranger intervenes. The stranger is one who is always limen, on the boundary of entering and departing, and therefore never truly understood.[9] He is capable of radically altering the traditional system, of bringing about changes which may have originally seemed unacceptable—the woman says in the narrative, 'Look what happens when you harbour strangers'. The narrative also expresses the idea that mime can reproduce the function of language. The monk never speaks yet is always clearly understood; if he is not understood, it is at some cost to the other, as in a hamlet being destroyed. The transitory nature of these visits by the prelates of the Middle East to the Christians of Malabar is also expressed. They came, according to tradition, to ordain priests, to consecrate the Holy Chrism, and to re-establish customs of the Eastern Church which may have lapsed. Further, the narrative expresses the continuing power of the *Bawa* (Holy Father) so that lapses of religious etiquette (commemoration services) result in the elaboration of his curse. Hospitality denied through the negation of mortuary feasting could result once more in the annihilation of the group through disease. Hereditary occupation is also given a sanction which is related to the myth of origin.

Narratives also express certain honours and privileges attendant on status which may otherwise be forgotten. Family remembrances, for instance, often express the fact of royal patronage, the services rendered to kings by loyal Christian subjects or such honours as were given to them by the rulers. According to tradition, the Syrian Christians were often in favour with the royal family in whose principality they lived as soldiers, traders or agriculturists. The following is a typical story of the patronage of the king towards a Syrian family for services rendered to him by a *vaidyan* (doctor). This incident, said to have happened six generations ago, is recounted by a ninety-six-year-old woman:

> The king had a hair, a tiny hair growing inside his eye-lid. It gave him great pain and no one could do anything for him. A Christian *vaidyan* (doctor) had come to him and seemingly cured the ailment. The king was pleased and gave him much money but in no time the hair grew back, troubling the king. In fact, the *vaidyan* had only cut the hair with a pair of scissors. Then my grandfather's grandfather went to the king and pulled the hair out by its root. He also put some ointment of his own making on the eyelid, and recommended that the king be enclosed in a dark room for three days. At the end of this time, the king was cured, and came out of the dark room. He gave the *vaidyan* a gift of land and instructed his *asari*s (craftsmen) to build on it a *nallu kettu* (a house built in the prestigious and complex architectual style which is a privilege of the high caste).

This narrative also expresses how a few Syrian Christian families are in possession of certain medicinal remedies which are usually sacred-properties of the *Namboodiri*s.

Similarly, an ancestor of an *angadi* family, Eruthikkel Thomas, is thought to have migrated from the north on the invitation of the *thekkumkur rajav* or the ruler of the southern kingdom. Thomas was a renowned swordsman and warrior and was employed by the king as a battalion commander. In stories associated with the Karot and the Ullatil families emerge similar motifs of royal patronage. Both families are shown by a genealogical chart to be offshoots of a family now extinct but once of some importance called Konopadam. Legend has it that these people were once so rich, their children played with gold coins. The narrative of this Konopadam family goes back to the time of the *thekkumkur rajav*, and the riot among the Christians (described by the Thekkaethallakal family) following the indignity inflicted upon the corpse of the woman of the Poonathra family.

Among those who ran away from the wrath of the king were the members of the Konopadam family. When the king realized that fear of punitive action was sending away the most prosperous of his subjects to other kingdoms, he forgave the Christians. The Konopadam family preferred to live some distance from the *rajav* and so shifted from Thazhathangadi (near the king's palaces) to Puthenangadi. The Konopadam family consisted of three generations: Valiya Korala, his son Kochu Korala, and grandson Thommi, with whom the patriline died out as he had two daughters and no sons. The first daughter was given in marriage to Kollatu Paraekkal Cheryan, and as dowry received land on top of a hill which came to be called Karot, later becoming the name of the family. Land at a lower elevation was given to the other daughter who is said to have married into the Palathinkal family, and this house came to be called Ullatil. Both the Karot and the Ullatil families belong to the *pathnettu veetukar* (the eighteen dominant households) though neither of these families have reached the level of prosperity attained by their common ancestors. Konopadam Thommi who gave land to his two daughters, gave to Kurisu Palli the land that lay between the two plots.

This narrative expresses the nature of inheritance and succession: the death of Konopadam Thommi results in the extinction of the Konopadam patriline. However, it continues in a submerged fashion as, for instance, the Ullatil branch of the Konopadam line. The husbands of the daughters of Konopadam Thommi are adopted but do not keep the house-name of their wives, changing it to a new house-name which is based on location.

When the Ullatil branch of the Konopadam line became impoverished, they sold the rest of their land to a family called Malliakal.
This family came to the *angadi* five generations ago. Now, because of
the manner in which their numbers have increased and their continuing material prosperity, they claim a place as one of the older
families in the *angadi*, and when this privilege is denied them, they
express anger. But the *angadi* families have a good memory with
regard to latecomers, and generational depth is a matter of status
hierarchy. Thekkaethallakal in this respect stands first, since their
genealogy is known for as many as thirteen generations. Varrikat is
both old and numerically predominant—in fact, the greatest number
of households belongs to the Varrikat lineage. An interesting story
relating to this hierarchy of families was narrated by an old lady of the
Thekkaethallakal *kudumbam*.

My husband's younger brother to whom the *taravat* came through
inheritance fell on hard times and found that he could not afford
to keep the house. Things came to such a pass that he was forced
to sell and Ittycheryan of Padinjerakara wanted to buy it. But his
mother would not allow him to do so because she thought that
the house should continue to remain in Thekkaethallakal hands
since it was an ancient house. Then my husband, realizing the
importance of what the old woman of Padinjerakara was saying,
somehow borrowed the money and managed to buy it from his
brother and so it remained with the family.

The importance of the family name to a large extent lies in its
genealogical age or depth. This is evident in the fact that all Syrian
Christians frequently hark back to their myth of origin—to AD 52 to
Thomas, and the legendary conversion of brahmins. Evidently assimilate across caste lines did occur, particularly in conversions of Nair
families. There are also instances when lower castes were absorbed
into the community of higher status Christians, though most Syrian
Christians deny this vehemently.

Just as some households may be associated with an 'ancient name',
certain families are associated intimately with the conflict in the
church, and their very name evokes a controversial response, depending on which side of the battlelines the informant speaks from.
The Orthodox Syrians in Puthenangadi believe one particular family
to be under a curse because, from once being in the position of a

premier family, it is now quite ordinary and without distinction. These are 'Patriarch's people', and those who belong to this group treat members of this family with respect because they gave away so much wealth to the *sabha* that the descendants are now poor. A member of this family said:

> My grandfather gave everything he had to the church, fighting the forces that chose to break the traditional bond with Antioch. That was his faith and for this he sold all his lands and died in debt. He asked for nothing in return. Out of more than 2000 acres of paddy land he sold everything except 505½ acres. Of that he asked that 5½ acres be kept aside and gifted to the church should there be union again. In 1958, when 'peace' returned to the *sabha* these 5½ acres were given to the *palli* (local church).

When families are so closely identified with one *katshi* (party) or another, their very name conjures up certain clearly defined associations. Thus Plaveddekal is closely identified with the Patriarch's party and most people of this *kudumbam* are Patriarch's people. To come across a Plaveddekal family which is affiliated to the Catholicos is unusual, and an instance of this has a personal reason behind it:

> My grandfather was Paulose Eapen's elder brother. Since he had a lot of land and property, for financial considerations and management, he put some in his younger brother's name. Later, when he requested that the deeds be returned to him, his brother said, 'Let it remain as it has been till now'. So automatically my grandfather lost a lot of property because of this misappropriation. Later, when the church quarrels began in earnest, we remained aloof, though all the Plaveddekal families went with Paulose Eapen. My grandfather would have nothing to do with them. So for this reason we remained with the *metran*.

Variations in narrative about a dominant household appear when the narrator is of low caste and has been intimately connected with a particular family through service. The history of a family offered through a servant's eyes depicts a picture that the members of the Christian family would perhaps never provide. Acharya Chovati belongs to the *Izhava* caste (traditionally toddy tappers), and for generations

her family has worked for the houses of the Syrian Christians in Puthenangadi. Of one particular household she said:

> There is a curse on them. Their house is full of corpses, and the
> curse of their sins will remain on them for some time (*korae
> naal*). My father used to tell me that Chakko Saar was a *muthalali*
> (landlord) of the old type, of the old days. He was the only man
> who had permission to enter the raja's courts without prior
> permission, and in those days Christians were rarely permitted,
> but he had power and money.
>
> How that family treated us Chovans: we had to stand there
> with heads lowered and hands folded when spoken to, otherwise
> remain silent; we were like the dust under his feet, my father
> said. He told me that once Chakko Saar went to the *paddam*
> (rice fields) where his people were working and, having seen
> to all matters, he said that the unhusked rice should be brought
> to his house by ten the next morning. But the wind was against
> the boats and by the time they reached, it was evening. So they
> tied the boats and went to the back of the house, not having per-
> mission to enter through the front. One of the servants looked
> out (he had eight or nine of them in the house) and told the
> master that the workers had come with the *nellu* (unhusked
> rice). They were kept waiting for a long time—do you know
> why? *Sameyam theti poyi* (they were late in arriving). So he kept
> them waiting though they were tired and hungry; after all, they
> had been rowing through the *kayel* (backwater/lake) for many
> hours in the hot sun.
>
> After some hours had passed, as they were sitting in the yard,
> they heard Chakko Saar saying '*Arriyum sammanavum koduku*'
> (give them rice and provisions). They were then given rice, some
> dried fish and the things with which to cook it. Tired though
> they were, and the time was now 11 o'clock, they set about
> building a fire, washed and scrubbed the cooking vessels and
> cooked the food. There were ten or twelve of them, and by the
> time the rice was cooked, it was almost one o'clock. No one paid
> any attention to them, so they got *kacci* (hay) from the boats and
> slept there. In the morning they asked for some *kattam kapi*
> (concentrated or black coffee) but Chakko himself came out
> and shouted at them (*Chadichu*) saying, 'You were told to
> come at ten in the morning, and you have come at night. You
> were given food to eat; that is all that you will get. Next time it

will teach you to come on time as you are told'. Now there was
one among them who was a 'man' and not frightened of the
muthalali. After all it was no fault of theirs that they were late; so
he told the other men, 'Come, let us go, there is nothing to be
had here, some others will untie the boats and unload the grain'.

But they needed the money, and were also afraid of the
muthalali. In those days there were no trade unions. The *thozhilali*
(workers) were bonded to the *muthalali*. This man went away
and then he unleashed Satan (*Satane ayrichu vittu*). There was
trouble which never ceased at Chakko's house after that. Stones
fell on the roof all through the night, and the food was full of all
kinds of terrible things as soon as it was set on the tables—faeces,
hair, stones, paper—there was no end to it. A few days later the
master of the house had to go somewhere. His wife approached
my ancestors who were well-versed in the art of 'tying up the
devil' and asked for their services. They told her, 'We will need
such and such a thing and you must have these herbs ready and a
big vessel in one of the inner rooms'..

At night, my father's father and his brothers all gathered in
Chakko's house to perform the magic. The pounding of the
herbs and the preparation of the medicines began. They say
there was just one *villaku* (lamp), and the men started singing
and beating the drum. Just then there were loud shouts at the
gate. Chakko Saar had returned without warning. His wife
started shivering and trembling; after all, she had wanted this
done behind his back. She had wanted Satan to be tied up
before her husband returned. Chakko Saar came in with his big
stick and said '*Eddo aa ra?*' (Hey, who is that!), and began to
swing the stick around. Everyone left in a hurry except my
grandfather's brother who was beginning to leap, having
become possessed by the devil; as Chakko Saar descended on
him with the stick, my relative said, 'Have you recognized me?'
in a very menacing tone. For the first time Chakko Saar felt fear,
for the question kept being repeated. 'Have you understood me,
do you know who I am?' He said, 'I will give whatever you ask;
but go away'. So the devil said, 'Ask my pardon.' Chakko Saar
did so, and after that the curse was removed, and life returned to
normal. Since it had been my grandfather's brother who had
been responsible for tying up the devil, we were given a privilege
for two generations—our family's needs for rice were met by
them.

This narrative expresses in exaggerated form the traditional relation between Syrian Christian masters and their lower-caste Hindu servants. It approaches the problems of hierarchy in terms of the relations of power. In the first case, the master is one who has wealth (much land, many servants), and being prosperous, controls his workers through the use of repressive measures. They must obey his will, and delays, errors and misdemeanours are calculated in terms of disobedience rather than the effect of the vagaries of nature or physical tiredness; he has the power to keep them waiting, to withhold food, they being the 'dust' under his feet. Further, he is portrayed as a man who has royal patronage, and therefore more powerful than the ordinary Syrian Christian.

Secondly, the worker, who has no rights, bows to his Christian landlord because he is dependent on him for work and wages. This precludes the possibility of asserting his identity against the master except by one who has courage and is therefore a 'real' man, as opposed to the others who are subjugated.

The 'unleashing of Satan' expresses the traditional fashion by which a repressed person could express his anger. Witchcraft is the unofficial sanction in a traditional society, the manner by which the angry subject exacts vengeance. However, it would seem that the *muthalali* (landlord) is not unduly perturbed by the consequent inconvenience. In fact he 'goes away for a few days'. It is his wife who expresses fear against the play of the devil and invites the exorcists, but this must be done behind her husband's back. His return frightens the woman who dreads being rebuked by her husband for giving in to superstition. How would a fearless Christian deal with the presence of Satan in his house? Chakko Saar is an archetypical *muthalali*. He is not afraid of anybody and is willing to 'swing his stick' at intruders, drum beaters and medicine burners, though it be dead of night. However, the menacing voice of 'Satan' forces him to change his stance; he accedes out of necessity to have Satan 'tied up'. Further, the man who performs this office is given a privilege that is passed down to the next generation ('Our family's needs for rice were met'). This payment is typical of an agricultural society, and expresses the alliance between two hierarchical levels where a favour is paid for.

The corpus of narratives discussed here are of three kinds— genealogies, family histories and episodic accounts. They are symbolic statements which structure relationships between individuals, and which are assertions of social identity. Similar narratives are found which relate neighbourhood life and dominant families to the churches around Puthenangadi.

THE LOCAL CHURCHES AND THE SOCIAL NETWORK

In Puthenangadi spaces are mapped by their relative distance to the *palli* or church which, as can be seen, is the most important of the symbols that tie (or divide) the Christians in neighbourhood life. In the relatively small space that constitutes the land area of Puthenangadi (0.50 sq. km.), there are three churches—Kurisu Palli, Simhasana Palli and Puthen Palli. Pazhenthe Palli and Cherya Palli lie off the main road where the houses of Pazheangadi and Puthenangadi face each other. These two are incorporated into the neighbourhood's consciousness even though technically they are in another quarter or *kara*. The churches, then, are like signposts depicting ideas of direction and space so that persons are referred to as living north, south, west or east of a particular church, people are described as seen going in the direction of or coming away from any one of these churches.

The churches are the central landmarks on the neighbourhood map—from these cardinal points the neighbourhood marks its spatializations. Accounts of the history of the six churches that structure the geographical space in and around Puthenangadi are coherent, and describe the relations between the people's past and present as Christians in a neighbourhood. The people's representation of who they are—the Christians of Puthenangadi—constantly refers to how their neighbourhood came into being, who the dominant families were, and how the six churches were built.

According to popular belief, when the first families migrated to Kottayam, they had no church and the nearest was at Kaduthuruthy and Kuravilangad. The only time that people went to church was in the week before Easter, spending all of Passion week there. In the period after Easter they celebrated the life cycle rituals of marriage and baptism, many of them being done collectively. Those who had none of these ceremonies to perform returned directly after Easter.

These families went to Kaduthuruthy or Kuravilangad by boat, carrying with them rice, provisions and servants. Since this long journey created a disturbance in the routine of their lives and was very inconvenient, the people decided to have a church of their own. Help came in the form of a man named Kattanar Cherian Mathu of

Kaduthuruthy, who brought with him some families who needed land in order to begin a new life. These immigrants were accepted by the king himself, who gave them the status of *athithi* (guests) and provided them with land on which to settle. (The kings were always pleased to have Christian subjects because they were a prosperous and hardworking people.) The ruler also gave them land for the church and is believed to have himself arrived and staked the boundaries with a trident (*trikai*). This was in 725 ME (AD 1550) according to an ancient song still remembered by Kurisumootil Lukose.

However, it so happened that Cheryan Mathu gave precedence in all matters relating to church affairs to those families who had accompanied him from Kaduthuruthy. This was because they were *thekkumbhagar* (southists) or Canaanites. Therefore, the other Christians decided to build a church for themselves in Puthenangadi where a wooden cross had accidently been discovered. They were mocked by the rival group of Canaanites who, according to the song, are believed to have said, 'Defeated, you move south'. The Puthenangadi Christians wanted to remain in the same area but there existed a royal order that there could not be more than one church in any one quarter or *kara*. The solution came from some friends at court who demarcated the boundaries so that the first church was now in a different quarter technically from the plot for the new church, while actually each was only a stone's throw away from the other.

Cherya Palli

The Christians who had moved away from the first church now gathered under the leadership of Ouseph Kattanar and received permission from the king and the prelate to build another church; thus Cherya Palli was born. It is the 'mother church' for Puthenangadi residents regardless of whether they belong to the Patriarch's party or to the *metran*'s. This church was built with the basis of the choice of place and the manner of construction in accordance with the conventions of the Hindu science of building as typified in the *Thaccu Shastra*.

First, a site was found as prescribed by the *shastras*. A black cow was let loose, and the place where it dropped dung without passing urine was to be considered the ideal place where the church should be built. [According to a song, the new church, the result of a quarrel, was built twenty-nine years after Vellya Palli came into existence, i.e., in 1579].

Everyone watched as the cow circled the field; then at the very edge of a precipice it dropped dung in the required manner. The site was accepted and a great stone wall was built to protect the church from the precipice. However, the beginning of the construction was not auspicious. Every wall that was built during the day was dismantled at night by unidentified miscreants. The people complained to the king who said that they must give him proof or a sign (*adayalam*). One night the wife of the watchman saw a hand on the wall dislodging bricks. She hacked it with her kitchen knife thus providing proof, for the next day all knew the identity of the man, a *thekkumbhagar* Christian. As a gift, the watchman and his wife were given nine cents of land which was in the possession of that family till recently, and the land was known as *kai vettya sthalam* (land or place where the hand was hacked).

When the building was nearing completion, the chief *asari* (carpenter) found that the ends would not meet, the measurements had been wrong. On examination, it was found that miscreants had cut short the ends of certain crucial poles with such care that the destruction had gone unnoticed, and the error in measurement had not come to sight till the last. The *asari* killed himself, hanging himself from the church roof.

This sacrifice is seen as an ill omen by the people who say its evil influence has never lifted. The church has always been afflicted by dissensions and quarrels.

The external aspect of the Cherya Palli resembles a Hindu temple. It is surrounded by a courtyard on all sides, and the walls are similar to Hindu temple walls in height, width and design. Further, like the temple, it has a *patippuram* (a threshold space) which is a small tiled shelter, a gate which mediates between the outside world and the outer courtyards surrounding the church. Motifs such as the peacock or *maile* (associated with the Apostle Thomas, who, according to one myth, was killed accidently by a hunter who was aiming for a peacock) and two robed Assyrian figures adorn the outer walls. There are also representations of a big fish which recalls Jonah and the Whale, angels, a lamb (the symbol of redemption) and a tiger (for which informants could not give any explanation).

There was no cemetery attached to the Cherya Palli for it was the custom to bury the dead under the floor of the church since this signified nearness to God, the body being rolled in a mat and then buried. An alternative space for burial was the *nedashalla*, a kind of 'second' space, a continuation of the nave, extending outside the main portal of the church on the western side. It was here that the *anyajyadi* (other *jyati*s or castes) were in the habit of standing when visiting these churches. Small children were buried behind the walls, proof of which emerged as late as 1981 when the floor of Cherya Palli was being given a mosaic surface. The practice of burying in the church was stopped through the office of a foreign *metran*, who said that by doing this the churches were being desecrated. Subsequently land around the church was used for this purpose.

Kurisu Palli

The story of how Kurisu Palli (the Church of the Cross) came into existence is closely tied to the history of the family called Kurisumootil. There are two versions of the story, of which one has greater credibility for the Syrian Christians:

> An ancestress of the Kurisumootil family saw a wooden cross floating in the *thode*, which was swollen by the monsoon floods. She pulled it ashore and left it in the cattle shed to dry. During the night the cows began to call without ceasing and the family, attributing the disturbance to the sacred character of the cross, brought it into the house and kept it safely in the *ara*. Later, the cross was anchored to the ground, people passing by stopped to pray in front of it, and miracles slowly began to be associated with it. It was first placed under a shelter of thatch (*olla*) and then later under a field roof. Its reputation as a sacred place grew. Some believed that it was one of the crosses which St Thomas had established and that in the flood it had been swept away from its home church.

This 'establishment of the cross' (*Kurisu sthabichue*) is thought to have occurred in 1650. By the effect of the sun and rain, the original wooden cross was destroyed, and a stone cross was put in its place. Since it was a *Kurisumootil* ('beneath the cross') ancestor who had discovered the cross, this family enjoys certain privileges which include the keeping of the keys to the church, the lighting of the 'inextinguishable lamps' (*kedathe villakku*), and the greatest privilege of all by which they receive at the time of festivals a pot of sweet rice (*pachor*) which has been taken into the *madabaha* (sanctuary) of the church and blessed.

The other version of how Kurisu Palli was established is offered by a *Chovan* or *Izhava* (lower caste Hindu) family, and it is laughed off by the Syrian Christians as *verde aa* (nonsense). This version, however, shows the significance of Kurisu Palli to believers who are not Christians, the link between the dominant Puthenangadi families and the church, the relationship between Syrian Christians and their lower-caste servants. Kurisu Palli is often referred to as being the 'property' of 18½ families. Eighteen families are Christian, the oldest inhabitants of the *angadi*. The half family is that of the *Chovan*. Being lower caste, they are afforded the status of only 'half' a family.

One night, one of my forefathers (*vellyappen*) was returning home after work. He was a *Cetan* (toddy tapper). At that time, there were few houses here; it was *kaadu* (forest). At the place where Kurisu Palli now stands it was difficult to find a path; however, he was in the custom of cutting his way through. That night, he saw something large and gleaming in the dark. In those days, *Chovan*s were lacking in intelligence, it was the Christians who had the brains. Fortunately, that has changed and now the *Chovan*s can look after themselves. So my ancestor, seeing this object gleaming in the dark, ran all the way to the house of Ulhannan Saar and folding his hands said, '*Acca, Acca,*' (Sir, Sir) 'There is something bright in the forest'. To this, Ulhannan Saar said, '*Chooroot kethiyir*'. ('Light a fire made from dry leaves'—to be held in the hand like a torch). They went to the forest and sure enough, the gleaming object was still there. 'It must be some fireflies,' said Ulhannan Saar. Then he said to my forefather, 'You go and get a *chembu kalam* (large copper vessel) and we will cover it so that tomorrow morning if it still exists, we will find it'. My ancestor went back and returned with the *chembu kalam* which Ulhannan Saar took to cover the object. Then he turned around and urinated a little near the *kalam*.

My ancestor, being the fool he was, thought that the Saar had done this because he felt the need. But the Saar knew that if you spit or urinate near an illusion it will disappear. If it is not an illusion it will remain firm on the ground. He sent away my forefather who, being a fool, picked up his bag and knife and went his way. What the Saar found was a priceless gem which he took home and hid in the *ara*. But it gleamed and gleamed with such a light that the next morning he threw it, and where it fell, they built a church. This gleaming jewel was one that belonged to Shiva—it was in the possession of the temple at Thirunnakkara (the famous temple a furlong from Puthenangadi) and had been lost in the flood. So the church is based on the property of the Hindu gods—and that is why Hindus too come to worship here, though they cannot themselves explain the cause of their attachment.

The church belonged to the eighteen dominant families in the *angadi*, but they gave privileges to one more family—that of the *Chovan* who had directed them to the stone.

But since we are *Chovan*s and not Syrians, we were counted as only 'half' a family. The privileges we were given were the right to celebrate in the *peryanal*s (festivals) of the Kurisu Palli and the gift of food on such days. In fact, one *kalam* (a large earthenware vessel) of *pachor* (sweet rice) was set aside for our family with our name written on it with *chunam* (white lime). This tradition continues, and it is one of my father's brother's sons who receives it on our behalf.

These are the two legends which describe the establishment of Kurisu Palli in Puthenangadi. However, because of its importance to the neighbourhood, there are other accounts of how it came into being. Kurisu Palli is often referred to as the 'heart' of Puthenangadi, and this sentiment is articulated further by the oral traditions associated with the Errithikkel family which explain the origin of priesthood in this family and simultaneously describe the history of Puthenangadi's Kurisu Palli.

In north Kerala, perhaps four hundred years ago or more, there was a brahmin family by the name of Errithikkel Illam. By the invitation of the *thekkumkur rajav*, they came as priests to a temple in Kottayam at Thiruvaddakal (very close to Puthenangadi). There were two brothers serving as temple priests and one of them took the path of Christianity. This was the ancestor from whom the present Errithikkel *kudumbam* takes its origin, though genealogical information is provided only for five generations. Nothing is known of the other brother who remained a Hindu. Around the same time there was a major migration of Christians from as far as Kodungaloor to as near as Kuravilanged, because of either Portuguese or *pandanmar* persecution. They came seeking the protection of the *thekkumkur rajav* who was only too glad to patronize the prosperous and hard-working Syrian Christians. For them, the king set apart the best of his lands, close to his palace, and so Thazhathangadi and Velyangadi became predominantly Christian centres.

The Errithikkel family provided priests to these Christians. By the nineteenth century, they were very powerful, and had priestly rights over Cherya Palli, which was the 'mother church' for all Christians living in and around Kottayam. It was here that they came to celebrate festivals, and when possible they came to take part in the *Qurbana*. Cherya Palli came into existence after twenty-five years of quarrels between the Canaanites and the indigenous Christians, and the land for this church was given to the latter by the *thekkumkur* kings. It lay between Thazhathangadi and Velyangadi, the two commercial centres of Kottayam, which were dominated by the Christians. Thazhathangadi had a cross which sheltered it from harm at a place called Kurisumood. It still stands there, a guard against evil and its dangers. Some families from these older *angadi*s wanted to be near their rice fields and coconut groves, and set up their houses there, and thus became Puthenangadi.

Another cross was established similar to the one in Thazhathangadi and there was faith in its power to shelter them. 'Among us there is always a great respect for the *devalayam*—for the place where God dwells, for that which is God's place.' So when the new *angadi* (Puthenangadi) was established, there appeared with it a new cross, which was respected by not only the Christians but also the *Porajyathikal* (non-Christian castes). There were miracles associated with this cross, and over it, in 1735, a church was constructed, an *olla palli*—a small church made of wood and a thatched roof—soon to be replaced by one with small scallop-shaped tiles made by the local potters. At this time, Cherya Palli was served by seven or eight priests belonging to the priestly lineages of Poonathra, Errithikkel, Mekkat, Oopootil and Venkadath, and each of them took turns celebrating *Qurbana* at the Puthenangadi Kurisu Palli. Since the number of devotees around the Puthenangadi Kurisu continued to grow, it was decided ('perhaps two hundred years ago') that *Qurbana* would be celebrated at the cross on Saturday, and one of the priests associated with the Cherya Palli would offer prayers and celebrate the Eucharist. Soon the *Qurbana* was also conducted on Sundays at the Kurisu Palli. However, the great festivals (*moranaya peryanaal*) of the church—the birth, death and resurrection of Christ, the feasts associated with Mary and the saints—continued to be celebrated in Cherya Palli as also, till 1958, the rituals of life cycle. The church as it presently stands was completed in 1898 in the Gothic style at the suggestion of Andros of Kattapurath who went to Alleppey and enlisted the help of English architects. He is remembered because he travelled all over Kerala visiting churches, and only after careful consideration of designs, particularly with reference to ventilation, did work on the church begin. (More than one informant remembers the darkness and the bats of the early twentieth century churches.) It was built by traditional Hindu craftsmen (the *asari* family of Puthenangadi), and then purified and blessed by the priest. The church was dedicated to *Kurusappoopen* (The Old Man of the Cross) as St Thomas is popularly called. The eighteen dominant householders of Puthenangadi, the *pathnettu veetukar*, contributed the most toward the building of the church, and by this act they became the *avakashigal* (heirs) to certain privileges of Kurisu Palli. This includes the fact that only representatives of the eighteen families could become trustees of the church.

Kurisu Palli is the heart of the neighbourhood. The other two churches in Puthenangadi do not share the same importance, are not characterized by this sense of power, of *mysterium tremendum*. But Kurisu Palli is not visited by all the Christians of Puthenangadi, and certainly not by the Patriarch's followers, since it is under the aegis of the Catholicos.

Pazhenthe Palli

Following the schism three generations ago, the properties of the Jacobite Church were divided by a decree of the Royal Court and very little came to the Reformist Mar Thoma, who were seen as secessionists. The church of the latter had to be built up again, mostly with the help of the laity and the donations and gifts that they gave. Just outside Puthenangadi, across the main road which separates it from Pazheangadi, is the St Thomas Church which belongs to the Mar Thoma. The location of the Mar Thoma Church (often referred to merely as *Pazhe Palli*), very near Puthenangadi and a stone's throw from Cherya Palli, was described as a clever tactic on the part of the Reformists:

> Pazhenthe Palli stands where it would be seen, so that all those who could be swayed, whose minds were not yet made up could be tempted. If the church had been built far away, who would leave the mother church?

There were many people in Puthenangadi who were in two minds about identifying themselves as Conservatives or Reformists.

We stood between the Mar Thoma and the Yakoba when the church was divided, and there were many people here of the same disposition. From our mother's side we were related to Chandapilla Kattanar, one of the most predominant Reformists. From our father's side we were related to the chief follower of the *bawa*'s supporters. When Cherya Palli was under the Reformists, we all belonged with them. Most of our fathers (*appenmar*) were swayed by their ideas. But then the Reformists lost the case and they lost Cherya Palli where our ancestors were buried, so we moved back to the Conservatives. The Mar Thoma, accepting the Royal Court decree, built St Thomas Church on the periphery of Puthenangadi, close to Cherya Palli, which they had considered to be rightly theirs. But they had no burial grounds and 'a church without a burial ground lacks strength' (*shakti*). Finally, deeds were procured for land in Puthenangadi, adjacent to the Jacobite *Puthen Palli*, which is the Jacobite cemetery. On the day the deeds were acquired, a child died and was at once buried there so that there could be no further quarrel regarding the use of the land.

Puthen Palli

The Mar Thoma cemetery thus lies adjacent to Puthen Palli, a church which functions for the Yakoba almost entirely as a cemetery church; rituals relating to the dead take place here, including funerals and ceremonies of rememberance. Puthen Palli too grew out of a quarrel, and it pre-dates the St Thomas Church. It was built during the time of the court cases between the conservative and reformist parties of the nineteenth century Syrians. At this time, Cherya Palli was locked up, and the Jacobites were not sure to whom the church would go once the decrees were passed. So Puthen Palli was built inside Puthenangadi with its attendant graveyard. The graveyard itself was a later addition; till the last century, according to informants, the dead were buried inside the church.

Families had burial spaces under the floor of the church which was covered by tiles removable at funeral times. The reason for this was that the dead were believed to be 'safe' there. Besides, there were people (competitors, people with grudges, hostile to Christian interests) who wanted to damage the *Nazranis* (as the Christians were often called) who would steal the bodies and dishonour Christians, as is evident from the story relating to the Veloor *kudumbam*. But this practice was given up. Then one of our *bawa*s came from Antioch and he said that it was insulting to the dead to stand on them while we prayed and from then on, we started burying our dead outside.

Simhasana Palli

The later quarrel within the conservative party was to result in the building of yet another church in Puthenangadi in the early part of the twentieth century. An old priest in Puthenangadi said:

When in 1085 ME (1910) Cherya Palli was first locked up because of quarrels, Joseph Kattanar, my uncle, and the father of the present Thomas Kattanar, built a chapel for his use where he celebrated *Vishudha Qurbana* But the remaining Kattanars who had till then served Cherya Palli were left seeking new churches. Joseph Kattanar treated the chapel he had built as his own property and had wanted to keep it under his *bharanam* (rule). So Simhasana Palli was built by some of us, the land being donated by Akara C J Kurian. It was here that those belonging to the Patriarch's party gathered to celebrate *Qurbana*, while those of the *metran*'s party had to go to Elias Chapel in the town. Simhasana Palli was ready for occupation in 1094 or 1095 (1919 or 1920). Venkadath Joseph Kattanar, who had been one of the priests serving in Cherya Palli but had privileges at Manarcaddu Palli (family rights to serve there as priest), returned to Puthenangadi and became the priest for Simhasana Palli.

This church too grew out of the Patriarch's people's need for a place to worship, and from donations and gifts. Families traditionally felt such an obligation. To give the land on which the church was built, to donate a door to it or the pulpit was an honour which even grandchildren remember.

The neighbourhood churches show the concretization of events in architecture, for each church is a mnemonic which encompasses within it a story of the neighbourhood's past. Each of these churches was spawned of a quarrel, and represents a particular historical moment or opinion. The church is the centre of neighbourhood life; affiliation to one church or another underlies community identity. Each church reflects a shared sense of faith and yet at the same time it expresses separation through divided loyalties.

Notes

1. Topographically, the distinction between town and country is blurred in Kerala.
2. See Max Weber, *The City* (Illinois: Free Press, 1958).
3. See e.g. Pierre Bourdieu, 'The Berber House' in Mary Douglas (ed.), *Rules and Meanings* (Harmondsworth: Penguin, 1971) and *Outline of a Theory of Practice* (Cambridge: Cambridge University Press, 1979); Daniel, *Fluid Signs*; Raymond Firth, 'Postures and Gestures of Respect' in Ted Polhemus (ed.), *Social Aspects of the Human Body* (Harmondsworth: Penguin, 1978), p. 88; David Pocock, *Kanbi and Pattidar: A Study of the Pattidar Community of Gujarat* (London: Oxford University Press, 1972).
4. See Arnold Van Gennep, *The Rites of Passage* (London: Routledge and Kegan Paul, 1977), p. 18.
5. Lucien Febvre and Henri-Jean Martin, *The Coming of the Book: The Impact of Printing 1450–1800* (London, New Left Books, 1976).
6. Zemon Davis, *Society and Culture in Early Modern France*.
7. Gabrielle Spiegel, 'Genealogy: Form and Function in Medieval Historical Narrative', *History and Theory*, vol. xxii, 43–53, 1983, p. 50.
8. There is the *nillavillaku*, a floor lamp often with as many as 28 wicks in seven rows of basins. The *kuthu-villaku* is a commonly found hanging lamp, often ornamented with an animal's or bird's head which is the point of attachment for the heavy link chain from the rafters. The *kole-villaku* is used particularly at the time of marriages, being a lamp with a long horizontal handle, so that this oil lamp is held as one would a ladle.
9. Georg Simmel, *On Individuality and Social Forms* (Chicago: University of Chicago Press, 1971) See also Van Gennep, op. cit.

4

Marriage, Birth and Death: The Rituals of Passage

The ritual life of Syrian Christians can be understood in terms of two aspects: the ceremonies of the house, and the ceremonies of the church. Domestic rituals reveal a Christian community which is in consonance with the wider Hindu cultural domain; particularly in the use of ritual substances (for instance, coconuts, areca nuts, oil lamps and rice). However, the two faces of ritual—domestic and canonical—are in their own way inextricably linked. Domestic rites prepare the key celebrants for the canonical rituals through the codes of food, prestation and formalized language; a particular state is induced whereby celebrants are 'marked off'[1] as different and separate, and this mood prepares them·for the rite of passage into which they are about to enter within the sacred space of the church.

The death rituals of the Syrian Christians are somewhat different from the life-affirming rituals of marriage and birth. In the death ceremony, the church enters the domestic space in a much more pervasive sense. The domestic rituals of death prepare the Christian for a mortal end which is unique to the Christian association of believers, and in this sense there are fewer similarities with the dominant regional culture of Hinduism.

While the domestic rituals for the main part show similarities with the wider cultural domain, the canonical rituals express one basic theme. This is the parallel between the life of Christ and the life of the Christian, expressed through the liturgical language of ritual. Marriage, birth and death, the key events in the life cycle of individuals and groups, are treated here as a set, and the questions of ritual, relationships, and property rights discussed.

MARRIAGE

Marriage is seen as a sacramental and permanent bond, and the arrangement of a match requires the serious attention of elders. Till about thirty years back, denominational endogamy was strictly prevalent, and those who broke the code had to pay a fine to the church. Even today, marriages within the same denomination (if not the same 'party' or *katshi*) remain the practice. Inter-religious marriages are taboo, as also marriage to a deceased wife's sister, a deceased husband's brother, and to all relatives up to seven generations.

The initiative in arranging a match is taken by the girl's family. Kinship and friendship circles continue to play a great role although the service of the *kothan* (professional matchmaker) is gaining in importance. A preliminary statement regarding the possibility of a match is made by the girl's family which is represented by the elder paternal members of the household. *Stridhanam* (dowry) is one of the basic issues discussed during this negotiation, and if the sum offered is too low, there is available the language of implicit refusal with its characteristic formulae. The two phrases which are used most often are 'Our son is not yet ready for marriage' and 'We have received another proposal which we are considering'.

A return visit, part of the ceremonies of negotiation, is scheduled, and made by the father and the elder paternal kin of the boy and his mother's brother. Here, a more formal declaration regarding the *stridhanam* is made. The pact is made entirely between the *appenmar* (fathers). The exclusion of the key actors in the negotiation is clear in the stock phrase used at this time, 'Let me see the girl, otherwise what shall I tell the boy'.

Once matters have been settled to some degree, the ceremony known as *kalyana orappu* takes place, governed by a very formal and restrictive code of behaviour. The date of the marriage, the *stridhanam* and ornaments the woman must bring, and the number of wedding guests to be invited are now decided. The boy and the girl are again not present, the dialogue taking place between the elder paternal kinsmen on both sides.

The next ritual event is the *virunnu*, an occasion of formal feasting when the *stridhanam* changes hands. It is an important ritual event for it expresses the entry of two families into an affinal relation with each other. The *stridhanam* changing hands becomes the symbol of the prospective incorporation into the family of the *marimakkal* (daughter-in-law) through marriage.

On this occasion, the *karnavan* (elder) of the girl's house stands on a mat in the centre of the room; his elbows are crossed horizontally, his *kavani* (silk shawl) tied across his waist like a sash. All the important details are announced by the speaker: whose children are going to be married, the date and hour at which the event is to take place, the amount of money (*thoka*) to be given as *stridhanam*. The language of announcements formalizes the relationship and establishes for witnesses the terms by which the relationship has been arranged. After the *stridhanam* has been given, and the presentation formally concluded with an embrace between the two *karnavan*s who have given and taken the money, a prayer is said by the parish priest asking for prosperity and blessings. The ceremony is concluded with the lighting of the *kole villaku* (a long-handled oil lamp) by the girl's sister, her father's sister, her mother, mother's sister or brother's wife.

The marriage may only be solemnized after the girl's family gifts four per cent of the *stridhanam* to the church. The bride's departure from her natal church is symbolized by a letter called the *desakuri*, stating that she has no dues toward the church and that she has not been excommunicated at any time, without which she cannot be affiliated into her husband's church. *Naddavarkam* is the second step, whereby the woman takes membership in her husband's *sabha* and here too a percentage of the *stridhanam* must be made over to the church as a gift. The last of the rituals in the arrangement of a marriage pertains to the invitation of guests. The formalities are extremely strict, and each person to be invited to the marriage must be personally visited by representatives and formally called to participate (*kalyana koodanam*). A male and female member of the household have to go together, of whom at least one is a person of mature years. Intimacy with the family is no criterion for neglecting the extension of a formal invitation.

Domestic Rituals: Preparations for the Marriage

Traditionally, the month before the wedding was a time of hectic preparation. Coconuts, spices and rice were prepared and packed away by kinsmen and servants. The pickles and *palharam* (sweet or savoury fried foods) were also made ready. Everything was made at home, and in the act of preparing food together lay the essence of celebration, the expression of family feeling and neighbourly ties, substituted today by the services offered by caterers.

There were many celebratory songs which were sung at the time of communal preparation before a marriage.[2] Informants remember some of these songs as describing the girl going for her ceremonial bath before the day of her marriage, the act of wearing fine clothes, and the journey in the boat (the traditional mode of transport till early this century) with all the wedding guests.

On the day before the marriage, the servicing castes attached to the Syrian households came and settled in the house—the *thattan* (goldsmith) who made the *thali* or marriage locket and other ornaments, the *pannen* (tailor) and the *asari* (carpenter). The goldsmith would place the *thali* or *minnu* in a small shallow bronze vessel containing rice as a symbol of the fertility of the union. The locket, traditionally, was a fleck of gold, ornamented with a cross made of seven or fourteen tiny gold beads. Like the other servicing castes, the goldsmith was paid in cash, and given gifts of betel leaves and areca nuts signifying that the patron–client relationship was not merely an economic one. The servicing castes were also acknowledged by gifts and payments in kind on the occasion of marriage, baptism or the great annual feast days of the church (*moranaya peryanaal*). At the time of marriage, the blacksmith (*kollan*), the carpenter (*maray-asari*), the goldsmith, the tailor, the barber (*shavvarakaran*) and the washerwoman (*parathi*) were given a measure of rice known as *edang-ari*, a bunch of raw bananas (*oru padalla pachakai*), oil (*enna*), a coconut and the symbolic ceremonial fee or *dakshina* of one rupee.

The rituals of bathing and ornamentation were of extreme importance the night before the wedding. The barber and the washerwoman were in charge of the groom and bride respectively, and were gifted with food, clothes and a bowl of sweet rice (*pachor*). *Korava villikuga* or hooting accompanied the rituals of ceremonial bathing.

On the night before the marriage, the groom's sister's husband removed seven threads from the *mantrakodi* (ceremonial sari presented to the bride by the groom). The threads were twisted into a single thread, on which would hang the *thali* or marriage locket. This was followed by feasting (*sadhya*) where kinsfolk, neighbours and servicing castes were all fed ceremonially but separately.

Weddings even now for the Yakoba often take place on Sundays which are considered most auspicious because it is the day Christ rose from the tomb. On Sundays, too, *rahu kalam* (an inauspicious time by astrological reckoning) is over early. The marriage ceremony is usually conducted in the morning, and in the afternoon the feast is held.

On the morning of the wedding, the priest is called. Facing eastwards, he prays for everyone in the house, particularly the bride and groom. Following the wedding breakfast, the ritual of *guru dakshina* takes place. The groom and bride, in their respective houses, gift a sum of money wrapped in a betel leaf to his or her first teacher. This is part of the rituals of separation called *yatra choikuga* (asking leave to depart on a journey), and after the teacher or guru blesses him or her, all the senior relatives of both patri- and matrilineages will come to bless the bride/groom.

On approaching the church for the ceremony, the boy must enter from the western door and be seated on the left of the aisle, facing the altar. Unless he has arrived and taken his place, the girl cannot enter (her role is passive, she is 'married' [*ketichu*], and does not marry [*ketti*], which latter verb is assigned to the male in grammatical usage). The bride sits on the right of the aisle. The groom's sister's husband stands with him, expressing the solidarity that exists between a woman's brother and her husband (*alliyan*). The bride is assisted by her sister, her father's sister or her father's brother's wife. The groom's sister's husband must place the *mantrakodi*, the *thali* and the ring on the table before the marriage service begins.

The Marriage Service

In the first part of the marriage service, the bride stands next to the groom, on his right, before the altar. The bride's attendant (*thozhima*) who may be her father's sister or father's brother's wife, stands on her right. The groom is accompanied by his sister's husband who stands on his left. The preparatory prayers express the fact that the marriage ceremony is clearly held in analogy to the spiritual bond that links Christ and the Church.

After this preparatory worship follows the service of the blessing of the ring, which signifies the ceremony of betrothal. The imagery expresses the lyrical theme that He freed her (the Church) from sin by becoming her groom, and that He sheltered her from the devil. The song says that to the wedding all are called: those of the chosen race and those who are of the other.[3] The wedding ceremony clearly becomes an occasion for establishing the correspondence between the life of Christ and the life of the individual Christian. Further, the dominantly male symbolism of Christianity is adopted in that the relationship expressed by Christ: Church is synonymous with groom:bride. The Pauline symbolism of marriage is implicit, and provides most systematically the basis of a Christian understanding of the body in sexuality, which for St Paul is to be understood in terms of the more general principle of sanctity and spirituality rather than of erotic love. 'Because Christ is the bridegroom of the Church, marriage should be held holy.'[4] By this homology, marriage is a mystery, carrying within it implicitly the nature of grace.[5]

This homological relation has its origins in the Old Testament. Johnston has argued that the most effective symbol of the relationship between God and His people in the Old Testament was that of marriage.[6] So also, the fulfilment of the Messianic era was spoken of in terms of a wedding feast, and Christ referred to himself as the bridegroom.[7] In Paul's writings, the relation is reversed: 'In order to drive home the obligations of married persons he (Paul) points to the relationship between Christ and the Church which the marriage symbolizes'.[8] The man in his specific character as husband represents Christ, the woman as wife represents the Church, and in matrimony they represent the mystical body. Thus, marriage becomes a sacrament where the microcosm of the Church in union with Christ is produced.[9]

The rings are blessed by the signing of the cross thrice, and prayers are said for the happiness of bride and groom. The ring symbolizes their fulfilment and is the symbol of completeness.[10] The priest places the ring on the fourth finger of the right hand of the groom, with the prayer that the right hand of Jesus may be extended over the couple in blessing, and the same is done for the woman.[11] We know from the comparative ethnography provided by Hertz that the importance of the right over the left expresses symbolically the dualism of the sacred and the profane, where, in most cases, the right is associated with the sacred and the auspicious and is superior.[12]

The ceremony described above, culminating with the placement of rings by the priest or bishop on the fingers of the bride and groom respectively, is called the *vivaha nischeyam* (betrothal). Prayers follow which refer to Isaac and Rebecca and the gift of gold ornaments that sealed their engagement.[13] These prayers also ask for a righteous life for the couple, for true love, that their life together be more fragrant than the Susannah flower, that they have freedom from evil, for many blessed children and a life of fortune filled with good works.[14] This is followed by a song which describes in first person the relationship between Christ and His bride, and the longing of the bride for the groom.

The reading from the Gospels: Eph. 5 follows, including the verse, 'Therefore as the Church is subject unto Christ, so let the wives be to their own husbands in everything. Husbands, love your wives, even as Christ also loved the Church and gave Himself for it'. Thus the love of wives must be submissive and dependent.[15]

The blessing of the crowns now begins. This rite consists of making a circular motion with a gold chain representing the crown, and the signing of the cross thrice around the head of first the groom and then the bride. The groom then ties the *thali*, here referred to as cross, around the neck of the woman. For a Syrian Christian woman this remains the chief symbol of her marriage. Then the *mantrakodi* (veil or sari gifted to the woman by the man) is placed over her head and shoulders. The girl's attendant, usually her father's sister, stands aside and is replaced by the groom's sister. The third step, the joining of hands of bride and groom by the priest, now takes place and blessings of the saints, Mary, and Christ are called upon the couple.

The relationship of the husband to his wife is articulated in the verses that follow: the bride must leave her family for her husband who in turn must love her and treat her with kindness. If naked, he must clothe her; if hungry, he must feed her, if thirsty, he must give her to drink. As she loves her own life, she must love him and, adhering to the commandments, she must live with him in love and tenderness.[16] The couple then recite the creed (*Visvas Pramanam*) together, articulating their faith in Christian precepts.

When the service is over the couple returns to the groom's house for the feast. The bride must change into the *mantrakodi* or *viripavam*, the sari given to her by the groom. It symbolizes that she now belongs to the groom and his family. It is essential that this ceremonial sari be worn unwashed.

Domestic Rites of Celebration and Conclusion

Once the bride and groom return home, a cup of milk anticipating the fertility of the union and its sustenance is served to them by the groom's brother's wife, his sister or any other close female relative. On reaching the house the groom takes his bride's right hand and together they enter with their right feet placed first. The groom takes the bride to his mother (customarily not present at the marriage ceremony) and gives her to his mother and/or grandmother. This is called *ammae epichu* and means to put in the care of the mother. It symbolizes the importance of bilateral kinship in a strongly patrilineal society. The mother and her kin play a role of great affectual importance on all occasions. On entering, the couple are once more greeted by a close female relative (father's sister or groom's sister) who holds in her hand a miniature *kindi* (a bronze vessel with a spout) containing water, a *kole villaku* (bronze lamp with an extended handle) which is lit, and a small *kinni* (shallow container) which holds a betel leaf, some water and a fine muslin cloth containing a small amount of finely powdered rice and some grains of unhusked rice. A small hole is made in the cloth. The sister or father's sister, with her head covered by a *kavani*, faces the couple who turn to the east, associated with the rising sun and with Christ. She dips the muslin containing powdered rice and unhusked grain into the water, and touches the brow of bride and groom three times. The rite is one of fertility and auspiciousness, the separate elements of which constitute the symbols of sexuality, procreation and domesticity: the *kindi* for the masculine, the *kinni* for the feminine, the unhusked rice for reproduction, the powdered rice for consummation.

Having put his bride ritually in the care of his mother, the groom with his bride returns to the *pantalam* (marriage canopy) where the bride's kinsmen are fed first. The groom and bride are expected to eat with them in a place of honour. The meal begins with a ritual preface. The priest or an elder of the boy's house will ask 'Have all arrived?' and the answer must be an assent before he can continue. Then he will ask, 'Have all sat?' If these ceremonially prescribed enquiries are omitted, serious quarrels can result. Etiquette is a point of high honour, and in seating and serving not a slip must be made for fear that some one will be offended.

After the meal the priest asks the ritual question 'Have all eaten?' Each person must sit with his or her fists closed (*kai madakki*) and wait for everyone to finish eating. As the guests depart from the *pantalam*, they are sprinkled with rose water, presented with lemons, flowers, sandalwood paste for the brow; the men are given areca nuts and betel leaves.

After the feast the rituals of gift-exchange take place. The bride's mother's brother who is the first recipient, ties a turban on his own head. There are jeers and hoots from the audience. He receives a gift of cloth, slipping a gold ring on the groom's finger in exchange. Then the bride's mother, paternal and maternal grandmothers also receive gifts of cloth, and give in return gold rings.

A ritual called *nalla vadil* (the good or auspicious door) exists whereby the bride formally enters her husband's house placing her right foot first while stepping in. She is accompanied by primary kin as well as by her father's sister and mother's brother. It marks the return of the bride and the groom after a stay of four days at the bride's house in the first week of the marriage itself. It is compulsory for the bride and groom to participate in one more rite: they must attend the church where the marriage took place and see the Eucharist celebrated on the Sunday following their wedding.

Prestations continue to flow unidirectionally from the woman's house to the man's house in a ritually prescribed way. After the marriage, the woman must provide many things for the household. These are usually bronze vessels (*ottu pathram*), earthenware cooking vessels (*chatti*), storing vessels (*kallam*), brass or bronze vessels with spouts (*kindi*), wooden cots (*kattil*), mattresses and pillows (*metha thallavanna*), knives (*pitchati*), baskets and brooms (*kotta, chool*), wooden chests (*kal petti*), etc.

Another ritual called *adakla kannuga* (seeing the kitchen) occurs sometime between the marriage of the daughter and the birth of her first child. The mother of the bride, her brother and his wife, and other close kin must take gifts of *palharam* (foods symbolizing festivity) and a gold ring or chain for the groom. *Adakla kannuga* signifies the incorporation of the bride into the conjugal unit, her natal household members having come to see her settled into her own kitchen, or what will one day be hers. The final incorporation occurs with the birth of a child, and after this event, gifts from the woman's household will take on an optional and non-obligatory character, being for the most part gifts of food, including agricultural or garden produce.

Stridhanam: Women's Wealth or Groom Price?

Stridhanam (female wealth) is the sum of money that a Syrian Christian woman brings with her at the time of marriage. It is not seen as a gift but falls under the category of prestations. Symbolically, it must be seen as the severing of economic ties for a woman from her natal home and her incorporation into the conjugal household.

Stridhanam is generally a very large sum of money (often running into lakhs of rupees) given by the father of the bride to the groom's father. The woman no longer has a share in her father's property. The Orthodox/Jacobite Syrian Christian idea of dowry does not correspond to the notion of dowry as defined by Goody and Tambiah,[17] who define dowry as part of a financial or conjugal fund which passes down from holder to heir. Goody prefers to classify dowry under the category of 'diverging devolution' where familial property is transferred from father to daughter who becomes, in this case, full heir, semi-heir or residual heir. Goody does refer to Yalman's distinction between dowry and inheritance where dowry is the result of a bargain and has a specific intention of linking a daughter with a desirable man.[18]

In the Orthodox/Jacobite Syrian Christian case, *stridhanam* ideally comes under the category of pre-mortem inheritance. However, the manipulative aspect has become empirically dominant and money is used in order to contract marriages with desirable families. The 'spirit' of the prestation however demands that there be no questions regarding its expenditure once money has changed hands. The woman has no control over her wealth and while there is often suppressed violence, in the majority of cases women tend to accept the entailed subjugation.

Stridhanam, according to informants, is a woman's share of her father's property (*avakasham*). It may be more than what the sons receive, as often happens in middle class houses where the entire property may be sold or mortgaged in order to marry off a daughter. Usually it is less than what the sons (particularly in the large estates) receive as inheritance when the father dies. The *stridhanam* given to each daughter will also vary depending on the time and circumstance of the marriage. There is a 'rate' (in informants' terms) for each economic class, and this rate increases from year to year.

Through such prestation status may be consolidated and maintained, and avenues for upward mobility created, but then *stridhanam* loses the character of the gift or even of pre-mortem inheritance. The sum of money paid is according to a prevalent rate with the possibility of compromise (bargaining) over the sum. The economic status of both families, the educational qualifications of the bride and groom, the kind of employment they may have or even the colour of the woman's complexion are important factors in this negotiation. The frequent 'market' quality of these arrangements is highlighted by the presence of the marriage broker (*kothan*) who receives a percentage of the total *stridhanam* from both parties. Many potential alliances have not taken place because the *stridhanam* offered was not sufficient or could not be produced in time. As a norm, the amount is always first decided upon before the marriage is fixed and money changes hands in a ceremonial and public manner.

Partly in deference to the anti-dowry stand that the government has taken, the practice of openly stating how much is given or accepted is losing ground. Since the old ceremonies such as the *virind* and *ora* (where ceremonial feasting and public declaration of the marriage contract took place) are losing importance, their function as safeguards are concomitantly lost. There are now several cases of fraud and cheating known to many informants. Formerly the tithe (*passaram*) paid to the church from the *stridhanam* had a significant function as a record of the amount given or received. Now almost all informants say that people try to 'trick' the church (*palliae kalpikkan okkum*). So, today, church records are no indication of the amount that really changes hands.

The obligation to provide *stridhanam* for a daughter at marriage is frequently a financial strain on her parents. The prestations have to continue, although varying in nature, even after the birth of her first child. A daughter was therefore seen as a burden (*pennungal chelavu annu*: 'Females are an expense'). The staking of conjugal rights and privileges is a function of this payment. As one informant said, 'In a crisis one can say, "I did not walk into this house like a beggar. I brought *stridhanam*"'.

Amongst Syrian Christians it is admitted that though rates are high, it is nevertheless a morally controlled system. Instances of methodical harrasment of the women were unknown to most informants. In cases where money has not been paid in full, the woman may be sent back to her natal household and asked to 'remind' her fathers or brothers. According to informants, this is perfectly honourable since the parents of the groom and bride had settled upon a certain sum, and payment was due. If tensions do develop between a girl and her affines, it is her relationship with her husband that settles the case. If this is weak, then increased demands may force her to return home. A separated woman, however, has no place in Syrian Christian society. Informants say that if a woman has any moral courage (*chov ollathu annangil*), she will remain in her husband's house despite all constraints. The relationship between husband and wife may remain affectually weak if the marriage has been contracted mainly with consideration to the dowry. The old values attributed to family name and individual character (which were once the most important criteria) are being replaced by the idiom of whom one can get for the amount one has in hand. Does *stridhanam* among the Syrian Christians of Kerala then begin to look more like groom-price than dowry? The facts seem to suggest this.

Stridhanam expresses, then, the nature of relations between two households which have entered into a relationship of affinity. By their consent to pay a certain sum, the wife-givers acknowledge the usually hypergamic situation whereby *stridhanam* is the means by which a befitting marriage may be concluded. It takes on the character of groom-price, for only by the payment of *stridhanam* can a marriage be fixed: it is controlled not by the woman as dowry is, but by her husband and his kin. It is used either for buying rights for sisters or daughters into other domestic groups, or invested in land; by allowing this, the woman bringing *stridhanam* has rights of maintenance in the conjugal household.

Goody has argued that the allocation of property to women, whether as money or land, always threatens the notion of patrimony. A balance has to be struck between that which is given to the bride in order to have her married, and a share of the estate which does not damage the interests of other siblings. Such an allocation was the condition of the preservation and possible extension of family interests as well as the status system itself.[19] Goody also takes into account the work of D D Hughes, who argues with reference to Mediterranean Europe that the dowry was a form of 'disinheritance' rather than diverging devolution, and accounts for the impossibility of a woman's claim to a share of her father's property at his death.[20] On the other hand (as with Syrian Christians), it encourages the early break-up or mortgaging of the estate. *Stridhanam* expresses the delicate balance that certain allocations of property involve, particularly the opposition of bilateral and patrilineal tendencies and their emotional contexts. Lastly, Goody's discussion of Hughes's material suggests that the dominance of cash dowries tended to place control in the hands of the men—the husband or, as has been expressed in the Syrian Christian case, the *father* of the husband, since it is he who controls property and the interests of his son.

The tensions within the system are explicit—the great affection for the daughter who *must* be sent away in marriage is defined through the seeking of hypergamous alliances (in terms of status and class) and the payment of high *stridhanam* towards this end. In the same breath, the daughter is 'disinherited'—she has no further share in her father's wealth. The language used by informants clearly expresses the nature of 'buying' one's way into a household. The moral code underlying these transactions is based on contract and not on gift-giving.[21]

The most evocative examples of the tensions deriving from the obligation to pay *stridhanam* and the Syrian Christian rules of heritance (so successfully challenged by Mary Roy *et al* and the Supreme Court judgement on Christian inheritance in 1986) are those cases where fathers have died intestate, and brothers do not feel morally compelled to provide for their sisters. In this sense, the relation between a woman's right to a share in her father's property and her brother's obligation to actually provide for her are very tenuous.

Domestic Relationships Arising Out of Marriage

The incorporation of the bride into the household soon after marriage expresses itself in terms of her relationships to the other members of the domestic group. The contribution of her labour power is acceptable only after she has been integrated into her conjugal home. She is first a guest, and then gradually an involved and labouring member. The act of childbirth is the most emphatic expression of integration. Here I am interested in the emotional webs that the payment of *stridhanam* and marriage create, acts whereby a woman receives the right to work and to reproduce. (It is virtually impossible to marry without *stridhanam*.) These rights should not be taken for granted, and we have to be sensitive to work and reproduction as conjoined privileges expressing the symbolic integration of women into their conjugal households.

For forty-one days after she entered her husband's house, the bride had to be ornamented and dressed in her finest. Household work was taboo and, in this sense, the new bride was seen to be in a state of liminality, for exclusion from domestic chores underlined her status as 'guest'. Rites of inclusion mark the majority of the wedding rituals, since by this event a woman is 'brought in' by marriage (*kettichu konduvaruka*). These rituals help individuals to slip into the social roles allocated to them by society, and articulate what is required of them.

The relationship between husband and wife was ideally one of respect and collaboration to the extent allowed by the man's mother. Male and female worlds were separated by the nature of daily work. The bride spent most of her time with her husband's mother. Husbands in the early years would hardly speak to their wives, partly because they were diffident, but also because they were out for the main part of the day in the fields and business houses. Close relations between husband and wife, specially in the early years, were thought to be unseemly. According to one elderly informant, it took as much as three years of marriage for a man and woman to be at ease with each other. The diffidence always remained to some extent right through their married life in a woman's relationship to her husband. This was partly due to the difference in ages which was usually (and ideally) five to seven years. It was when they moved into an independent household with the birth of children that husband and wife complemented each other. We shall look at fission more closely, but it must be noted that household fission affected only the elder sons, for the youngest remained in the ancestral house with his parents.

The most important of the affinal relationships that a woman entered into at marriage was with her husband's mother. Not surprisingly, then, as one woman pointed out, a father enquiring about a potential son-in-law would first ask the most searching questions about the boy's mother. The closeness of family bonds that has been the traditional mark of the Syrian Christians is a tribute to the relationship between a woman and her son's wives. A daughter-in-law who is ill-treated is the greatest source of misfortune both to her natal family, to whom she may be forced to return, and to her husband's house if she cannot live in amity with them. For the first year she is like a guest in her conjugal home, all her clothes and personal needs being provided for by her parents. Traditionally, she was provided at the time of marriage with all manner of personal possessions including utensils, furniture and linen, it was a question of *mannam* (self respect) that she came with such goods.

The generosity of the husband's mother at this time was of crucial significance to the new bride, particularly as in the early years of the marriage the bride spent much time in her company. An informant said:

In the old days it was not so much the case of a difficult mother-in-law (*amaiamma*) as a difficult daughter-in-law (*marimakkal*). If one was obedient and willing to learn, the first three or four years were the most important periods of education for a young girl. But during this period there was no independence, and none could be expected. One had to do exactly as one was told, and there was no place for individual desire and will. In those days, families were large, the servants were many, the guests were frequent. All had to be fed, and only after this could the women sit and eat. There would be days when lunch was bypassed because there was so much work to be done. No point complaining then that your husband's mother did not feed you. All this was an expected part of your life in a household. Today, who are mothers-in-law? Wives and husbands want only each other, no one feels there is anything they can learn from old women.

It was not merely cooking and the organization of the household that a bride learnt from her husband's mother; she was also taught the Christian virtues of charity and piety which, as a wife, she had to exemplify. The secrets of herbal remedies, of what the Christians call Kitchen *Ayurveda*, passed down to her not from her mother but from her mother-in-law.

However, there were often animosities generated between the two women, caught in their specific roles. It was a relationship of hierarchy, and conflicts had to be suppressed. There were particular situations which brought increasing strains upon the two roles. Ecclesiastical feuds were often reflected in conjugal life. A woman, always to be loyal to her husband's ecclesiastical affiliations, found this particularly difficult where natal loyalties remained strong. Sometimes a mother-in-law and her son's wife supported each other if they had the same natal affiliations, but this endangered the patrilineal ecclesiastical standing of the house in which they stood as married women.

The relation of a bride to her father-in-law was, by custom, one of respect and avoidance. While the father remained the head of the family till his death, by the time he was sixty, he would retire from an active social life. Responsibility then fell on his eldest son if the latter lived with him, or if he had set up house separately, on the youngest son who by ultimogeniture would inherit the house. As a man grew older, in an almost socially prescribed manner, he became more meditative and spent most of his time in the portico, reclining on an easy chair, reading the Bible or the newspapers. That he was still a moral force to reckon with was apparent in his sons' relation to him, and by the fact that many economic decisions were still formally taken by him. In all matters even if practical control was in the hands of a woman's husband, his father was treated with deference and his advice invariably sought. His symbolic headship was confirmed by the fact that it was he who lead the family at prayer, when after dinner the family knelt together on the carefully laid out reed mats.

Further, it was the father who gave formal permission, economic assistance, and the blessings necessary when a couple wanted to set up house separately. The relationship between sons and fathers was one marked by deep filial devotion, affection, obedience and respect on the one side, and by patronage and authoritarianism on the other. This relation, fraught with tension, was reflected also in the relation of the bride to her husband's father.

Since ties with the natal home remain strong through the entire period of married life, a woman frequently returns to her father's house. During the first year she may return for every festival and every celebration. As the years pass, these visits may become somewhat less frequent as her responsibilities increase, involving the care of aged parents, taking over the reins of the kitchen and rearing the children. Nevertheless, she returns to her natal home for her pregnancies and for the celebration of the rites of passage of her maternal and paternal kin. When these visits begin to decrease with the death of her parents, her brothers will continue to visit her sporadically to see that all is well with her. The ability to spend time in her natal home depends on her husband and his parents and the permission they give her to return home. Marital discord may result from too frequent returns to the natal household; the bride has often to contain her anxieties about her aging parents and their state of health since these are, in a strongly patrilineal society, not her concern, but that of her brothers and their wives.

PREGNANCY AND CHILDBIRTH

Domestic Rituals: Restrictions and Practices for the Expectant Mother

The next phase in a woman's life is the bearing of children. Pregnancy and childbirth have certain domestic rituals associated with them, as also specific dietary and other social restrictions. This would include a description of Kitchen *Ayurveda*, for Syrian Christian women make and use traditional medicines in great quantities for both ingestion and anointing. The mother and the brother of the expectant mother arrive at her conjugal home in the fifth or seventh month of her pregnancy to take her home. Even numbers are considered inauspicious, and if leave-taking were to take place in such months, then misfortune is bound to occur. When the mother of the girl comes to take her daughter home during the seventh month of pregnancy, she gifts one gold sovereign, either in the form of a ring or a gold chain to her daughter's husband. According to Yalman, 'affinity is a long-term alliance', and gifts may be drawn out over time to reaffirm continually the connection between a woman's natal family and their affines.[22] Sometimes this ritual prestation may coincide with *Adakla kannuga*, which is a rite normally occurring soon after marriage, symbolizing the girl's incorporation into her conjugal home; her relatives come as 'guests' to observe the manner in which she now lives. Her mother, brother and his wife are, by custom, the relatives who come to take her home. The oil lamps are lit and hung up, the family prays at the time of departure, and the custom is for the expectant woman's husband's mother to present her with a Bible (*Veda Pustakam*).

If the woman goes to her natal family in the early months of pregnancy, as in the fifth month, her husband's mother and other affines will come to visit her there. They are always feasted on such occasions. If they ask that the woman return with them for some weeks, she will have to comply, since her conjugal ties are based on a socially constructed primacy.

One reason why even the early phase of the first pregnancy is spent in the woman's natal home is because pregnancy is seen to be a difficult and transitional period, and the rest and leisure that a woman requires during this time is culturally recognized. It is also perceived that the girl has particular desires and urges, especially in the matter of eating. These desires of the palate for exceptionally sour, sweet or bitter things are called *jyakoon* and are a subject for jokes.

There are certain restrictions on behaviour that are imposed upon the expectant woman both when at her husband's house and at her 'mother's home' (*amma veedu*). She is not allowed to travel, or even to visit others. Particularly after dark, the girl may not walk alone, or even step out since this time of day is considered inauspicious. Further, while the Syrian Christians of Puthenangadi will not formally admit to a belief in ghosts or evil spirits, they associate nightfall with danger, particularly for the vulnerable, such as the old, small children and pregnant women. Although restrictions are placed on mobility, housework is encouraged till the final days of confinement excepting for lifting or carrying heavy objects. Sometimes the pregnant woman is given a black bangle to wear in order to ward off the evil eye.

For the baby to be fair in colour, certain precautions were taken by the expectant woman. One of these was the daily rite by which gold from the girl's mother's wedding ring was scraped off and put in milk, a herb called *kunnthoti* was washed, dried and boiled till the *rasa* or juice emerged. This potion was drunk by the woman. The mother-to-be was bathed after being anointed with a paste of green turmeric and given the juice of bitter gourd to drink. Fair colour is a preoccupation with the average Syrian Christian, reflecting, perhaps, a desire to be equated with brahmins who are conventionally perceived as fair-skinned, and from whom they believe themselves to be descended.

Oil baths are given before the delivery of the child but precautions are taken regarding the health of the expectant mother, since the suitability of herbs must be first established. False steps can lead to death since many of these herbs called *pacca maranu* (green medicines) have strong effects. Since a healthy and long life is highly desired, the post-natal health customs of Syrian Christians express a very great dependence on *ayurveda*. *Ayurveda*, the science of living to a ripe age, prescribes not merely curative treatment but also promotes health and longevity.

At the time of birth, it was not the custom for the child's father to be present since conjugal concerns were considered detrimental to the pregnant woman specially if it was the first pregnancy. The prescribed absence of the husband during the time of confinement expresses the formality between husband and wife in the early years of marriage. The physical pain of childbirth, by custom, should not be shared with the father of the child. It was in fact the reverse of the couvade, where the husband mimes the labour of his wife.

If the delivery is normal the mother is bathed as soon as possible. She is rubbed by the *vaittati* (midwife) with *ayurvedic* oils which were traditionally made at home. This practice still continues, although births now take place in the hospital. The water for these baths is boiled with herbs. The best of these are thought to be *vep* (neem) and *pooverishu ella* (thespesia). Both are easily procured either from one's own or the neighbour's back garden. They are put into boiling water with turmeric roots. The water is boiled the previous evening and then used the following morning. It is re-heated, since the bath must be taken in hot water. These baths are given for seven continuous days and then on alternate days for a month (i.e., 15 baths). The *vaittati* is usually the one who is employed to bathe the woman. Just as the boiling of the water and preparations of medicines are done in privacy and silence (being considered vulnerable to the evil eye), so is the act of oiling and massaging the woman. Secrecy is part of the traditional lore of the *vaidyan*.[23] The Syrian Christian women who know of herbal remedies also maintain this rule to the greatest extent possible. Frederick Dunn refers to the barrier to female practice in *ayurveda*[24] yet among the Syrian Christians it is the women who are the keepers of herbal medicine in the practice of domestic *ayurveda*.

The *kozhambu* (oil) may either be prescribed and brought from the *aryavaidyashala* or, more commonly, it may be made according to certain traditional prescriptions which are kept by the women of the house and passed down from one generation to the next. The *vaidyan* is consulted if there is any unusual circumstances of health but the average healthy woman uses one called *pinnathailam*. Ayurvedic preparations such as *kashayam*, *arishtam*, *lehiyam* and *nei* are given to the woman. *Kashayam*s are of different kinds, some for respiration, others for contracting the uterus, or for treating specific complaints. *Arishtam* too is used for specific and individual complaints such as bleeding or skin rashes, *lehiyam* for strength, for lactation, and for treating boils, *nei* (*ghee* or clarified butter) for strength.

The bath is supposed to be given on an empty stomach. After the bath, the mother is at once given some hot rice with *nei*. Food must always be hot and freshly cooked. Curds, buttermilk and pulses are not eaten. It is believed that if any ailment of the stomach occurs at this time, it will be slow to heal and may persist for a long time. *Kaachi-more* (seasoned and hot buttermilk) is given, so are vegetables like bitter gourd and snake gourd which are rich in iron. Root vegetables (tapioca and yam) are an accepted part of the diet.

No fish or sour foods are given to the mother. In the old days, not a drop of water was given since it was believed that the stomach would distend, and the rules regarding these prohibitions were extremely strict. The new mother was not allowed to eat curries and food was given to her after the water content evaporated from it. She was not even allowed to drink rice water (*kanji vellam*) which was a normal part of the daily diet.

Sometimes the only recourse was to steal water but the *kallam* (earthern pot for water) was so jealously guarded that elderly informants admit, while reminiscing, to opening their mouths when being bathed, so that they could drink the bitter herb-treated water trickling down. Fried bitter gourd and *thoran*s (finely cut vegetables cooked in salt, turmeric, coconut scrapings and a teaspoon of oil) were the only permitted foods.

Remarking on the fact that they were put on a very rigid diet and given no water at all to drink for a period as long as three months, an old woman said, 'This was the time when our mothers were like strangers. We would beg them to give us water or a piece of fried fish but they were like strangers in their ability to refuse us, to reject our pleas'. The result of this preoccupation with health, with strong bodies and slim figures is evident in the older generations who rigorously followed these rules.

If the *kashayam*, *kozhambu* and other *ayurvedic* oils which reach the child through its mother's milk seem to disagree with it, it is discontinued. These days it seems *ayurvedic* medicines suit children less than they did sixty years ago, since constitutions have undergone changes over time.

For fifty-six days after childbirth, a woman was not allowed to do any work and was expected only to lie in bed. This was the only real period of rest that a woman got during her active years. Her stomach was tied very tightly with a cloth to tighten the uterus, and she was expected to wear a *mundu* (sarong) since such a garment would stay in place only if it was gripped tightly around the waist. An informant said that *arogyam* (health) was a preoccupation, traditionally, in a way that it is not today. Consequently, women today have a capacity for much less work and suffer from pain and tiredness much more frequently.

THE CHILD

Certain domestic rituals also governed the early life of the child. Directly after its birth, after the first bath, usually given by the mother's mother, the child was placed in a banana leaf, or in the smooth white spathe of the coconut. The first ritual that is enacted for the benefit of the newborn child is the feeding of gold and honey to the infant. The gold is obtained by scraping the mother's wedding ring against a rough surface; this is then mixed with honey. The mother's mother, mother's father or mother's brother then places a drop of this mixture on the child's tongue, simultaneously praying for 'its health, for joy in its life, for love of god (*deva bhakti*) and service of men; that he or she should run like a deer and sing like a sweet bird'. The person who first prays for the child in this manner and who feeds him gold and honey is thought to pass on his character to the child. The ceremony integrates the newborn within the circumference of human existence by the ritual act of the transmission of qualities from adult to infant.

Once the child has been bathed, and fed with honey and gold (*thenum sornam*), it is taken to the mother so that she may breast-feed it. Soon after, word is sent to the child's father's house and as soon as possible, members of the infant's father's family arrive. Traditionally, the first question that was asked when the child's cry was heard was 'Is the child male or female?' If it was a boy there was rejoicing; if a girl, no further questions were asked.

At least five or seven people from the boy's house arrive, including the father of the child and his primary kin. They are given a festive meal (*sadhya* or *oon*) which include various kinds of meat and fish as well as coffee (*kaapi*) which is served with traditional *palharam* (sweet foods like *chooroot*, *avlose oonda* and *mav oonda*, and salty fried foods like *achapam* and *korallapam*).

The child's father and his kinsmen bring gifts such as baby powder, soaps, toys and clothes. While the expenses for childbirth have been paid for by the woman's natal household, five per cent of the dowry is placed in the child's hands. This is expected to cover the needs of the child and the mother, the expenses of the midwife, the medicines and the hospital.

On the twenty-eighth day after the child's birth, the mother's brother ties the *arrinanam* on the child's hip. At first this may only be a black thread, and the ceremony is called the *irruvathi ettu kettu* (the twenty-eighth knot). At this time the child is also gifted with a gold waistband (the *arrinanam*), a gold chain, a gold ring and two gold bangles by the mother's natal household. Those who have daughters describe such 'optional' gifts to the child as a necessity for the maintenance of status and honour. The gold *arrinanam* differentiates symbolically the sex of the child. The male child is given an *arrinanam* which has an ornamental elongated tassel called the *koombu* while the female version has a flat disc attached to it.

BAPTISM

The sacrament of baptism entails a discussion of the corpus of ideas relating to the initiation of the child into the Christian Church and the establishment of the homology between Jesus's life and that of the Christian child as an initiate. The baptism rite is customarily held fifty-six days after the birth of the child. This is the length of time which is thought to lapse before the menstrual cycle is re-established. Before these fifty-six days are over, the woman is considered to be polluted (*asudha*). Menstrual pollution is to be found not only among the Hindus, but also in the ancient Judaic tradition.[25] That birth pollution existed among the Syrian Christians some decades ago has been testified to by many informants. In some houses even now, men will not eat in the house where a birth has taken place. Arrangements are said to be made with some other nearby family for a period of fifteen days. However, I myself never observed such an instance. During this time everything around the house is believed to be *asudham*. Bathing is a purificatory ritual of great importance for this reason.

The mother may enter the church with a male child after forty days of birth, since after the birth of a son the period of pollution is less, but only after fifty-six days in the case of a girl. Early baptisms may take place in the church if the child is ill, or its designated godparent not expected to live long. In such cases, the mother may not attend the service since she is polluted. During periods of Lent and mourning, no baptisms may take place.

Among the Yakoba, the child is confirmed into the Church at the time of baptism unlike many other Christian sects and denominations. Not only is he washed and anointed with the holy oils, but bread and wine are also given, as at communion.[26] The holy oil (*muron*) with which the child is anointed is made with great care from various herbs, and its preparation involves many complicated rituals. The child's clothes are taken off, it is bathed in perfumed water and anointed with oil. The water that has been used to bathe it must not be polluted (*asudham akallae*) or thrown where feet may step on to it. It is sometimes thrown into a well or buried deep in the ground.

The Baptism Service

On the day of the baptism, the infant's father's family (seven or nine people, never too many) arrive at the infant's mother's house. There is no fixed custom as to whether the child is to be baptized in its mother's natal parish or the father's, though it is usually the latter. However, the child must wear the clothes that its father's family has brought for it, a symbol of their claim. All the expenses at the church (the gift to the priest and the deacon, for example) are met by the child's father's household.

The child is taken into the church by its mother, or paternal grandmother or father's sister. In church, it is given to its chosen godparent who must be of the same gender as itself. Baptism may take place on any day that the Eucharist has been celebrated. The godfather (*thallael-thoduna-appen*, literally, 'the father who touches the head') holds the child in such a way that his head rests on his right arm. The child and its attendants (the godparent and another close female relative such as the paternal grandmother, mother's sister or father's sister) stand before the priest just below the *madabaha* or sanctuary. Then begins the first prayer or *prarambha prarthana*. The priest speaks, pleading that the soul be born again through baptism, in fire and spirit. He prays that the soul receive salvation, grace and mercy through the intercession of the priest, though he is himself sinful.[27]

Each life-cycle ritual recreates an event in the life of Christ. Thus, in the service of baptism, there is reference to the appearance of the Holy Spirit in the form of a dove at the baptism of Christ. George has argued that the Father's designation of the Son points towards the adoption of the baptized as son: baptism creates sonhood.[28] The twenty-third psalm is then recited, since it is a prayer for safe-keeping and refuge, for shelter from the 'valley of the shadow of death' from which the soul has emerged. Thus life itself is symbolized as the life of the soul as distinct from death or lifelessness. Baptismal symbolism is both spatial and temporal. St Paul said: 'The Father... has delivered us from the dominion of darkness and transferred us to the kingdom of the beloved son'.[29] But more often the symbolism is epochal, from one age to another, from Adam to Christ, from sin to grace. Baptism is the frontier between these two ages,[30] as it is the primary rite of initiation.

Following this, we find a reference to the 'sons of Adam' (mankind) who, condemned to death in sin, are born again through baptism. By this rite, man is made pure, and sin is washed away from the heart. The priest prays that this child, this servant of the Lord be made new, that he be clothed in the indestructible vestments of the spirit.

The gospel is then read by the deacon or *shemasha*. The text is invariably Rom. 5:20 to 6:4 and includes the verses:

> Know ye not that so many of us as were baptized unto Jesus Christ were baptized upto His death.

> Therefore, we are buried with Him by baptism unto death: that like as Christ was raised up from the dead by the glory of the Father, even so, we also should walk in newness of life.

Thus, the death of Christ is paralleled by the immersion of the infant into the water which is synonymous with the Resurrection, a return to air, to life and spirit.

Baptism is often referred to as *mamodisa mungnu* which connotes the act of drowning or total submersion in the water. At baptism a new ontological relationship is created. By 'putting on Christ',[31] the neophyte becomes one with him. From this sort of union with Christ springs the close union of the baptized with each other, 'for you are all one in Christ Jesus'.[32] Baptism thus stands at the point where past and future, the individual and the ecclesiological, the moral and the mystical meet.[33]

The ritual of baptism is a ritual of initiation whereby the child is homologous to Christ at Jordan. Here the priest echoes the words of John the Bapișt:

> I indeed baptize you with water, but one mightier than I cometh, the latchet of whose shoes I am not worthy to unloose: He shall baptize you with the Holy Ghost and with fire.[34]

The three elements, spirit, water and fire are symbols of the action of God, not burdened by the weight of the earth.[35] The other two sets of elements constituting the rites are the sacraments and the holy anointing oils. The first of these is linked to the bond of association with Christ, the second with divine purity. The priest then prays secretly that the child may be entered into the communion of worshippers, that the servant of the Lord have his name entered in the book of life, that God's glory should shine in his face. The act of baptism is the act of individuating a child by conferring upon him a name, and at the same time making him enter the association of Christian believers.

The priest breathes out (in the way a candle is extinguished) over the child, making with this exhaled breath the shape of a cross in the manner whereby God breathed life into Adam. The priest makes the sign of the cross three times on the forehead of the child saying, 'I make the sign in the name of the Father, Son and Holy Spirit'. He places his right hand on the head of the child, and there follows a long prayer for the rejection of evil spirits and all wickedness and asking for the shelter of God.[36]

In these liturgical texts, the ideas and images of the Christian faith are disseminated to the lay. The idea of sin is deeply encased in the language of baptism: *sakla pischachukallum dhustharum asudharumaya elle atmakallum orinjumarripokuan vendi*—for the removal of all devils, evil and polluted souls, the priest calls upon the name of God. The verses say that the body of the child is a temple for the living God, not a residence for the devil. The priest banishes the evil spirits in the name of God to the deserts, the 'waterless' places (*vellamillathathu-maya sthalakangal*), and to eternal hell-fire.

It is not surprising, in this context, that Christians desire baptism so earnestly for their children. If a child dies before it can be baptized, it is as if a terrible shadow has been cast over the family because, while being born in a Christian household, it does not die a Christian and cannot be buried in the church.

The godparent places his right hand on the right hand of the child and recites thrice on behalf of the infant the following vow, 'Lord, whatever has been received as law by your prophets, apostles, fathers, I will receive and believe'. He also recites the creed (*Vishvasa Pra-manam*) on behalf of the child.

The child is taken to the baptismal fount and all his clothes are taken off. The priest prays secretly (*rehsya prarthana*) that the child be established firmly in the Church, that he may be filled with the gifts of God, and be freed from sin and filled with light. The child is thus a receptacle into which mystical and social forces (God, priests, parents, godparents) pour their various influences.

The priest, using his thumb, makes the sign of the cross three times on the brow of the child. This is the seal of his membership in the Christian Church (*mudra*). The priest then places his right arm over the left; in the right he has a vessel of hot water, and in the left one of cold water. Pouring both together so that the water is the temperature of the human body, he says a secret prayer: 'Lord who is God, make this water through our weak mediation as indestructible fire. May the Holy Spirit enter it'.[37] He prays that the vestments of the soul (i.e., the body) be freed from the bonds of sin.[38] The water is then covered with a white cloth with the sign of the cross, and a hymn follows, describing the baptism of Christ, referring to the advent of the dove and the voice from heaven.[39] The priest prays secretly asking that the child receive Christ's breath in him as did the apostles. He stands west of the fount, facing east, and with his breath he blows the sign of the cross thrice on the water, saying, 'Lord make this water pure'. He pleads that the head of that great 'serpent' (*maha sarpa*) who kills men may be crushed by the sign of the cross, which he proceeds to make. At this juncture the *susrusakaran* (server) says: 'How great is the moment, how awesome, when the Holy·Spirit enters the water'.[40]

The priest then prays that the following qualities should be invested in the water: that it be comforting, joyful, a symbol of the death and

Resurrection of the Christ, that it should purify the soul and body, it should loosen the bonds of evil, forgive sins, give light to body and soul, and symbolize the baptism of rebirth.

The ritual expresses the nature of time as both cyclic and linear. Baptism announces the entry of another Christian into the association of believers. It is in that sense linear, biographical, non-repetitive. On another level it repeats, homologically, the baptism of the Christ. Every infant baptism is an initiation in the manner of the initiation of Christ, and by this act the child is adopted as a son of God. Third, the time of baptism creates a moment where the birth of the individual and the Second Coming of Christ are mediated. It is through baptism that the two are brought together and have meaning. It is in this sense that for Christians baptism becomes the mediation between present and future, for only the baptized may have an understanding of the Apocalypse.

The removal of the pollution and sin, which for Christians are innate in man by his very nature, is the primary expressive function of baptism. Thus the removal of clothes, the bathing and anointing become central symbols. The concept of the 'seal' or *mudra* is also of significance because, by this rite, the Christian becomes 'marked'. The expulsion of Satan and the acceptance or 'taking on of Christ' are central to the rite. Baptism is essentially a symbolic act but the nature of the sacrament is such that grace is inherent. Like marriage and death, it too is Eucharist-centred. Baptism, being performed on days when the Eucharist has been celebrated, enables the child from the moment of its initiation to partake in the body of Christ. The rite of baptism confirms the child into the Church at that very same instance.

NAMING, FEASTING AND GIFTS

The naming of the child follows explicit rules. The first child, if male, is named after the father's father, the second, if female, after the father's mother, and if male, after the mother's father. The priority of naming the first male and first female child went to the father's parents, the second set to the child's mother's parents. After this order was complete, a fifth child, hypothetically the third male among the family's offspring, would be named after the paternal grandfather's brother or any such respected relative. Lineal continuity is thus ensured by the process of naming.

Gifts and property play an important role in structuring social relationships after the birth of a child. The child's father's household by custom gives gifts of gold bangles, a waistband, a gold chain with a cross usually worth about five sovereigns (forty grams of gold). If gold is not given, then money worth five per cent of the dowry received is given, and this money is 'put in the name of the child' and not used for household expenses. This ritual of gift-giving is called *perr kanuka* (seeing the birth).

The child's mother's household also sends along with the woman on her return to her conjugal household the things necessary for an infant's care: copper and brass vessels, plates, buckets, basins, towels, bottles; and even a cow and calf, if they can afford it. Status considerations were deeply attached to such systems of gift giving. These were unilateral prestations primarily because gift-giving in these contexts, as Vatuk has argued, underlines one set as perpetual 'givers', and the other as perpetual 'recepients', re-echoing the context of giving and taking a woman as bride.[41] We have already noted how a woman's natal family make gifts of gold and food to the man's household when they come to take her home in the last months of pregnancy. The child will receive more gifts of gold on the twenty-eighth day.

While arguing that prestation is unilateral, reciprocity nevertheless plays its role in relation to the life cycle. The father of the new-born child is given a piece of land, and the materials and men with which to build a house. The gift is made by a man to his son, and therefore at one level it may be seen as a type of pre-mortem inheritance. Informants frequently state that there is a correlation between the amount of *stridhanam* received at a son's marriage and the kind of land and house given to the seceding son. The level of reciprocity operates here not between wife-givers and wife-takers but between the woman and her husband's father. By giving over control of the *stridhanam* she receives through her husband rights to maintenance in the conjugal estate. *Stridhanam*, over which the husband's father had controlling rights, is now translated into property which the woman enjoys as her husband's partner. This is analytically separate from what her husband will receive as post-mortem inheritance. The *stridhanam* thus does have the power which Mauss called the *hau* of the gift.[42]

For the Syrian Christians the house or *taravat* is a mnemonic, and a carrier of legend and tradition. Houses born out of fission after the birth of a child are all called by the same family name except that each is distinguished by the Christian name of the owner or by the direction in which the house lies. *Thekkaeveetil* (Southern House) pinpoints at once which household is thereby meant. By shifting residence, the son continues his membership in the patriline though by this event he too becomes the originator of a potential lineage. Thus every house, once set up, becomes at some point an ancestral house, inherited by the youngest son. From the very beginning, the building of a house, while being associated with the most elaborate ceremonies and restrictions which are related to the larger cultural domain of Hinduism, is also an important event in the Christian sense, for the Christian sees in the house an abode for the family which will continue for generations. Christianity is patrilineally organized, and the house in a system of transmission becomes the symbol not merely of habitation but also of religious values and their expression.

CHANGES IN THE PATTERN OF RELATIONSHIPS

Like marriage, birth constitutes an event which creates new roles and relationships. We will examine these along the two traditional axes of lineality and descent, and bilaterality and filiation. In this community of Christians, households undergo fission at the time of the birth of children, when expansion takes place. Donald Pitkin cites the work of Sydel Silverman on life in an Italian hill town to show that while people may live in nuclear households, the ideal family that they generally desire is three-generational, in which the sons all bring their brides into the paternal household.[43] Again, Pitkin defines the extended family not solely in terms of shared residence but in terms of the quality and quantity of relationships that the members of the separate households exhibit together. The Syrian Christians patently exemplify this aspect of patrilocal residence, close ties between households of the same name, and the notion of 'shared substance' as the concrete link between them. This link—being of the same blood—is expressed through the symbols of sharing, particularly of food and the rituals of celebration and commemoration.[44] Goody's work on devolution and its relation to the development cycle of the family has stressed the critical role of timing in the event of fission. Thus late fission meant large households, while early fission meant small households.[45] An informant, when asked why he had shifted out of his father's house at the birth of a child, said to me, 'My brother was getting married. In time he would start a family of his own. How could we all live together in the same house?' Where authority is clearly demarcated in the presence of the father tension is less evident than where brothers and their wives live together. While the norm of the joint family is maintained ideologically, the majority of the houses are nuclear, with a surviving parent or unmarried sister.

With the setting up of a house, the husband and wife now come into their own. This is however different in the case of the youngest son, who normatively does not separate from his parents with the birth of children, but 'replaces' at their death the earlier generation. Thus fission and house building is related to age *and* marital status, as well as the order of genesis in the fissioning group.

The rearing of children is almost entirely the responsibility of the parents. However, the grandparents play an important role because they are available and close at hand, and, in the case of the youngest son who inherits, they are co-resident. The paternal grandmother is an important person in the life of the child, particularly as it grows up. The child spends most of its time with its grandmother either in the same house or in the ancestral *taravat* where she lives with its father's brother. Even before they go to formal school, children accompany their grandmother every day to the parish church, and it is to her that they invariably recount the events of the day. A casual and teasing sort of relationship often exists between grandmother and grandchild, and it is here that the 'merging of alternate generations' is most clearly evident.

With the grandfather, on the other hand, the relationship is almost one of ritual avoidance. Children do not disturb the meditations of their grandfather. Further, while passing on the practical daily control of property to his sons, the father does not in actuality abdicate authority. Accounting, the keeping of careful ledgers with regard to daily expenses, is a prevalent custom among the Syrian Christians. Thus the son, though of mature age, will still account for every coin that he has spent during the day to his aged father. Such account books can explain every major expenditure for several decades including sons' education, repairs to the house, births, marriages, hospitalizations, dowries sent out and brought in. They are also a symbol of actual control. Children are aware of latent tensions that exist between their father and grandfather, and this creates a barrier that is not conducive to merging. It is the consequence of authoritarianism and patrilineality: the paternal grandfather is one who chastises the child's father, who can say, '*Edda*' (untranslatable—a casual way of summoning one's inferior in age or status) to him. The grandfather, while alive, is the *griha nayakan* (head of the house), and this notion of domestic authority is pervasive: from the leading of family prayers to priority in being served the best at meal times to the making of all important decisions regarding property, money and marriage.

For the Syrian Christian, the patrilineage is important, and the continuing significance and priority given to a man's house-name over his Christian name is an example. It is more significant in this sense to be known as Vazhapallil or Pallivadikal than as Jacob or John. Lineage identity carries with it the notion of jural and moral rights associated with property or privilege.[46] Family and lineage are closely co-ordinated and integrated.

In contrast to descent is filiation which is universally bilateral.[47] The relation of children to their mother is in striking contrast to their relationship with their father, and is expressed almost entirely in affectual terms even while she remains an important disciplinarian. Traditionally, the men were away for long periods of the day at their places of work, and only returned in the evening to a meal, family prayers and sleep. Further, the influence of a child's father was mitigated by the even more dominant and authoritarian figure of the father's father. It was only after the latter's death that his son, often past his first youth, came into a role of authority. At this time, his mother, who did not express herself at all during her husband's lifetime, now becomes a powerful matriarchal figure to whom her son will defer.

It is to the mother that the young child turns for every need, and she mediates between the child and the father, the latter being always a distant figure. In this context, the cult of Mary, Christ's mother, who is a major influence in the life of these Christians, is easy to comprehend. There is a degree of emotional honesty that men display before their mothers which they would be ashamed to in the presence of their fathers or others.

The position of Syrian Christian women is made clearest by the attitude of sons to their mothers. While there is a bond between them, it can only be expressed through joking. Mothers are helpless, they know nothing about practical things, they are overly concerned about mundane events. Such treatment is the consequence of the way women were treated and expected to behave in the traditional family. They were never *formally* included in the affairs of the external domain, in matters relating to property inheritance or dowry. Even with regard to marriage, it was the fathers who met, discussed financial and practical matters and fixed alliances. The mother never saw her son's wife till her son ritually placed his bride in her care (*ammae epichu*). Women cooked, cleaned, took care of children and were devoted to the religious life. There were enough males in the household and in the lineage to take care of all financial matters, even the mundane buying of household provisions.

Just as the mother is the source of affection, so also the mother's brothers are of primary importance to the children. Gifts from the mother's brothers are prescribed on the occasions of marriage and birth. It is the mother's brother who ties the waistbelt on the new-born child. It is her brother who comes to enquire about a woman and her children on behalf of the natal household; who brings abundant quantities of fruit, vegetables and *palharam* (festive foods). Many summer holidays and Christmas vacations are spent at the *amma-veedu* (mother's house) with the maternal grandparents. Here the children are honoured and beloved guests. They have the run of the house, the fields and the *thattampuram* (lofts) where the bananas, jackfruit and sweet foods are stored.

As they grow up, however, their father's house grows in importance; it now becomes the centre of their consciousness particularly when they are sons. It is of this house and property that they will be heirs. This is 'their' own house as opposed to their mother's house. When living patrilocally, this distinction between the child's father's house (of primary significance to his sense of identity) and his mother's house is most apparent, since he is living in his father's house with paternal grandparents, near paternal uncles.

OLD AGE AND DEATH

For men, old age is a time of meditation and increasing detachment from the affairs of everyday life. The influence of Hinduism which associates renunciation with old age is clearly present. While some men continue to manage property, most pass it on to their sons. An old man will spend the major part of the day reading in the portico or the verandah, legs stretched out on the *char-kasera* or easychair. The Bible, prayer book and the newspaper are his main sources of reading. Involvement in church and neighbourhood activities continue but, for the most part, men tend to retire into a private world of contemplation. In the domestic group, the authority of the father is still paramount.

The sons refer to him in the making of decisions and are guided by him in even the most trivial of matters. This combination of detachment as well as implicit authority creates a relationship of deference and respect toward the head of the household which is found almost uniformly.

For women, hard work continues till such time as they are virtually bedridden. In those households which contain a widowed mother, they are found to help in the cooking, cleaning and care of the children. Far from a manifest renunciation of temporal affairs, they are active participants in all matters including the financial, which is otherwise a male territory. They wield authority by virtue of their age and experience.

Yet for both men and women, in spite of differing attitudes to life, old age is essentially a time of waiting for death. Most evocative, perhaps, was an old woman who showed me her wedding clothes, saying that soon she would be covered in them and laid to rest. For those who wait thus, anticipation of meeting Christ and the beloved dead is the most important feature of death. For those who are old, who have done their 'duty', there is no fear of death.

The Domestic Rituals

When a man or woman nears the time of death, the priest is called. In Puthenangadi, there is often no need to summon the priest, he will already be there, word having got to him the first instant that an ailing or elderly person takes a turn for the worse. The family turns the individual so that his face is turned towards the east (associated with the Second Coming of Christ), with his hands folded on the chest in an attitude of prayer. All the members of his family gather round him. The priest recites the creed of faith, and he who is dying must either recite parts of it himself, or be recited to in a loud voice by someone near him. *Thaila abhisekham* (the anointing oil) is administered. It is the last of the rituals of life.

An informant said:

People think that if *thaila abhisekham* is performed, then the end has come. In actuality, it is a stimulant for the spirit and must be given when the subject is fully conscious. When the *thailam* (holy oil) is rubbed on the body, it is believed that peace pervades the spirit and flesh.

The anointing oil is put on the eyes, nose, ears, mouth, hands, legs, feet and the stomach. If it is early morning and the dying person has eaten nothing and is therefore in the required state of fasting, the Eucharist is administered. When these rituals have been concluded and the person breathes his last, it may be said that an individual died in the faith (*visvasa pramanathil marichu*). The manner and dignity with which one dies is of great importance.

Following death, the eldest son has the duty of closing the eyes of the dead person. As soon as there is knowledge of a death in the neighbourhood, the kinship network tightens considerably. Neighbourhood ties too become analogous to kinship ties. All those who are associated with the family in any way arrive in the household where the death has occurred, and the family is given the freedom to mourn as others take over routine tasks. No fires may be lit in the kitchen, and neighbours and kinsmen must cook food, bring coffee and tea, and look after the small children in the house. The relatives and friends help wash and anoint the body; the deceased, if male, by men; and if female, by her own sex. This last ceremonial bath is a duty of love, and the corpse is dressed in clean white clothes. It is not unusual to find that the deceased may have set apart a set of clothes during his or her own time.

Shavam samskaram refers to the manner in which the corpse is treated before burial. The body must be treated with respect: *shavana-thine bahumanikkum*. That a person must be dressed in his best at the time of his own funeral is constantly reiterated. Although the time of waiting for the return of Christ is spent by the soul in a shadowy region (*padallam* or *sheol*, the land of the dead) of which there is no clear idea, informants are confident that when they meet Christ, they will be dressed in their finest, their lost limbs will be restored, their ailments cured. Their bodies will have the aspect of thirty-three years of age, since it was at this age that Christ died and was resurrected. A woman who had her leg amputated is said to have had it interred in the family tomb since she believed that when Christ came, she would be restored to a perfect body. Whether true or false, the story has symbolic significance. In another case, a woman washing her mother's sister's daughter's body suggested that the newer, brighter *kavani* (drape) be used to cover the deceased since that would be visible to the mourners, and the older one used to actually dress her in. An old lady assisting her said, 'No, she must wear the best when she meets Christ, she must be in her finest, the older one will not do'. In the case of a woman her *minnu* or marriage locket is removed, either then or at the church where the last rites are performed, and, traditionally, this is supposed to be gifted to the church.

A table is positioned near the head of the corpse, and on it are placed two crosses (a wooden one and a silver one, both of which are borrowed from the church), a prayer book and a Bible. The deceased is laid on a bed which lies west to east, so that he or she is facing the east and can await the Second Coming. The hands are folded in an attitude of prayer and a cross and candle placed between the fingers. This symbolizes the event of welcoming Christ with a lighted candle as well as with a symbol of affiliation, the cross, during the Second Coming. All those who come to mourn sit around the deceased and read from the Bible or the prayer book. On all four corners of the bed, candles are lit and incense sticks burnt.

The Funeral Procession

Someone is sent to the church to ask for the umbrellas, the flags and the canopy. If the dead person is someone very old, who has craved for release for a long time, death is seen as joyful. A long and fruitful life has come to a peaceful conclusion, and all the celebratory umbrellas and canopies are taken out. On the other hand, when untimely death occurs, the black umbrellas alone are taken out. The body is laid on a ceremonially designed hearse (made of solid wood decorated with scroll work) and after the prayers in the house, the body is taken to the church to be buried.

An eighty-three-year-old lady had died in Puthenangadi when I was there. A woman watching the procession from the gates of her house said to a younger neighbour:

She has seen everything of life that there was to see. Thirty-five years ago her husband died. It was a feast day at the church and some people were drunk. A fight started, he fell, there was a stampede and he died. His wife brought up six daughters and three sons, we don't know how. Some people passed by our house and they said that all the daughters were crying as if their hearts would break. Who cries so much and so loud for an eighty-three-year-old lady, even if she be their mother? Not one of us will ever be able to understand the relationship this mother had with her children.

The music that accompanies the funeral procession as well as the synchronized lamentations of the priests could be heard in the distance. All the Christians came out of their houses. Word had got around early in the morning that there was a death in the neighbourhood.

First came a young boy carrying a silver cross about three feet in height on a wooden pedestal. Then two boys appeared, carrying big candles on silver sticks. There followed four elderly men with black umbrellas decorated with small silver tassels hanging ceremonially from the rim. Six priests in black robes and skull caps walked in measured steps under a large silk canopy that was held up by four young men. The priests chanted in Syriac, their books held aloft before them. The sons of the deceased followed close behind, accompanied by fellow mourners with solemn and composed faces. Last of all came the women, most of whom were weeping but with restraint, since the Christian believes that too much sorrow ties the soul to its earthly home. In earlier times, a wife could not accompany her husband's cortege. If she did so, people would contemptuously say 'She has gone to bury her husband'. This attitude is no longer prevalent. Recently, a priest said to his parishioners that it was the duty and privilege for a woman to be by her husband's side till the moment he is interred.

After the procession, when the coffin reaches the cemetery, there is a ritual called *kuzhi kannuka* or seeing the grave. The son of the deceased kneels in the chancel and puts some money on the place where he has knelt, with his head touching the ground. Only when this has been done can the body be taken to the burial place. The money amounts to whatever the giver feels that his family owes to the church, and varies according to the age and social status of the deceased. This is also the time when all debts are paid. Obligations to the church which have not been met with earlier are fulfilled now; otherwise, this may result in the delay of the burial, which is a source of great embarrassment. Such delays do not occur frequently as Christians generally never fall behind in their payments to the church. Priests and their children are exempt from the *kuzhi kannam*. So are families which have given land to the church as a gift.

The Rituals of the Church

The rituals of death express the relation between the body and the soul, and the symbolic relation between the living and the dead.[48] All

death ceremonies are specifically for the 'good' Christian, who has
followed the rules and tenets of the faith. Those who have broken the
law are excommunicated and denied a proper funeral.

Shav samskaram (the ceremony for the deceased) begins with the
statement made by the priest that death is freedom from the struggle
of life, that the soul on its way to a distant place where there is peace
and happiness.[49] The songs of the service speak of the resurrection
promised by the Messiah to the Sons of Adam. The deceased is told:
'Do not weep when you leave; you will live in the light of Christ. The
guardian angel of paradise will show you the way. As Lazarus was
resurrected by the voice of Christ, so will you'.[50]

It must be affirmed here that official theology states that the departed are 'quick'.[51] Prayers for the dead are beneficial primarily
because the soul which is separated from the body is still alive. The
theologian cautions against questioning 'where' paradise is, or where
the soul goes to after death. Whatever its nature, whether good or evil
or working towards perfection, the soul must wait for the general resurrection before it is damned or liberated in the full experience of
God. The *Shav samskaram* can be seen to oscillate between two forms
of speech: one, an indirect reference to the soul which has departed
from this life; the other, directed to the soul, in the first person. In the
latter case, the soul continues to be present, and to be directly affected
by the prayers and services that are held for its benefit. Two spatial
metaphors are implicit—on the one hand, the dead go to the city of
ghosts;[52] on the other, the dead are still with 'us', invisibly present,
partaking in the Holy Eucharist.[53]

Sometimes the people refer to paradise (*perdeesa*) as the waiting
place or to *padallam*, the place of the dead. People pray that the soul
be saved from darkness, from evil spirits, and that it be guided to the
place of light. It must be clarified here that the Syrian Christians of
Puthenangadi do not believe in ill-motivated ghosts and spirits primarily
because they see themselves as 'good Christians'. No 'good Christian',
according to them, was ever harmed by evil powers. However, all the
rituals of the church affirm the presence of Satan and his powers.

Much of the funeral service relates to the idea of the Second
Coming of Christ. With every death and funeral attended, the people
have the abstract quality of the afterlife spelt out to them in vivid
terms, based on the Book of Revelation. The rituals express the
continuity between life and death, between the historical event of
every life and the apocalyptic event which will lead to corporeal

destruction and spiritual regeneration, to universal annihilation and the Last Judgement.

Thus, when the destruction of earth occurs, accompanied by the trumpeting of the angels and the appearance of God, the soul of the departed one should be sheltered from anger, from punishment, from hell-fire.[54] In this destruction of the earth, the sun, moon and the stars are without light, sepulchres crash open, all creation becomes annihilated, the dead are resurrected. This is the moment when Judgement comes.

This fearsome image of catastrophe is replaced by the optimism of the Second Coming of Christ. From the time of Adam to Christ, there was death, but with the death of Christ, there is victory and redemption.[55] When Christ is judge, those who are victorious are blessed. In the light of this, the people are warned:

> Today, we are happy, tomorrow, we are silent in the grave. He who remembers this every day is blessed. Listen carefully: wealth, beauty, commanding power become as nothing. He who has eternal life is blessed.[56]

It is the separation of the body from life, from the soul, that the Christian most fears. The idea of resurrection is therefore of central significance. The priest says, 'Do not fear for your destroyed bodies. He who has created you will resurrect you'. But the resurrection and the shelter are conditional. Only those who have rested in Christ will have life.[57] The dead man speaks to the living in stanzas which echo the belief that the living and the dead may speak to each other for their mutual benefit.[58] The reading from Deuteronomy refers to the death of Moses and his exclusion by the Lord's commandment from the promised land. 'I have let you see it with your eyes, but you will not cross over into it.'

The necessity to be well prepared for the Second Coming is stressed in 1 Pet. 3: 3–13. ·

> The scoffers will say, 'Where is this "coming" He promised? Ever since our fathers died, everything goes on as it has since the beginning of creation. . . ', but with the Lord a day is like a thousand years and a thousand years are like a day. The Lord is not slow in keeping His promise as some understand slowness.

The reading of the verses from Corinthians reiterates to the listening Christian the nature of the resurrected body:

> All flesh is not the same: men have one kind of flesh, animals have another, birds another and fish another. There are also heavenly bodies and there are earthly bodies; but the splendour of the heavenly bodies is one kind, and the splendour of the earthly bodies is another. . . If there is a natural body, here is also a spiritual body.

The act of burial is likened to sowing whereby the corporeality and putrefaction of death is transformed through the imagery into a seed out of which glory, power and the spiritual body are raised.

The soul speaks constantly for the blessings of memory and prayer on the part of those it has left behind:

> Come, close to me, pray for me, sing songs of sadness for me. Christ has sent a messenger for me. Out of sadness I say I must leave. Those of you who are still alive, live well. Those who do not believe in Christ will receive nothing. I am going to settle my account with the Lord who knows all secrets. On the barren land grow the Susannah flowers. We will wear clothes not stitched by hand.[59]

This song expresses many things: the suddenness of death, the sadness of departure from the pleasures of life, the hope of resurrection after death captured in the imagery of flowers growing on barren land.

In the last of the rituals of death, *thailam* (the holy anointing oil) is poured over the body. The priest prays that:

> You who have removed him from the temporary earth, send your army from heaven to escort him there. Through this *thailam*, may the evil spirits have no baneful influence, may he be sheltered from them.[60]

The holy oil is poured on the face, the chest and the knees in the form of a cross; the priest prays for the deceased and asks that he receive shelter and rest from this world's cares, win the battle with evil spirits, and live in happiness with the saints.[61]

I

When the body is lowered into the grave, after the face is covered with a *sosofa* or the veil used in covering the sacraments, the priests speak of the body being resurrected without defects. Though Lazarus, the brother of Martha and Mary, had grown corrupt with death, yet he was brought back to life. It was so with the daughter of Jairus. 'Returned to dust to the state of Adam, so you who have died be not sad.'[62] The priest takes a handful of earth and puts it on the body in the sign of the cross: 'Returned to dust, you become dust. The desire of God is fulfilled'. The priest says:

> Blessed is He who gives Death, and brings Life. In the moment of the Return, Christ will destroy the reign of death and Satan. Like lightning He will return. And the dead will arise singing songs of happiness. Go in happiness, close the door that links life with death. Christ will return and open this door.[63]

The cross is symbolized as the bridge between the chasm that separates Man and God. The creed is recited, and the concluding prayers refer to the soul's entry into the garden, the table and the bridal chamber (*mannavra*) of the Lord.[64] Further, the priest prays that the hearts of those who stand here should be made happy as were Martha and Mary at the resurrection of Lazarus.[65]

Two themes run parallel to each other in these mortuary rituals. At one level, death is closure. The rituals signify that the mourners are separated from the deceased by the closing of a door. Their tears are desired, departure must be mourned, 'Sing songs of sadness for me'. The anniversaries of death commemorated by prayer and feasting and with visits to the graveyard underline this separation. Mourning is a way of remembering and recreating what is now over.

On another level, it is the liminal aspect of death that the funeral service is most concerned with. For the Christian, death marks the beginning of a liminal phase which cannot be understood by social time or space because it evades such expression. The dead and the living orient their existence to the Second Coming of Christ. Those who are alive experience time and their lives in the context of that which is to come; the dead must wait in *padallam*, that unimagined place, for the Judgement of Christ. In this time of waiting, they continue to experience temporal life. The soul of the deceased may be prayed for, and the living through their services may alter the fate of the deceased's soul. While not as fully formulated as the notion of purgatory, the Yakoba in their concept of *padallam* and commemoration rituals come close to such a concept.

Post-Mortuary Rituals: Adyantra, The Prayer for the Soul and Qurbana

After the funeral services in the church were over on the occasion of the death of an old woman of Puthenangadi, most of the neighbours and friends who had come wandered around, looking at family gravestones, lighting candles at the heads of these, commenting on the new stone slab that had been laid over some grave or a cross which had been installed recently over another. After the burial, the solemnity of the occasion is somewhat eased for all those who are not chief mourners. The rite of separation is not fully concluded but for the majority who are not affected by post-mortuary rituals, the return from the cemetery signifies the return to profane time, symbolized by the partaking of a meal.

When the mourners return to the house after the funeral service, all those who are present are given food called *pasini kanji* (starvation gruel) which has been cooked in a nearby house by neighbours and distant kin. It signifies the breaking of the fast, since after the event of death no one consumes anything other than black coffee. The food that is served is usually gruel (*kanji*), bean sprouts/pulses (*payr*), and *pappadam* (wafers) which are not fried in oil but roasted over hot coals—*chuttu edukuga*. Meat, fish, eggs, curds, milk and *ghee* (clarified butter) are never served. Black coffee is provided for everyone. The priest returns to the house of mourning with the censer (*dhoop petti*) and the blessing of the house takes place. On the third day after the death the mourners celebrate the Eucharist in memory of the soul of the deceased kinsman. For forty days the household is in a formal state of mourning signified by fasting and abstinence (*noimba*). It is believed that the soul of the deceased remains on earth at this time, unable to free itself from the bonds that held it down during life.

Adyantra, a mourning feast, may be held on the third, ninth, sixteenth or thirtieth day. This meal is again completely vegetarian. There is a custom, almost forgotten now, that on the ninth day after death, a tender coconut must be offered to the deceased. An informant said that they had had a prayer meeting and a meal in honour of their father but had forgotten the matter of the coconut. Just then one fell from a tree, of the right size and maturity, as if it had been carefully picked. The priest officiating at the ceremony said, 'It is *Achayen* (the deceased parent) who pushed it down to remind us'.

By belief, the soul after death does not go straight to heaven or hell but waits for the Day of Judgement when Christ will return. During the forty days that the spirit of the person is still on earth, hovering around loved ones and remembered places, there is *noimba* (abstinence) in all respects. *Qurbana* must be celebrated every day if possible for the soul of the dead. If death has taken place during the weeks of Lent, then *Qurbana* for the deceased can be celebrated only on Saturdays and Sundays. A lamp must be kept constantly lit for all of the forty days (*keddathe vellaku*), and then it must be the priest who puts it out, not by blowing on it, but by snuffing it out with the tip of his thumb and forefinger. For sons, particularly, the forty-day fast is compulsory. If it is a woman's father-in-law or mother-in-law who has died, *noimba* is only for sixteen days for there is no blood tie (*raktha bandham*).

If death should occur in the middle of one of the Great Lent periods (i.e., the fifty-day Lent (*Ambadha Noimba*), then the forty days are calculated from the day of death onwards. For example, should the person have died on *Pakthi Noimba* (Half Lent, or the twenty-fifth day of the Great Lent) the family must fast for fifteen days beyond the Great Lent, except on Easter when the fast compulsorily must be broken for that one day, to signify the joy of Christ's resurrection.

For forty-one days, the bed on which the deceased was laid must be left untouched in the centre of the room, with the foot of the bed towards the east. This becomes a room apart. No one is allowed to use the bed, which is kept covered with a clean white sheet on the centre of which is placed the Bible. The lamp on the table behind the headboard or in one of the corners of the room is kept constantly lit. If possible, the priest must come every day and pray for the dead person, and the censer swung about so that incense fills the room. This signifies that the body and soul are separate, and that for forty days the soul still remains in the house where it has lived, the incense representing prayers for the soul. Informants say that this refers to Rev. 4:7: 'Golden vials full of odours which are the prayers of saints'. The importance of *kundrikam* (incense) lies in that it was one of the gifts of the kings to the infant Christ, and has always been associated with Him. The importance of wearing white, which is the customary colour for even everyday use, has its context in Rev. 3:4.5: '...And they shall walk with me in white, for they are worthy. He that overcometh, the same shall be clothed in white raiment'.

If the *sadhya* is given on the forty-first day, the time of *noimba* is

considered over and non-vegetarian food is served without restriction
or inhibition. It is the responsibility of the daughter of the deceased to
bring *nei-appam* (a sweet food made of rice, jaggery and clarified
butter) which she must cook herself. Bananas cut into small pieces are
also put in a dish which the priest blesses and serves to all those who
were most closely related; but everyone must be given a little, if only
the crumbs in the basket (*kotta podi*). The importance of making and
eating *nei-appam* is expressed in the statements made by neighbours at
childbirth. If a daughter is born, they say 'There is one now who will
cook the *appam*' (*Appam choodan allu ondu*) and when a son is born
they say 'There is one who will eat the *appam*'. Food (and its eating)
becomes a symbol of shared blood. Commemoration ceremonies
become the central events around which lineage members congregate.
The priest, when leaving after prayers of blessing, touches everyone's
head with his small handcross. This is symbolic of the Kiss of Peace
(*kai muth*). People put a little money as offering towards the income of
the priest on a plate. If it seems too little, the bereaved family will
contribute some more money. Like the gift at baptism, this is not a fee
but an offertory to the priest.

The Rites of Commemoration

The rites of commemoration which occur every year are expressions
of the Christian ideas regarding the soul. While the Christians in
Puthenangadi do not give credence to the existence of frightening and
ill-motivated ghosts and spirits, nevertheless there is a concern for the
dead, and the state of the soul awaiting judgement. This is the reason
for the emphasis on the *Qurbana* compulsorily said in the name of the
deceased on the *Orma divasam* or commemoration day.

The central feature of the commemoration day services are prayers
for the dead. The rites on this occasion have to be understood in the
context of lineage membership (including bilateral filiation), and the
ideas of the Christian relation to the soul. The prayers for the dead
central to the ceremony are explained thus:

When your father lives in the same house as you, you say that
you love him. Then when he is dead, how can this bond of love
be broken? For us, our love goes beyond death and physical
separation. Somewhere, our fathers are gathered, and as long as
we can, we pray for them and remember them.

On commemoration day, a memorial service is held in the church. *Qurbana* is said in the deceased's memory. Those of the family who are to partake of communion do so, and then the family, accompanied by the priest, goes to the grave where candles are lit and crosses placed; the deacon lights the *dhoop petti* (censer) and the priest circles the grave saying prayers in honour and remembrance of the dead person. The family returns to the house for a vegetarian meal, and the priest is always formally invited. *Nei-appam* is prepared by the daughter. These may be seen as oblations in memory of the dead since they are even brought to the church on the commemoration day of holy men, blessed by the priest, and eaten by all the parishioners.

The *Orma divasam* is an important day for the living. It is a day when close cognates of the deceased congregate. The day may not be necessarily melancholic, particularly if the event of death occurred a long time ago or if the person was old enough to have merited eternal rest. It is a day when kinship ties are reinvigorated and, ideally, antagonisms forgotten or blurred. In one particular case, the daughter of the family who had differences with her brothers did not arrive for the service. Further, when she put in an appearance at the close of lunch, she refused any food saying that she had eaten at home. This was clearly an index of her resentment, since it is imperative that those who are present should share food. To refuse food from a kinsman is tantamount to severing links. We shall now turn to the Syrian Christians' concern with inheritance, and the transformation of relationships following a death in the household.

INHERITANCE

So long as the household continued to exist without breaking up after the death of its head, the problem of succession was not a complex one.[66] In many cases, the youngest son was in possession of the house, the daughters having been married with *stridhanam*, and the other sons settled in patrilocally situated residences of their own.

Till February 1986, it was the Travancore Succession Act of 1916 and the Cochin Christian Inheritance Act of 1921 which governed the intestate interests of the Syrian Christians. These were of particular significance in the case of women's right to property. The Travancore Act of 1916 had fixed *stridhanam* at one-fourth the son's share or five thousand rupees, whichever was less, for a daughter, in the event of a man dying intestate. Female heirs who were paid *stridhanam* did not inherit paternal property. Quite clearly, women were at the mercy of their brothers who, as it often turned out, did not provide for them beyond the nominal five thousand rupees. Intestate division of property now follows the Indian Succession Act of 1925 which establishes equality between the sexes in matters of intestate succession.

In many middle class Syrian Christian households, the concept of gift transmission would sometimes seem more useful than inheritance. Here pre-mortem transmission of property may result in divided ownership, the donor retaining a residual title to the property while the recipient may acquire working rights.[67] Thus, in actuality, very little property remains to be inherited on the death of an individual.

There is also a material dimension to filiation, which is what inheritance of any kind is basically about. As Madan has clearly shown, *stridhanam* expresses the father–daughter relation while inheritance expresses that of father to son.[68] I have dealt with the problem of *stridhanam* as a form of pre-mortem inheritance, and have also stated that it is not merely devolution of wealth but, in fact, disinheritance. Let us then look at inheritance as an expression of the father–son relationship, where the implicit morality of kinship is all the more underlined. Julian Pitt-Rivers asserts that here was a moral obligation to forgo self-interest in favour of another, to sacrifice oneself for the sake of someone else.[69] This is expressed in the manner in which patriarchs carefully account their expenses, save as much as they can so that they may leave something for their children. Thrift and economy are very specifically values associated with Syrian Christians.

The setting up of house for an elder son at the time of the expansion of the latter's household implies necessarily the sharing of decisions, of food and leisure, and the closeness of father–son relations (in spite of actual emotional distancing). Death, in a sense, then, does not create the turbulence through post-mortem division of property that it otherwise would. Therefore, it is not surprising that rights of inheritance are made known very early in life. Small boys glibly say 'The house is mine' or 'That particular piece of land will be mine'. Property then does not have the connotation of belonging to 'another' (father or grandfather) because in time it will devolve upon oneself and is therefore potentially one's own.

Inheritance customs express the dominant place of the patriarch in the Syrian Christian household. Traditionally, the concept of an equal share was never of importance to them and property was divided quite often according to whim or personal need. One brother may receive more than the other brothers because his family had not been able to rise to the same income level as the others or because he had more children to educate. 'Give the depleted ones a little more' (*Sheenam ollavaraku ichuroode koduka*) was a frequently-heard phrase from informants.

Settlement of property being vague and ill-defined,[70] it reflected personal interpretation by the father of the conduct and needs of his heirs. The question of manipulation and preferment did frequently arise. A will was necessary particularly when there was a chance that the brothers would quarrel among themselves. Usually, agricultural land was partitioned only after the death of the father but sometimes, if sons and father quarrelled or went 'separate ways', partition would take place earlier. This is against the norm relating to father–son relations and such pre-mortem partitions are accompanied by acrimony. There is no fixed rule that the youngest son must inherit the house though this is a norm born out of the particular function of ultimo-geniture, where the old age of the parents and the coming into maturity of the last born coincided. If, however, it was the elder son who took care of his parents, by common consent he *may* remain behind in the *taravat*. Fraternal joint family in its fullest sense is virtually unknown, is perhaps even distasteful. But to live in adjoining houses is very common, though divided by house and garden walls.

The role of women in the matter of allocating inheritance and property is not of formal importance. However, the written will is an important institution among the Syrian Christians. It expresses in-dividual desire, and women may change the opinion of husbands about particular offspring. However, the patriarch's brothers play a very important advisory role here in seeing that custom is followed and that each son receives what is right and just. Variables such as the amount of *stridhanam* brought in at marriage by a son, payments made to the father by the son during household financial crises, his role in paying family debts or educating other siblings or help in marrying off the sisters are all considered at this point.

Before the 1986 Supreme Court ruling on Christian inheritance, a woman who received a *stridhanam* at marriage could not have any farther claim upon her father's property. It is too early to engage in any analysis of the impact of this ruling at the level of everyday life. Journalists, however, reiterate that high rates of *stridhanam* prevail, creating intensely pathological situations; further, that written wills safeguard patrimonial interests.

The father's death before a daughter is settled results in the role of the brother as guardian of his sister, and responsible for her marriage and the concomitant settlement of estate upon her. The problem of disinheritance arises most acutely when women have been evicted from their *taravat*s with a payment of five thousand rupees as their share of the estate, which amount, according to the Travancore Act of 1916, was a legitimate equivalent to the payment of *stridhanam*. The two cases of Mariakutty Thoman and K C Aleykutty which appeared before the Supreme Court regarding women's rights over property, describe the cases of women who had been 'legally' evicted by their brothers. By the judge.nent of 24 February 1986, a daughter has rights to equal shares with male siblings. The changing inheritance laws may have an impact upon father–daughter relations as well as the brother–sister relationship. More importantly, the role of the affines—the daughter's husband and sister's husband—will change drastically with the repealment of the Travancore Act. When *stridhanam* was paid, informants were vehement that by giving away a daughter's share the possibility of affinal interference was precluded.

It must be noted here that where daughters were sole inheritors, the practice of *deth keruka* (a form of affinal adoption) existed. Thus, while the older daughters would be married off in the traditional manner, the youngest daughter would remain to look after her parents, and only such a groom would be found for her who would be willing to live uxorilocally. This implied living with affines rather than with agnates, which was never, in a strongly patriarchal society, a very comfortable position for the man. It might even imply taking on the house-name of his wife. Thus, the conditions imposed upon the husband in the institution of *deth keruka* was to act as if he were an adopted son. The material advantages were balanced out by the mild social discomfiture that was involved.

The right of the widow to her husband's estate till 1986 was one primarily relating to maintenance. In the case where the father died of old age, his wife continued to live in the household, normally cherished by her son, his wife and their children, with her other sons in the neighbourhood frequently visiting her. She would be a person with much influence over her sons, wielded in a purely affectual manner. While it is veiled by laughter and teasing, sons are more readily influenced by the logic provided by their mothers than by their wives.

However, if the widow is young and without issue, the consequences can be very different. In one particular case, the woman's parents took her away after the untimely death of her husband. They also reclaimed her *stridhanam*, although she had been married for three years. This ended the relationship between the two families. It was only at her death at eighty-six that her husband's brother's son, a priest, came to attend the funeral. Seventy-odd years had passed since contact had ceased between the woman and her conjugal house. Her *stridhanam* had been used to help educate three of her brothers. She, in turn, had lived with one of her brothers and after his death with his son in a respected and honourable position. The intensity of emotion displayed at her death, albeit silently and with restraint, was an indication of the love and affection they felt for her. The money that had been used for educating her brothers had been returned to her in time. It did not amount to much in 1982, but it was divided equally between her brother's son's sons, by a written will.

The fact that this woman returned to her father's house at eighteen, a young widow, relates to the attitude of wife-givers to wife-takers. If there are no children, what stake does a women have in her husband's house if he dies? With her husband's death, traditionally, a woman had only maintenance rights by law. Withdrawal of *stridhanam* implied a lack of trust by the woman's parents in her conjugal household, and this, while perhaps justified in many cases, created deep and bitter wounds.

Conclusion

One problem clearly asserts itself and remains to be analysed. This is the change in inheritance laws that have recently come about. What effect will this have on marriage prestations? Ideally, it should bring to a close what has become over time pathological prestation, where demands for *stridhanam* leave many women and their families in a piteous condition. Will there be a gradual decline in the giving of *stridhanam*? How will the church receive this order, when it seems that it too will financially lose its tithe on amounts given and received? Is patriarchal ideology really threatened? While the chief actors in this law court drama were three marginalized and courageous single women, it is interesting to note that even in 1981, when I undertook a survey on behalf of two local seminaries, I found that the majority of women believed that 'equal share' would not only be materially advantageous, it would be in keeping with the modern ethos of gender equality, in which they believed in principle.

Notes

1. See Roman Jakobson and Krystyna Pomorska, *Dialogues* (Cambridge: Cambridge University Press, 1983).
2. See e.g. Ananta Krishna Ayyar, *Anthropology of the Syrian Christians*.
3. The text of the marriage service is published by Mar Julius Press (MJP), Pampakuda, 1979. See p. 71.
4. W Guenther, 'Marriage' in Colin Brown (ed.), *The New International Dictionary of New Testament Theology* (Exeter: The Paternoster Press 1976), p. 581.
5. Eph. 5:31.
6. L Johnston, *Sacraments in Scripture: A Symposium* (London: Geoffrey Chapman: 1966).
7. Mark 2:19.
8. Johnston, op. cit., p. 239.
9. Ibid., p. 245.
10. MJP publication, p. 81.
11. Ibid., p. 83.
12. Robert Hertz, *Death and the Right Hand* (Aberdeen: Cohen and West, 1960).
13. Gen. 32–53.
14. MJP publication, p. 87.
15. Eph. 5: 22–33.
16. MJP publication, p. 135–7.
17. Jack Goody and S J Tambiah, *Bridewealth and Dowry*, (Cambridge: Cambridge University Press, 1973).
18. Nur Yalman, 'On the purity of women in the castes of Ceylon and Malabar', in *Journal of the Royal Anthropological Institute*, vol. 93, p. 25–58; Goody and Tambiah, op. cit.
19. Jack Goody, *The Development of the Family and Marriage in Europe* (Cambridge: Cambridge University Press, 1983).
20. Ibid., p. 255–6.
21. Mauss, *The Gift*.
22. Nur Yalman, *Under the Bo Tree* (Berkeley: University of California Press, 1971), p. 123.
23. See A L Basham, 'The Practice of Medicine in Ancient and Medieval India' in Charles Leslie (ed.), *Asian Medical Systems* (Berkeley: University of California Press, 1977), p. 26.
24. Frederick L Dunn, 'Traditional Asian Medicine and Cosmopolitan Medicine as Adaptive System' in Leslie, op. cit., p. 149.
25. II Sam. 11:4; Lev. 15:25–30.
26. Kadavil Paul, *The Orthodox Syrian Church, Its Religion and Philosophy* (Puthencruz: K V Pathrose, 1973).
27. MJP publication, p. 3.
28. A George, 'A Literary Catalogue of New Testament Passages on Baptism' in *A Symposium: Baptism in the New Testament* (London: Geoffrey Chapman, 1964).
29. Col. 1:12.
30. D Moliat, S J, 'Baptismal Symbolism in St Paul' in *A Symposium: Baptism in the New Testament*.

31. Gal. 3.27.
32. Gal. 3.28.
33. See *A Symposium: Baptism in the New Testament*, p. 208.
34. Luke 3:16; Matt. 3:11.
35. *A Symposium: Baptism in the New Testament*, p. 35.
36. MJP publication, pp. 21–3.
37. Ibid., p. 35.
38. Ibid., p. 37.
39. Ibid., p. 39.
40. Ibid., p. 43.
41. Sylvia Vatuk, 'Gifts and Affines in North India' in *Contributions to Indian Sociology* (n.s.), vol. 9, no. 2.
42. Mauss, op. cit..
43. Donald S Pitkin, *The House that Giacomo Built: History of an Italian Family 1898–1978* (Cambridge: Cambridge University Press, 1985).
44. See Andrew Strathern, 'Kinship Descent and Locality' in Jack Goody (ed.) *The Character of Kinship* (Cambridge: Cambridge University Press, 1973), p. 21–33..
45. Jack Goody, *Production and Reproduction* (London: Cambridge University Press, 1976), p. 20.
46. Meyer Fortes, *Kinship and the Social Order* (London: Routledge and Kegan Paul, 1970) and *Time and Social Structure and Other essays* (London: Athlone Press, 1970).
47. See Meyer Fortes, ibid., p. 253.
48. See e.g. Veena Das, *Structure and Cognition* (Delhi: Oxford University Press, 1977); Robert Hertz, op. cit. Meena Kaushik, 'The Symbolic Representation of Death' in *Contributions to Indian Sociology* (n.s.), vol. 10, p. 265–92; 1976; Ralph Nicholas, 'Sraddha, Impurity and Relations Between the Living and the Dead', in *Contributions to Indian Sociology* (n.s.) vol. 5, 1 & 2, Jan.–Dec., pp. 366–80, 1981; Jonathan Parry, 'Death and Cosmogony in Kashi' in *Contributions to Indian Sociology* (n.s.) vol. 15, 1 & 2, pp. 337–65, 1981: Lloyd W Warner, *Family of God* (Connecticut: Greenwood Press, 1975).
49. MJP publication, pp. 175–77.
50. Ibid., pp. 177–9.
51. Kadavil Paul, op. cit., p. 39.
52. MJP publication, p. 179.
53. Kadavil Paul, op. cit., p. 41.
54. MJP publication, pp. 185–91.
55. Ibid., p. 193.
56. Ibid., p. 197.
57. Ibid., p. 199.
58. Ibid., pp. 245–51.
59. Ibid., pp. 273–5.
60. Ibid., p. 275.
61. Ibid., p. 277.
62. Ibid., p. 279.
63. Ibid., p. 281.
64. Ibid., p. 287.
65. Ibid., p. 289.

66. T N Madan, *Family and Kinship: A Study of the Pandits of Rural Kashmir* (Bombay: Asia Publications, 1969).

67. See e.g. Ward H Goodenough, *Property, Kin and Community On Tonk* (Connecticut: Archon Press, 1966).

68. T N Madan, 'The Ideology of the Householder among the Kashmir Pandits' in *Contributions to Indian Sociology*, vol. 15, no. 1 and 2, 1981.

69. Julian Pitt Rivers, 'The Kith and Kin' in Jack Goody (ed.) *The Character of Kinship*, (Cambridge: Cambridge University Press, 1973).

70. Ananta Krishna Ayyar, op. cit.

5

The Eucharist
and the Person of Christ

The life-cycle rituals of the individual Christian and the annual rituals centring around the life of Christ are marked by the presence of the Eucharist as the central liturgy.[1] This service is the core of Christian worship. The service of the Eucharist or the *Qurbana* is viewed here as if it were a model of the life of Christ. In that context, it replicates a historical event which took place almost two thousand years ago.

THE EUCHARISTIC LITURGY AND RITE

The Eucharistic liturgy of the Syrian Christians of Puthenangadi derives from the Liturgy of St James, which is apostolic in origin. This liturgy incorporates within it the body of religious knowledge that every practising Christian must possess, implicitly carrying the doctrines of Christianity regarding the notions of the Trinity, the Incarnation, Redemption, the place of Mary and the saints. The main elements of Eucharistic worship are

I   The opening or prefatory prayers including censing and the Trisagion
II   The deacon's prayer preceding the apostolic reading
III   The reading of the Epistle by the deacon
IV   The gospel as read by the priest
V   The censing
VI   The creed
VII   The Kiss of Peace
VIII   The Invocation of the Holy Spirit

My description begins by viewing the space of the church as the stage on which the Eucharistic rite is enacted. As the believers enter the church, they leave their footwear outside: 'In reverence will I enter Thy house and offer my prayers'.[2] Prefatory prayers and the Trisagion ('that God is thrice holy') follow. The Lord's Prayer is recited as also a prayer to the Virgin Mary. The chancel is then unveiled, and heaven revealed to the people. The *namaskaram* or prefatory prayers serve to prepare the laity for the moment of revelation. At this time, they are between *bhumilokam* (earth) and *akasam* (sky).

The priest enters the chancel to offer the *Qurbana*. He asks for leave to perform the sacrifice in Syriac–Aramaic: *Barekmore All Shub'kono* (Bless my Lord, for leave). Without divine grace, the sacrifice or *Qurbana* has no effect. The priest is, with the laity, human, and while in office, he is their leader. The chancel is again veiled, so that the priest may prepare himself for the Eucharist. The deacons enter, and after asking for blessings while assisting in the sacrifice, one of them lights the candles. The priest places the objects to be used in the *Qurbana* on the altar. The paten (a shallow dish) cover, the sponge and the spoon are placed on the celebrant's right. He places the chalice cover, the *sosafa* (a veil) and the cup for ritual ablutions on the left-hand side of the altar. The priest places the Host (the bread that is blessed and eaten at holy communion) in the paten, and looking upwards he prays that the sacrifice be accepted:

O Thou First Begotten of the Heavenly Father, accept this first born from the hands of Thy weak and sinful servant.[3]

Here, the complexity of the Trinity, the nature of the Eucharist as sacrifice which replicates the original sacrifice, is clearly expressed. The priest offers to Christ the sacrifice which is at once a replication of the first sacrifice, and a new sacrifice. He mixes water with wine in the cup saying, 'O Lord God, as Thy divinity was united with Thy humanity, so unite this water with this wine'.[4]

Pouring the wine and water into the chalice, he recollects that at the crucifixion of Christ, water and blood flowed from the side which was pierced by the spear, and these washed away the sins of the universe. A complex set of correspondences is made available here: water is equated to wine (in Cana) which is paralleled by wine which is synonymous to blood (the Last Supper). The celebrant covers the paten and the chalice. He then recites the Service of Penitence. This has one main theme: the priest offering the sacrifice is both mortal and a sinner.[5]

The vesting of the priest in the sacred garments of his office takes place with special prayers. He removes his outer garments and puts on the *hamnikho* (stole), the *zunoro* (girdle), the two *zende* (sleeves), the *masnafto* (head cover) if he is a prelate, the *phayno* or cope, as well as the cross for the neck, the handcross, and the crozier or crook (if a prelate). Each of these symbolizes the power of the sacred over the profane life. The priest washes his hands, kneels down before the altar and prays inaudibly. He beseeches God for strength and purity, underlining that he is a servant of God, both mortal and sinful.

The priest once more kisses the altar and ascends the altar steps. Taking the covers off the paten and chalice, he takes the paten in his right hand and the chalice in his left. He stretches out his hands, crossed, right over left, and lifts them up above the *Tablitho* (altar stone). In the general prayers that follow the priest 'commemorates at this time, upon this Eucharist that is set before us' the entire life of Christ:

> His glorious conception and His birth in the flesh, His baptism in Jordan and His fast of forty days. His saving passion and His crucifixion, His life-giving death and His venerable burial, His glorious resurrection and His ascension into heaven, His sitting on the right hand of God the Father.[6]

At this point, the persons for whom the Qurbana is offered may be prayed for, and the intercession of Mary the Mother is requested.

The priest lowers the paten and chalice, placing the former to the east and latter to the west of the altar stone. The censer prayers follow where the priest, ascending the steps, raises the censer and swings it over the Mysteries (the bread and wine), east, west, north and south, and then in a circular motion, twice from the right and once from the left, intoning prayers for the acceptance of the sacrifice.

After the Trisagion, where the priest says three times 'Holy art Thou, O God, O Almighty, O Immortal', the Lord's Prayer and the Nicene Creed are recited.

The public celebration now begins. The sanctuary curtain is draw aside, the priest burns incense and censing the altar, says loudly:

> Mary who brought Thee forth and John who baptized Thee shall be suppliants unto Thee on our behalf. Have mercy unto us.[7]

The people respond with exaltations, and with devotions to Mary, and the Trisagion is once more chanted.

The readings from the Epistles which follow are usually undertaken by the deacons. The reading of the Evangelion or New Testament is performed by the priest and is done in a very celebratory way. Two servers stand on either side of the priest with lighted candles symbolizing the light brought to the world by Jesus. The priest says:

> With calm and awe and modesty, let us give heed and listen to the good tidings...[8]

The people respond with the prayer that they be made worthy. This reading aloud of the Bible must have been of extreme significance at a time when the Bible, being unprinted, had not been available to all, and thus it is most elaborately framed with rituals, particularly in the way the Book is ceremonially placed on the artistically engraved lectern in the centre of the sanctuary. The priest now vests himself with a beautiful surplice.

The Blessing of the Chains of the censer takes place. It is an important rite because it symbolizes that while the Trinity is one, it is simultaneously three. This is particularly significant in terms of the role that the priest plays in the Eucharist, because at different moments, he expresses the different manifestations of the Trinity, and functions in the context of these differences. He holds each of the three chains of the censer separately, with prayers to God the Father, the Son and the Holy Spirit, then he holds them together symbolizing their unity.

After the prayers of the censer, the priest censes the sanctuary and the congregation. The creed is recited by the people, and the deacon cries *Stomen kalos* (stand well) for inattention is sacrilegious. The people respond with *Kyrie eleison* (Lord have mercy).

The priest washes the tips of his fingers praying that the filth of his soul may be washed away and 'that with pure conscience I may offer unto Thee the living sacrifice that is well pleasing to Thy Godhead and is like to Thy Glorious Sacrifice, Our Lord and Our God for ever'.[9]

Here I would like to argue that there has been a subtle shift in the identity of the priest. He has moved from the sinful mortal being who asks for leave to perform the sacrifice to one who may offer the *living sacrifice* which is similar to 'Thy Glorious Sacrifice'. He is now the sacrificer and, therefore, in function similar to God the Father. I argue here that the priest substitutes at this point in the Eucharist liturgy for God the Father, not homologously but analogously; and that in taking the place of God, he accepts not deification of any kind but the sacred function of offering the sacrifice. Where God sacrificed Jesus, His only begotten Son, the priest sacrifices the Mysteries, which are not bread and wine merely, but body and blood as 'living'. By its very nature, the offering is both sacrifice and oblation.

The Kiss of Peace follows. This is an ancient custom based on the words of St Paul: 'Greet one another with a holy kiss'.[10] The priest gives the *kaimuth* to the highest deacon, who passes it on to the other deacons, who in turn pass it on to the people. On giving the hand of peace, each one says to the other, 'The Peace of our Lord and God'.

The priest then lifts up the great *sosafa* and waves it three times over the Mysteries. Having removed the veil that covers the Mysteries, he prepares the people for what is at the heart of the celebration, the partaking of the bread and wine.

After calling upon the heavens, the sun, the moon and all the stars, the earth, the seas and the first-born, the angels and the seraphim to proclaim His holiness, the priest takes the Host from the paten with his right hand. He puts it on the palm of his left hand and, raising his eyes skywards, commemorates in a loud voice that moment when Christ blessed, broke and gave bread to His disciples saying, 'Take, eat of it, This is My body, which is broken for you and for many, and is given for the remission of sins and for life eternal'.[11] Then the priest takes the chalice with both hands and similarly commemorates the moment when Christ said, 'Take, drink of it, all of you. This is My Blood which is shed for you'.[12]

Following this act of commemoration, the priest invokes the Holy Spirit upon the Mysteries by waving his hands like the wings of the dove that descended at the moment when Christ was baptized. Here, the function of the priest is similar to that of the Holy Ghost; the fluttering of his hands symbolizes the dove which descended on Jesus and was the bodily form of the Holy Spirit.[13] The deacon says:

How full of awe is this hour, and how perturbed this time, my beloved ones, wherein the Holy Spirit from the topmost heights of heaven takes wings and descends and broods and rests upon this Eucharist here present and hallows it. In calm and in awe were you, standing and praying. Pray that peace may be with us and all of us may have tranquillity.[14]

The priest cries loudly,

Hear me, O Lord, hear me, O Lord.
Hear me, O Lord, and have mercy upon us.[15]

The priest is again clearly only the sacrificer, a mortal. Without divine intervention, the *Qurbana* cannot have meaning. He stretches out his left hand and waves his right hand over the Body and says,

May He (the Holy Spirit) abiding here make this Bread the life-giving Body, the Redeeming Body and the True Body of our God and Saviour Jesus Christ.

He repeats this formulaic prayer substituting blood for body, as he waves his right hand over the chalice.

After the consecration of the bread and wine which occurs secretly behind the veil come the diptychs. Here, kings, rulers, statesmen, prelates, saints, doctors of the Church and the dead are remembered. Through the diptychs the Church as an institution is related to the social and political world around it. After the priest blesses the people, the veil is drawn over the sanctuary and the Mystery is hidden.

Behind the veil, the priest silently recites the Prayer of Fracture and Commixture:

Thus truly did the word of God suffer in the flesh and was sacrificed and broken on the cross, and His Soul was departed from His body while His Godhead was in no way departed from either His soul or from His body. By His blood He reconciled and united the Heavenly hosts with the earthly beings, and the people with the Gentiles, and the soul with the body. The third day He rose again from the Sepulchre and He is one Immanuel, and is undivisible into two natures after the unity indivisible. Thus we believe and thus we confess and thus we confirm that this flesh is of the Blood and this Blood is of this flesh.[16]

As Christ broke bread[17] saying that it was His body, so also the priest breaks bread symbolizing His suffering and crucifixion. Here he substitutes for Christ, replaying as actor the role of the central character. Christ is represented through the priest but is objectified in the bread and wine. The first is a relation of analogy and substitution, the second of homology.

In the rite of the Orthodox and Jacobite Syrians, the bread and wine are given together, not separately, symbolizing the unity of the body and blood which is the living Christ.

In the next prayer, the priest offers this living sacrifice to God, as sacrificer, mediator between the people and God:

O Father of Truth, behold Thy Son, the well-pleasing sacrifice. Accept Thou Him who died for me that I may be forgiven through Him. Receive this offering at my hands and reconcile me unto Thee. And remember not the sin I committed before Thy Excellence.

Behold His Blood, shed on Golgotha by the wicked, pleads for me, for its sake receive my petition. As great are mine offences, so great are Thy mercies. Look upon the sins and look upon the offering for them, for the offering and the sacrifice are far greater than the sins.[18]

In these two prayers, the priest clearly defines his own sinfulness. Yet again, by the power of his office and calling, the function of these, he has been made worthy of offering the supreme sacrifice to God himself. While the Trinity is indivisible, yet it is manifest as three. I interpret this sacrifice as the return, for it can only be understood within the framework of the gift and its inherent spirit.[19] Not everyone can take upon himself this function of returning to God what God has given man. They may participate in it, but cannot mediate the return.

The return which is the sacrifice or *Qurbana* is the institutionalization of memory. Only through this return can the gift of God (the sacrifice of His begotten Son) have meaning. The priest substitutes for God in his separate manifestations, yet he is never God. He makes the same sacrifice that God made, yet it is only because it was first made by God that the priest can in turn offer it. Because the Trinity is indivisible, God's sacrifice is also Christ's sacrifice; the priest who is neither God nor Christ is yet made worthy by his office to invoke the Holy Spirit and offer the sacrifice of the Living Christ. The priest says of the bread and wine,

Thou art Christ the God who was pierced in His side on the heights of Golgotha in Jerusalem for us.

Thou art the lamb of God that taketh away the sin of the world. Do then pardon our offences and forgive our sins.[20]

Here he washes his fingertips and dries them. Then follows the litany of supplication. There are prayers by the people for compassion, tranquillity and to be made worthy of partaking of the Mysteries.[21]

The curtain or veil is drawn back. Prayers for preparation to receive the Mysteries follow. Incense is offered, and the elevation of the chalice and paten take place. The priest uplifts the paten ceremonially with both hands so all may view it. Then he puts it down slowly on the *tablitho* or altar stone. He repeats the same action with the chalice. There are prayers for Mary and the saints; for the dead who are always remembered in the Eucharist. The veil is again drawn over the sanctuary. The priest kneels before the altar and prays silently for forgiveness of sins after which communion takes place.

He ascends the altar steps taking the *Gemourto* (the particles of the Host) with the spoon. Receiving it, he says,

Thee I hold Who upholds the borders of the World; Thee I grasp, Who orders the depths; Thee, O God, do I place in my mouth; By Thee may I be delivered from the fire unquenchable.[22]

He takes the *Gemourto* with the spoon from the paten, and puts it in the chalice. Thus the bread and wine are one. He fills the spoon from the chalice and drinks it, saying:

By Thy living and life-giving Blood which was poured on the cross, may my offences by pardoned and my sins remitted, O Jesus, Word of God, Who came for our salvation and will come for our Resurrection and of our race for ever and ever.[23]

The priests and deacons in the sanctuary receive communication with prayers. The veil is drawn back once more. The prayers of the people are now joyous and triumphant rather than supplicatory.

In the ritual of communication the priest says to each one receiving bread and wine,

The atoning *Gemourto* of the Body and Blood of Christ, our God, is given to this faithful believer for the remission of debts and for the forgiveness of sins in both worlds.[24]

The communicant responds with 'Amen'. Following this are the Prayers of Thanksgiving and then the *Huthoma* or the prayers of the exit. The priest blesses the faithful. The priest also asks the people to pray for him:

> And may I, thy weak and sinful servant, be favoured and helped by your prayers. Glad and rejoicing, go now in peace and pray for me always.

The people say in turn,

> Amen. May the Lord accept your offering and help us by your prayers.[25]

The sanctuary is veiled, and the people leave the church. The priest must ceremonially consume whatever remains of the bread and wine. The sacred, awesome properties of the Mysteries are delineated here, which must not be reused or contaminated:

> If there be a remaining particle, it remaineth to Thy knowledge, which created the Worlds, and if there be a member remaining, the Lord be its keeper and to me absolver and forgiver.[26]

After several prayers accompanying the consumption of the contents of the paten and chalice, the priest washes the sacred utensils and wipes them. With prayers, he washes his hands, wears his ordinary garments and takes farewell of the altar, kissing the middle, the right and the left sides.

The priest says:

> Farewell, O holy and divine altar of the Lord. Henceforth, I know not, whether I shall return to Thee or not. May the Lord make me worthy to see Thee in the church of the First-born, Which is in heaven, and in this covenant do I trust.[27]

With other similar prayers and hymns from the deacons signifying closure, the priest exits.

THE STRUCTURE OF THE EUCHARIST

The Eucharist must be seen as a construction positing a relation between three elements: myth, ritual and liturgy.

The mythic dimension is that of the oral tradition. The origin of the liturgy according to informants is based on the crystallization of memory by those who shared the life of Christ (*Yesu Christue Kanda-varde Orma*). Informants speak of the first commemorative service that took place in which Mary, the Mother of Christ, also participated. Here, the apostles, disciples, and the Mother of Christ congregated 'in a small room' to carry out the wishes of Christ who had departed from their midst, but was yet ever present.

Such ideas are part of the structure of folk imagination, brico-leurian, hazy but in existence. However, the historical dimension of the formulation of the liturgy is not known to common people who treat the text synchronically and do not imagine that it is a piece which can be segmented according to the history of its development. In the same way, scriptural tradition represents a closure and is unquestioned veracity. It is the codification of memory, as opposed to the un-structured, open, mythic quality of apocrypha. Before I examine some elements of the liturgy in its aspect of text, I shall offer some com-ments on the category of myth as it exists in the form of the 'pale shadows' of belief which accompany the individual in all that he does.[28]

The Eucharistic service has meaning because it is related to the already existent idea that the Christian has about Jesus Christ. These derive both from scriptural and apocryphal traditions. It is because the Christian knows the history of the life of Christ that he can interpret for himself the liturgy and rituals which condense this life. Thus he relives Christ's birth with the opening phrases of the public celebra-tion 'May Mary who bore You...'. Later on in the invocation, the priest flutters his hands like the wings of the dove, and the people remember the Baptism and the Divine Acknowledgement of Sonhood. The central motifs of the Last Supper, crucifixion and resurrection are re-enacted through the language of the rite (consecration, elevation and communion).

Within such a framework, the myths underlying the practice of the Eucharist concern themselves with the person of Christ.

These myths and legends pass down orally from generation to generation or are crystallized in the literate tradition through the offices of the colporteur. Church festivals, particularly, are occasions when tracts describing the life of the saints are sold to pilgrims. This again is reinterpreted by the people in their own idiom. History and myth often tend to coalesce in the conception of the present. There is complete lack of clarity in such accounts regarding geographical and historical detail. One woman insisted that Antioch was the land from which Jesus and Mary came, and thus it was the duty of Christians to revere the Patriarch, who came from Antioch too. Antioch and Nazareth can converge geographically because they are places of mythic rather than geographical importance.

The lay Christian views and interprets the person of Christ very differently from the theologian and in terms of a paradigm born of lay experience. The latter results in a web of perception internalized over a long period of time, particularly through the many rituals (both individual and collective) that occur in a society where Christianity is still practised in a ritually effervescent manner.

People express ideas about the person of Christ primarily through conceptions about his mortality. Though theologically the unity of moral and divine are underlined,[29] lay perception has its own ways of rendering comprehensible what may otherwise remain mysterious and inaccessible. Here, presumably, the corporeal explains what is other-wise too abstract to be understood. Questions of theology dealing with the indivisibility of the Trinity are not available in lay discussions. In fact, people resent being asked who Christ is or what constitutes the nature of his body. The answer invariably is that the ethnographer ought to ask such questions of theologians (*seminary le anchenmar*) and not devotees or even parish priests. However indirectly posed, the question reappears in term of people's narratives, where the life of Christ is often located in terms of the life of mortals like his Mother, Joseph and the Apostles.

Besides liturgy and scripture, the people, in their attempt to under-stand the divinity and humanity of Christ, turn to the stories about Mary. She is the figure who is closest to Christ as only a mother can be to her son. If to some extent Mary can be visualized, then by that very exercise one is closer to an understanding of the nature of Christ. By referring for instance to the sorrow of Mary, the stories speak simul-taneously of the mortal nature of Christ. Her deepest pain is known through the words of a song where she cries,

For how long I have brought you up;
If I had known the desire of Judas for silver
I would have given it myself.

By this rendering, Christ's crucifixion could have been avoided if his
mother had satisfied Judas's greed. It is in this sense that the life of
Mary re-echoes aspects of the life of Christ; visualized through her
person, it is more clearly grasped.

Narratives are infused with empathy and describe how Mary gave
birth in a stable, with no woman to attend on her, in such poverty that
she had only rags to wrap the child in. Of course, the absence of
'women to assist her' appears in the context of how women perceive
birth even if this be divine birth. In fact, another narrative about the
birth of Christ includes the presence of a midwife, but one who was so
sceptical that she did not believe in virgin birth and, using her arm for
purposes of gynaecological verification, came away a leper. According
to another old female informant, the Christ child emerged from the
thigh (thus unpolluted), and having given birth in purity, the thigh of
the virgin was healed and no scar remained.

Similarly, Mary's emotions as she perceived her son dying are
actually songs about Christ's Passion.

As he hung on the cross
The mother looked at her son;
Like a spear in her heart,
Her sorrow was felt
With tears in her eyes
She watched the death of her son
She asked him
Have you redeemed man of
the sin of his birth,
Of the sin of Adam, Eve and the Devil?
Born from my womb you have paid the debt.

Adam ate the Fruit of knowledge
And it is for that you must suffer now
And I must see you die.
If I had died first
I would not have to see this
You had told me earlier and
asked my leave

But now you are
Bathed in your own blood.
While you were near death,
You looked down on us on earth.
The earth was soaked with your blood
And the earth was freed.

This song, sung to me by a ninety-five-year-old woman, with tears in her eyes and a voice quavering with deep emotion, portrays how Christ's death is experienced by his mother as a physical rupture.

Both the canonical and the apocryphal sources of myth pertaining to the life of Christ contribute to the details about Christ as a person living in a particular culture and time. He is Jewish, born to Mary and sheltered by Joseph. He grew up in a carpenter's household, had brothers whose blood he did not fully share since they were, according to informants' accounts, sons of Joseph from an earlier marriage.

Even Christ's sojourn at the Temple of Jerusalem is perceived through the pain of Mary. Here, according to informants, is the moment when Mary realized that her son would be claimed by His Father. There is pain and pride, and a deep sense of loss because Jesus will not live by the decrees of ordinary life. Virgin birth, however, is the primary event that symbolizes Christ's difference from other mortals.

Lay informants accept virgin birth as an essential element of Christian dogma. Some Christians, referring to apocryphal literature, describe the conception of Mary herself as *shudh* (pure, untainted by the lust implicit in the sexual act). So also the conception of Christ is mystical, whereby the word of God takes flesh. The relationship between Christ and God, Son and the Father is a philological relation. It is the Logos that becomes flesh. Christ is the male principle, the 'son' of God. In body, logically, Christ is entirely of the substance of Mary. We have a principle here where the flesh belongs to the mother and the spirit belongs to the Father. Leach argues that virgin birth is a myth compatible with social systems that are essentially patriarchal. More importantly, he argues that myths and rites do not distinguish knowledge from ignorance but establish categories and affirm relationships.[30]

In my analysis, the problem of sexuality, both in terms of the alleged mystical conception of Mary and the conception of Christ, is conveyed here as a continuing problem of the sin of Adam and Eve, which is transcended by the birth of Christ. Christ stands in a relationship of correspondence to Adam. As Adam was created without sexual union, so was Christ; as Adam was banished from paradise and with him Man, in reversal with the death of Christ, Man is allowed to re-enter paradise. If disobedience, sexuality and the loss of innocence was the condemnation of man and the rejection from paradise, then celibacy, abstinence, suffering and death become the mode by which re-entry into paradise becomes possible, but through the symbol of Christ. Christ is homologous to Adam but in reverse. Carnal knowledge, childbirth and suffering accompany Adam and Eve in their expulsion from paradise. The spiritual union exemplified by the marriage of Christ to the Church facilitates man's re-entry into paradise. This problem of sexuality continues as a central theological motif centring around the person of Christ both with reference to the ideas conveyed about blood relations and their subjugation to the spiritual kinship arising from the relation to the Father,[31] and the symbolic centrality of the celibate Christ.[32] The celibacy of Christ in fact becomes a symbol of the destruction of culture and temporality, the images of which conclude in the Apocalypse. In the hereafter, nature and culture are destroyed, and affinity is subsumed by the siblinghood arising out of the love of the Father for all redeemed mankind; all are brothers and sisters in Christ.

Although Christ rejects the primacy of biological ties for spiritual ones,[33] the figure of Mary continues to remain central in a lay interpretation of Christ. Christ's rejection of Mary is explicit in the narrative about the marriage at Cana and the changing of water into wine. Mary says to Jesus, 'They have no wine'. Jesus answers, 'Woman, what have I to do with thee? Mine hour is not yet come'.[34]

This seeming rejection is seen by these Christians as characteristic of the way in which sons may treat women in a patrilineal society. Here, verbal rejection of the mother is not to be read as a denial of the love a man has for his mother. Verbal contempt does not reflect the true nature of affectual ties. As one informant said, whatever He may have said, the mother at once bade the servants to do Jesus's will, knowing that a miracle would occur. In the same context, love for His mother which at the end made Jesus put her in the care of His beloved disciple,[35] is treated as an index of the personality of Christ. Similarly His anger at the Temple, His love for children, His compassion and knowledge are spoken of by the lay as if they are virtues of one known closely. The story of Christ is narrated too in terms of the details of His daily life; He is the son of Joseph in that He derives from the saintly protector (who is pater, not genitor) His lineage and occupation. He is a carpenter—Jesus of Nazareth, of the line of David; His brothers are the sons of Joseph from an earlier marriage. Mary in these accounts is immaculate and continues to be so because Joseph is both a widower and an elder whose role is to protect the mother and the child, born out of mystical union with the Logos. Jesus is then understood within the frame of two overlapping forms of experience— the empirical and the mystical.

The myths provide the narrative framework within which the Eucharistic rites may be understood, a reservoir for the purposes of the interpretation of any particular rite. Ritual becomes the mode of enactment of important aspects of the Christ's life, a theatre wherein the life is replayed. Both myth and ritual together appropriate time in several non-homogeneous ways. Time is not merely comprehended here as if it were historical, linear and irreversible. Christianity takes into account an idea of time which is divided into mathematically notated division which are irreducible qualitatively, but yet, para-doxically juxtaposes mythic time at two ends of the continuum— Creation and Apocalypse.

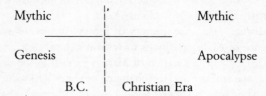

In this sense, time is linear and event-based, counted both in terms of the passage of years and the actions of men. It expresses at once the mortality of man and the immortality of the soul. Good and evil are in existence in the very nature of man, and reward or punishment come at the end of time when man confronts eternity.

It is this notion of mythic time which gives quantitative time its meaning; which, in fact, introduces into the notion of the passage of quantitative time the vitality of ritual life. The sacred calendar in this sense becomes superimposed upon the secular annual schedule of time.

The cyclic closed dimension of myth and ritual which captures the life of Christ through annual commemorations is also recapitulated in every Eucharist. The dissemination of Christ's life occurs through the Eucharist. It signifies that Resurrection is not closure but that Christ returns to the Earth (mysteriously) embodied in the bread and wine. Without this mysterious return, the life of Christ in history can have no religious meaning. This is particularly so in a community where Christianity as it is practised is Eucharist-centred. The time of the Eucharist is thus simultaneously mythic, linear and epochal. This multi-dimensionality of the nature of time occurs because myth, history, legend, and personal and traditional memories are caught within the same sacred framework. In both myth and ritual, in practice, there is very clearly a bricoleurian element, for variations in form at any one particular moment depend upon the elements chosen by the performer. In myth there is a greater emphasis on the need of the moment, and selection depends upon the audience who receives it. In ritual, there is a greater degree of codedness, but it must be affirmed that some priests say it 'better' than others, some chant in a higher pitch than others, some abbreviate, others do not. There is then an element of choice involved though in principle the element is negated. What I wish to emphasize here is the performative aspect of ritual.

While myth and ritual are interrelated, they are yet mediated by the closed world of the liturgy which exists not only as the point of mediation but also of transformation. Here, in the text, the pure rule of synchrony dominates. It lies midway between the amorphousness of myth and the codedness of the rite. The liturgy, as text, excludes in its fixity of inscription the diachronic dimension. (This is true in spite of the fact that the text may be academically dismembered in terms of its historical evolution). The text is a structured realm unlike the bricoleurian aspect that myth and ritual express. This closed structure of the liturgy best expresses itself in the synchronization of actors, by the learning of rules in the seminary. Standardization becomes here the primary principle.

Time, movement and harmony are set along a scale which is rigidly followed. The interpretation of the liturgy becomes an unequivocal one, and charges of heresy are clearly made if there are modifications and changes. We know from the instances of the nineteenth century that the first signals of discord came from parishes divided over the reformed liturgy.[36] Changes in the liturgy are thus difficult to bring about, take place over long periods of time, may result in schisms, and are made possible only through theological forms of discussion.

Just as the mythic dimension is codified and encapsulated in liturgy and enacted through ritual, changes brought about in the sphere of ritual (conversions, reform movements, ecumenicism) in turn affect the liturgy, leading to a change in the mythic consciousness. Thus the reform movements of the nineteenth century express this radical shift in the structure of the model. Changes in any one element are expressed in the transformation of the structure as a whole.[37] How this happens can be seen in a single mytheme; here, the place of Mary is considered. (*See p. 169.*)

The Eucharist is the central motif of the Christian ritual life. It represents the unity of event, the condensation of all the separate events that constitute the biographical rituals of the Christian calendar—the birth, baptism, works, death and resurrection of the Christ. In that sense, the Eucharist is the model of the life of Christ. The Eucharist, which consists of the communication of the Mystery, culturally transforms itself into the symbols of eating and communion that occur in the family and the neighbourhood. Thus the Eucharist, or the experiencing of the bread and wine as body and blood, is a feast. The food of the Eucharist represents the body and blood of Christ. What bread and wine are to the physical body, Christ is to the spirit.

CHURCH, NEIGHBOURHOOD AND HOUSEHOLD

There are three sets of signs which explicate the concept of the feast of the Eucharist. The Christian neighbourhood, the house and the Church are to be seen as representing the table of life. Just as the Church provides a frame for the Eucharistic celebration, so also the neighbourhood during feast days can become after the *Qurbana* a centre of communal eating, with the house becoming a third locus.

This 'sacred food', clearly differentiated from everyday food, expresses itself in various ways, primarily in terms of the nature and logic of the gift. During church festivals, the people take pancakes (*appam*) to the priest for blessing after which they are distributed. Such communal feasts commemorate the death anniversaries of saints and holy men. During the rituals of celebration (as in the Festivals of Mary), they may be elaborate, consisting not only of cereals and vegetables, but also of *palharam* or festive foods. Similarly, the household enjoys a celebratory meal on Sundays and feast days after the Eucharist. Each of these is only a more elaborate level at the syntagmatic plane of the presentation of food. Food as spiritual sustenance, as sacrament, has the fewest possible elements; at the level of communal feasting, the

Changes in the Liturgy: the place of Mary

Liturgy deletes prayers to Mary, suppresses her function as intercessor and turns references to her from Active to Passive

Conservative Theology believing in the Immaculate (Liturgy of St James introduced after 1664)

Ritual Reformation of the 1830s influenced by the CMS Missionaries; Changes in liturgy follow

Suppression of Mariology and its Myths in the Reformed Church

Affects the place of Mary in the liturgy and in ritual

Example
'May Mary who bore you, and John who baptized you, be intercessors in our behalf; have mercy upon us' is changed to 'Jesus the Messiah: Who took birth from Mary and was baptized by John, have mercy upon us'.

elements are numerically fixed by the local church; at the level of the household, the greater the elaborateness of the meal, the greater the financial ability that is expressed.

The symbol of the table expresses, then, a morphological structure. The *tablitho* is the altar, it is also the cradle, the table and the tomb of Christ. Similarly, the neighbourhood feasts present a metaphorical table were there is the communal preparation of food and communal eating. The household is also a table for the serving of celebratory food, with a fixed ritual place given to the head of the household, who like the priest (*Achen*, Father) blesses the food, which is eaten to celebrate a particular event.

Each of these separate morphological situations expresses a particular system of relations. The priest as head of the table is in a particular hierarchical relation with the servers and the lay. Similarly, the communal meal is an extension of the Eucharist, where the servers are like the deacons, assistants to the priest and the trustees of the church. The food served here is sacred to the extent that it may not be arbitrarily disposed of, must be eaten then and there, or taken carefully home to be shared with those who did not come.

The two occasions when food as a meal is most definitively served at the neighbourhood table are the occasions of Passover (*Pesaga*) and Good Friday. During Passover, besides the Eucharist in which all must compulsorily participate, there occurs the distribution of *aviyal*. It is an elaborate preparation of vegetables which essentially symbolizes the condensation of the fully celebratory meal, and the Christian is invited to feast with the Christ.

On Good Friday the Christian partakes of the food of mourning, commemorating the Crucifixion of Christ. This echoes the vegetarian meal associated with the death of a beloved person. On Good Friday, the Eucharist is not celebrated, and the food served both at the communally organized meal and at the house, symbolize death and bereavement. Rice, green pulses, *pappadam* (wafers) and pickles express the sorrow of the mourners who abstain from the use of preferred culinary items such as flesh, fish, yoghurt, coconuts and oil. When the Eucharist is celebrated, the family meal that follows is correspondingly celebratory. The father or head of the household blesses a meal that is elaborately and ceremonially non-vegetarian. A Sunday lunch is an *oon* (a feast) as opposed to *aaharam* (food as subsistence). It follows a period of fasting and the joyful celebration of the *Qurbana*.

The main event of ritual and communal feasting are in fact associated with *Kanji Nercha* (rice/gruel offering) which commemorates the establishment of Kurisu Palli in a new architectural design in the nineteenth century. On this occasion, the entire community of Orthodox Syrians contributes to the elaborate feast, bringing not only the raw materials required for cooking, but their knives and labour power as well. The communal effort involved underlines the joy that the residents feel in having Kurisu Palli in their midst. To that extent it may be interpreted as a sacred meal, uniting an association of believers.

It is not merely on feast days and at the anniversary of the establishment of the church but also during saints' days that the Syrian Christians are integrated through the sharing of food while commemorating the death anniversaries of holy men. For Mary, St Thomas and other important saints, *pal appam* (pan cakes) is given to all who come to church. This is a transformation of the Eucharistic bread, and only the saints receive these white pancakes as gifts for redistribution through the office of the priest. The holy men who are not officially canonized receive cakes of a different shape which consist of jaggery and coconut and are similar to the cakes offered in the commemorative services of deceased parents.

Thus food and its sharing have always provided an important framework for mediating the rituals of integration. The Eucharist enjoins all those who participate in it in mystical union with Christ. The community meal, whether abbreviated in the form of pancakes for distribution, condensed in the *aviyal* or syntagmatically elaborate in the *Kanji Nercha*, define the nature of ritual relations that are in existence in the neighbourhood. When some of the Patriarch's party followers refuse to participate in the *Kanji Nercha* though they may be trustees of the church, they are making a statement about the affairs of the church, the nature of schism, and the consequent rupture in the association of believers. The sharing of food becomes an important index of the solidarity of the community. When the Christian does not wish to participate in the *Qurbana* by partaking of bread and wine (often he does not), he is in effect saying, 'I am not worthy to eat at the Lord's Table'. When the Patriarch's follower refuses to participate in liturgical events organized by the Catholicos, he also refuses to share in the communal extensions of the Eucharist.

Given that the Eucharist is the primary feast, when it is withheld (as during Lent) domestic and neighbourhood feasts also foreclose. On the other hand, on the day that Eucharist is celebrated after a long gap such as after the fifty days of Lent before Easter, the meal that follows at the domestic table is a gargantuan one, symbolically expressing the closure of mourning and, through the consummation of the sacred, a return to a sacralized and more meaningful profane life.

Food is thus a central symbol of celebration and of closure as well as of liminality. The absence of certain elements and the abbreviation of the food code expresses mourning, ceremonial anticipation or liminality. The converse symbolizes joyousness. Where the Eucharist is celebrated, the breaking of the fast is imperative and this culminates in the elaborate meal or feast typified by the Sunday lunch. Where the Eucharist is remembered as instituted either through the Passover (*Pesaga*) or the establishment of the church, the event must be commemorated through the sharing of a meal. Where the Eucharist is withheld, as at the commemoration of Christ's crucifixion, the Christians are mourners around the newly interred body of the Christ.

Food symbolizes the nature of ritual relations which exist between the church, neighbourhood and family. It separates the private from the public, the house from the neighbourhood, the ecclesiastical from the familial, the partaker from the observer, the server from the receiver, yet it interrelates the three levels of neighbourhood, church and family in a system of continuities based on food and its distribution.

As is well known, Jewish sectarianism expressed itself through food. Thus in Christ's teaching and life, food became of central significance and it was through several 'culinary disasters' such as eating with sinners, with unwashed hands and so on, that a new interpretation of life and divinity could be established.[38] In this context it is both interesting and logical that Christ himself is analogized as food, implicit perhaps in the moment of his conception as flesh.

THE EUCHARIST: GIFT AND SACRIFICE

The Eucharist is perceived to be a thanksgiving, an offering, while at the same time it is *Vishudha Qurbana* or the Holy Sacrifice. It recaptures the life of Christ Who is understood through scripture to be given by God to Man in order to redeem him, and towards this end, underwent the sacrifice of His mortal life through crucifixion. Pain and suffering are for the Christian implicit in this life of Christ virtually enacted. Gift and sacrifice are inextricably interwoven: for, as the birth of Christ was a gift, His sacrifice was also a gift. As Marcel Mauss would argue, this gift of God given to man has its own inherent spirit which makes the return obligatory. The commemorative service, the concrete form of which are the myths, rite and liturgy, is the gift returned. Without this, the God would die.[39] That the Hebrew *Korban* corresponds somewhat to the English term 'sacrifice' while also meaning offering, shows this union between the two terms. The offering of bread and wine as the living sacrifice by the sacrifiers (believers) and the sacrificer (God or the priest) is thus both return as well as a replica of the original sacrifice.

Through the Eucharist memory is institutionalized, and from generation to generation the vicarious experience of the life of Christ is passed down. Through the experience of the Eucharist (participation by accepting the bread and wine), the soul is transformed and there is every effort logically to believe in the redemption of man through this second level (or ritual) participation.

Both Christ and the Christian are in a reciprocal relationship as giver and receiver. Christ receives the Christian, the Christian receives Christ. The gift received, however, is implicitly dangerous because it comes morally, physically and spiritually from a person; in this case more so because it comes from the sacred person of Christ. Here, then, is the importance given to the 'pure state' that is required of the participant whether he is priest, server or lay, and to the prayers asking for compassion and mercy, for the receiver is a sinner. The act of repentance through confession is one where the Christian enters into a state of optimism. It is this optimism as opposed to a state of despair that signifies the true Christian. By committing oneself entirely into the hands of Christ through the Church, the Christian receives both peace and salvation.

In the same way, alms, both for the poor and in the form of gifts to the church and the priest, are typical of this relation of reciprocity. Material goods are in fact exchanged for blessings. The reciprocal nature of the gift relation in its legitimate and sacramental manifestations (tithes, alms, payments for blessing children and the Eucharist fee) is the bond of culture and the base of the institutionalization of the church. It reflects the temporal dimension—the translation of ritual payments into concrete goods such as church property, expenditure at festivals, welfare institutions. The basis of the tithe—that grace will follow the giver—is the 'economic theology' that Marcel

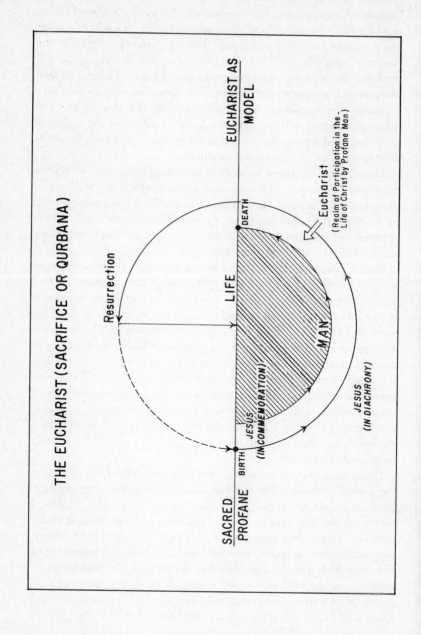

Mauss defines as being the subject of innumerable codes, epics and cantos.[40] The danger of the gift taking on the nature of contract is expressed in the nature of precautions taken. There is etiquette at every step—each stage in the process is regulated morally and economically.[41] It is perfectly understood that money transactions can become corrupting.

Basically, there are two kinds of gift exchange: the gift of the Holy Spirit, through invocation, where bread and wine become the body and blood of Christ, and simultaneously, the return made by man through the rites of commemoration. The two are inextricably linked and explain each other. The second is the material payment made to the church by devotees. Both kinds of gift exchange are understood only through the context of the sacrifice of Christ which occurred, by belief, in history, and is replicated through the liturgy and each ritual event of the Eucharist.

Sacrifice here consists of establishing a means of communication between the sacred and profane worlds through the mediation of a victim.[42] The destruction—participation in the sacrifice does not result in taking upon oneself the dimensions of the sacrificed. The sacrificed is only one: the Christ, the sacrifiers are the believers and the sacrificers are God and the priest. The relation between God (as the Father who sacrifices His only begotten Son) and the priest (as one who performs the ritual sacrifice) is a relation of substitution, not of homology, as we saw. The priest is the mediator, and the sacred rite of sacrifice is one performed through grace which comes about only through ordainment. The most important function of the priest as it appears through the liturgical service is to gradually prepare the lay to face the overwhelming quality of the sacred.

This transition from profane to sacred is the essence of the performance of the sacrificial act. The Eucharist is a theatre, where the limen of enaction captures the moment between the profane and the sacred. To 'see' the Qurbana (Qurbana Kannuka) is not a perfect moment of ritual purity—it is to see the heavens open, but not a full participation in the world of the spirit. True participation is possible only through the 'experiencing of the Eucharist': by partaking of the bread and wine, and to believe thereby that the spirit of the Christ has entered one's soul. The movement from the profane to the sacred state through the participation in the Qurbana is not to become the Christ but to participate in the nature of Christ. The purpose of the intermediary according to Hubert and Mauss is 'that the two worlds that are present can interpenetrate and yet remain distinct'.[43] Hubert and Mauss did not deny the existence of the 'other world' at least in terms of the logic of the social fact that ideas are things.[44]

The process of sacralization which sacrifice entails must perforce be accompanied syntagmatically by a process of desacralization. This is made possible by the act of returning to the profane world, explicated by the breaking of the fast after *Qurbana*. The ceremonies of exit in the sacrificial scheme prepare the sacrifiers for the return to the profane world since continued states of sanctity are not possible.[45] Hubert and Mauss also argue that 'the religious condition of the sacrificer describes a curve symmetrical to the one traced by the victim'. But the curves thus described while having the same general contours are not the same.[46] The sacrifiers and sacrificers may approximate the curve, they never attain it in the manner of the victim.

The return of the resurrected Christ as the sacrificial victim at the moment of consecration is a return to empirical time, resulting in a return to the earth, to the logic of ritual time which is a construct of culture. At the same time, the participants in the body of the Christ (*pars pro toto*) through the partaking of *Qurbana* return to the profane world carrying with them the sacred knowledge of Christ. It cannot be a perfect knowledge but an approximate one, and forms the basis of Christian life as a life of hope as opposed to despair. It is this opening of the heavens that *Qurbana* represents, symbolically stated by the parting of the *trisheela* or veil.

NATURE–CULTURE–SUPERNATURE

In conclusion, I shall attempt to analyse the Eucharist in terms of the relation between the categories of nature, culture and supernature. The Eucharist must be seen as a model which represents within it the life of Christ at three levels, each of which is a miniaturization, where aspects of the life are replayed but in a condensed fashion.[47]

In the first case, the Eucharist is a model in the dramaturgical sense. The life of Christ is re-enacted with all the parapharnelia of costume, elevated space and the physical properties which have dramatic and symbolic uses. The Eucharist replays Christ's life for the benefit of believers, and in each of these enactments they too have a part to play.

At the second level, the Eucharist involves the participation of the lay Christian in the category of man, both as homologous to the thief crucified, who repented and was redeemed, as well as to the life of Christ himself. Thus, specifically, Christ's mortality, symbolized by his life-cycle rituals, re-echoes itself in the rituals marking the transitions of the individual life. Thirdly, the Eucharist is the centre of the annual cycle of rituals which enact separate episodes of crucial significance in Christ's life.

The first is the level of history replayed, the second is the inter-pretation of Christian biography in terms of the life of Christ which offers itself as an ethical map, the third is the map itself, spread out, detailed and re-voyaged with the passage of every year. Thus, at one level, the Eucharist is always the same, because it is a model. At other levels it is different in every context and frame. For example, the manner in which it prepares individuals for marriage or for death are of an entirely different order. In the same way, the Eucharist that celebrates Christmas, the commemoration of the dead (*Dukha Shanyarcha*, the Saturday following Good Friday) or Easter are dif-ferent in their frames of reference.

The central liturgy of the Eucharist thus commemorates very dif-ferent kinds of events, all of which are fundamentally related and cyclically understood. So, while Christmas commemorates the birth of Christ, it also reminds the Christian, through the enactment of the Eucharist, that this birth may be understood only through what was to follow—His life, works, death and resurrection.

We saw that at the mythological plane (often submerged but in existence) the nature of kinship becomes of central concern. The relation between God the Father and Mary as the Mother of Christ is expressed in terms of a relation of conjugality. This relationship of conjugality is however homologous to the relationship of marriage that is expressed between Christ and his bride, the Church. The problem of sexuality is a suppressed category. Virgin motherhood and, therefore, virgin conjugality become a symbol of the relationship between Christ and his bride. This interpretation must be located within a conception of nature–culture–supernature.

Lèvi-Strauss has argued that the existence of the incest taboo dis-tinguishes nature from culture. Thus rules of marriage are to be found in human societies while no such rule of accessibility or inaccessibility prevails in nature. In the third category, supernature, what follows is that where God is father and all men are children of God, we have a (hypothetical) situation where all relations are marked by the incest taboo. All are brothers and sisters in Christ. This is a logical rela-tionship, not an empirical one; it anticipates what is to come in the hereafter. Thus the category of supernature resolves the duality of nature and culture through the person of Christ.

At the level of supernature, Christ is the begotten son of the mystical relation between Mary and God. There is thus a relationship of filiation which is expressed separately as a physiological relation between Mary and Christ, and a philological one between God the Father and Jesus. The unification of the Trinity in Jesus participates in the mortal flesh of Mary, as informants believe, and in the triune nature of the Godhead. The category of Jesus the man becomes a mediatory one because it represents within it the manifestation of the spiritual as well as the corporeal. This is also true of Mary who similarly belongs to three planes at once: the plane of history, of the model, and of that which transcends both these, supernature. First, of course, it must be accepted that nature and supernature are both cultural categories, so that nature ('out there') is still perceived through the conception and vocabulary of a given culture. Supernature, even more so, is a cultural construct.

The Eucharist as a model represents the plane of culture, yet on this axis, nature and supernature coalesce. On this axis, as exemplified by the liturgy, are always present the figures of the saints including Joseph and Mary; the central figure of Christ mediates between nature and supernature at the most exemplary level; Satan, too, is always present, but is a category conceived ideally as absent because the Eucharist symbolizes victory over evil; the priest, like Christ, mediates between Heaven and Earth (supernature and nature), deriving power through the handling of the Eucharist. The people by their participation make the Eucharist not merely a model of but also a model for the Christian life.[48]

The diachronic level which interpenetrates the mythic takes into account the lives of Jesus, Mary and Joseph as they were lived historically. Thus, as we saw, Joseph is according to the local myths the protector of Mary and Jesus; the brothers of Jesus were sons of Joseph from an 'earlier marriage'. Whether true or false, the credibility of the myth lies in the nature of mortality, where Joseph and the brothers of Jesus are of a different category from Mary, related to Jesus by affinity. Joseph provides to Jesus the mundane aspects of His existence— occupation, lineage and country.

On the plane of synchrony, where time in its linear sense is virtually absent, Mary acquires a different personality, drawn both from mythology (the Mother of God) as well as history (the mother of Jesus

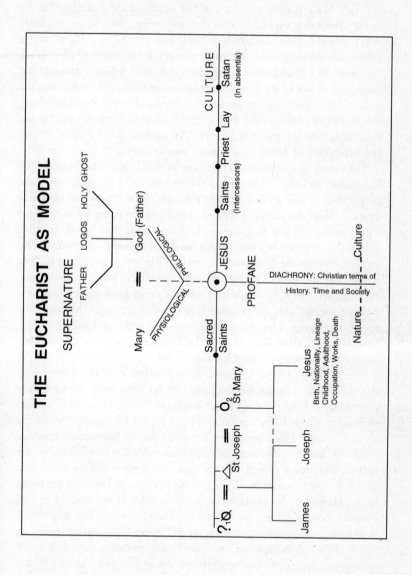

THE EUCHARIST AS MODEL

of Nazareth). The distinction between the two may not be theologically valid, but as a point of differentiation they do empirically exist. In this context, Mary is the mediator but her mediation acquires a different quality from that ascribed to Jesus or the priest. She did not celebrate the Eucharist even though it is 'well known that she took part in commemorative services'. She did not receive the power of priesthood, therefore the Eucharist may not be celebrated by any woman. Her mediation is not of the same order as that of the priest, and where the cult of Mary has been suppressed (as among the reformed churches), she loses her place on the axis of the Eucharist as model though she maintains it on the plane of history. Yet, among the Orthodox Syrians the mediation of Mary is of utmost importance.

The priest as mediator plays a central role in the enactment of the Eucharist, and shifts from being the servant of God, both sinful and unworthy, to one who is worthy through the transmission of divine grace to offer the sacrifice. Thus as mediator the priest substitutes for God, and offers the sacrifice of the living body and blood. But this substitution occurs at a temporally bounded moment—the sacred and explicit time of the *Qurbana* celebration. The priest expresses both in his person and his sacerdotal office the mediation between nature and supernature. He substitutes for God but never loses sight of his own profane being; this is expressed in all the prayers. This complex relation between suppressed profanity and expressed sacrality, particularly during the Eucharist, is the most characteristic feature, as a normative element, in the Christian priest.

The language of the *Qurbana*, Syriac–Arāmaic, draws attention to the fact that it is the sacred language which Christ spoke. Through the priests' knowledge of this sacred language, by the donning of certain vestments which carry symbols of the Christ's life (grapes, corn, the chalice, paten, lamb, shepherd's crook), by his separation spatially from the lay, he delineates his difference. In the hierarchies of the sacred, he is more sacred than the deacons, servers and the lay. These derive by the virtue of his office and his function in handling the living body. However, the problem of who the actor is becomes of crucial concern here. God is represented through the priest but it is Christ who is objectified through the bread and wine. These are two different kinds of sacred metaphors, one based on externality, the other on an internal structure of correspondences devised so that notions of difference may not be alluded to. The presence of Christ which activates the corporeal (i.e., the bread and the wine) into entering the realm of the *mysterium tremendum* (its transformation into body and blood) is made possible only by the manifestation of the Holy Spirit. Through the prayers of the priest, the Holy Ghost is called upon to descend.

However, whatever the sacredness imbued in his office, it is the manner in which the priest fulfils his role that most clearly demarcates the balance between sacred and profane aspects. In the traditional system, the parish priest was allowed to own property, engage in agriculture and be employed in some respected profession like teaching. This aspect locates the priest on the diachronic axis. It expresses the fact that roles may be fulfilled in divergent ways without detracting from the legitimacy and power of the office. The priests of Puthenangadi are not always seen in the best of lights by their parishioners. Sometimes it would seem that the mundane aspects of their life subverts the sacred, both in terms of their attitude toward church politics and money.

The disillusionment of the people and the priests themselves is a direct consequence of the church quarrel. It expresses the fact that the Eucharist and the resolution of the conflict that it captures, ending as it does in communion and Christian brotherhood, remains in the context of schism and its politics a form of ritual enactment rather than a charter for action. It contrasts, even for believers, theory and practice, model and reality.

Notes

1. I have used (besides the method of participant observation) two literary sources. They are both by themselves inadequate for a full understanding of the Eucharist service of the Syrian Christians. One is the Divine Liturgy of St James, according to the Rite of the Syrian Orthodox Church of Antioch (1967), and the other is the *Qurbanakramam* (1981) or the Service Book of the Holy *Qurbana*, provided for the use of the lay by the Malankara Metropolitan or the head of the Syrian Orthodox Church in Malabar. It is possible that there may be some prayers used here which are not found in the Syriac Malayalam text but such prayers would be very much in the spirit of the service as it actually occurs. It is also true that the liturgy in use is both condensable as well as expandable. This is testified to in its usage; when some priests are accused of cutting short the liturgy, others may be accused of making it too long. In that sense, it is necessary that the structure be maintained while prayers, invocations and hymns may be abbreviated or recited in full. I have engaged in a similar act of abbreviation since my purpose here has been to describe merely the central rite of the Syrian Christians.

2. *Qurbanakramam* (Thadiyoor: Oriental Printing House, 1981).

3. *The Divine Liturgy of St James* (published by Metropolitan Mar Athanasius Yeshue Samuel, Archbishop of the Syrian Orthodox Church in the United States and Canada, 1967), p. 6.

4. Ibid., p. 6.
5. Ibid., p. 8.
6. Ibid., p. 12.
7. Ibid., p. 20.
8. Ibid., p. 22.
9. Ibid., p. 31.
10. II Cor. 13:12.
11. *The Divine Liturgy*, p. 88.
12. Ibid., p. 39.
13. Matt. 3: 13–17; Mark 1: 9–11; Luke 3: 21–22.
14. *The Divine Liturgy*, p. 40.
15. Ibid., p. 41.
16. Ibid., p. 49.
17. Matt. 26:26.
18. *The Divine Liturgy*, p. 50.
19. Mauss, *The Gift*.
20. *The Divine Liturgy*, p. 50.
21. Ibid., pp. 51–2.
22. Ibid., p. 58.
23. Ibid., p. 59.
24. Ibid., p. 60.
25. Ibid., p. 63.
26. Ibid., p. 64.
27. Ibid., p. 68.
28. See e.g. Clifford Geertz, 'Religion as a Cultural System' in Michael Banton (ed.), *Anthropological Approaches to the Study of Religion* (London: Tavistock, 1966).
29. Kadavil Paul, *The Orthodox Syrian Church.*
30. Edmund Leach, *Genesis as Myth and Other Essays* (London: Jonathan Cape, 1979).
31. Matt. 10: 37–8; Luke 11: 27–8; 14: 26–7.
32. Matt. 19: 12.
33. Luke 11:27–8; Matt. 12:48; Mark 3:32.
34. John 2:4.
35. John 19:26–7.
36. See *Royal Court of Final Appeal.*
37. Claude Lévi-Strauss, *Structural Anthropology* (Harmondsworth: Penguin, 1977).
38. Gillian Feeley Harnik, *The Lord's Table* (Philadelphia: University of Pennsylvania Press, 1981).
39. Marcel Mauss, op. cit., p. 71.
40. Ibid., p. 55.
41. Ibid., p. 59.
42. Henry Hubert and Marcel Mauss, *Sacrifice: Its Nature and Function* (Chicago: University of Chicago Press, 1973).
43. Ibid., p. 93.
44. Ibid., p. 10.
45. Ibid., p. 48.
46. Ibid., p. 48.
47. Lévi-Strauss, *The Savage Mind.*
48. Clifford Geertz, 'Religion as a Cultural System'.

The *Angadi*

The *Nallu-Kettu* House

Cherya Palli: the *pattipuram*

Cherya Palli's wall paintings

Another view of the paintings. St Peter is represented as holding the keys

Cherya Palli: the western door (Note Assyrian figures and peacocks guarding the cross)

The Kurisu Palli Cross

Kurisi Palli's painted ceiling depicting the sun, a dove and cherubims

St Thomas the Apostle, with Christ represented above him

Puthen Palli and its attendant graveyard

Simhasana Palli

Marriage rituals: the *yatra choikuga*: seeking permission to leave from the head of the household

The priest blesses the crowns

The joining of hands. The *mantrakodi* is draped over the bride's head

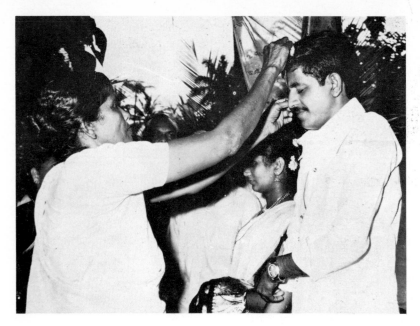

Nellum-nirum: the rites of fertility on entering the house

An old couple in traditional attire

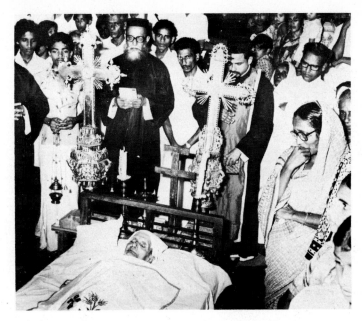

A funeral: priests pray in the house before the body is taken to the cemetery

The Evangelion is read by the prelate

The prelate holds paten and chalice

The prelate blesses the people

6

Syrian Christian Calendar Rituals

The calendrical rituals of the Syrian Christians are central to their perception of time, which is structured by the ceremonial activities marking episodes commemorating the life of the Christ. The Western calendar year (January to December) does not serve here as the point of analytical departure so much as the life of Jesus as interpreted through ritual. These rituals regulate the time perception of Syrian Christians in ways which are different from the Hindu calendar, even while the latter is used by the community for various practical purposes such as the building of houses or the making of horoscopes.

The event-based episodic Syrian Christian riaual calendar is a system of classification in which the nature of time and its usage is expressed in the context of the sacred. Since it is structured around the biography of Christ, it expresses the fundamental relation between man and the sacred world. Although lunar and solar calculations affect this classification of time, the seasons or natural cycles do not form its fulcrum. It is a 'technological classification' whose purpose is primarily to facilitate ritual action.[1] In more general terms, Durkheim and Mauss have argued that all classifications have a history which has to be understood in terms of a shift away from confusion to relative clarity and distinction.[2] In Christianity, we have to understand the ritual calendar as symbolizing the movement away from one clearly circumscribed ritual tradition (the Judaic) to another—the Christian perception of time and history. This raises the question of the plurality of the concept of time.

What the sacred calendar of the Syrian Christians commemorates is the origin of a new world-view, a mytho-historical event that is elaborated with every ritual celebration. Unlike the interlaced classifications of other cosmological calendars such as the Chinese where elements, cardinal points, colours and animals interweave in the 'marking off' of time, the Syrian Christian ritual calendar provides a charter of action dependent upon a triadic notion of time: secular and Western, Christian, and Hindu. The three elements in this categorization of time are discrete, and while they may coincide, they do not assimilate each other. Rather, they are like three different languages which while being perfectly understood are not commingled, spoken and interpreted in harmony. The translations are implicit but the use of each is different and identities are thus kept intact.

Like all systems of classification, time too has its rules by which its elements (moments) are segregated or aggregated. The Christian ritual calendar applies the rule of commemoration for structuring the year into segments. Particular days are marked out as ritually important in relation to either to Jesus or to Mary or the saints. The past, both historical and mythologized, interpenetrates the present, and through its implicit moral codes defines the nature of the future. Thus the Christian calendar is Janus-faced, and its present is understood only in the context of the historical but mythologized past, and the future which is revealed apocalyptically. Thus, while the calendar is a system of classification expressing the order of continuities and discontinuities between the sacred and everyday or mundane worlds, it must necessarily be a charter as well as a schedule.

Eviatar Zerubavel has shown how the calendar as a schedule structures the year according to events. In this sense, the classification is quantitative because time here is an entity which is segmented into various quantities of duration and is therefore countable and measurable. However, at the same time, it is qualitative because temporal symmetry is one of the primary expressions of the calendar in use. It synchronizes the activities of different individuals, and thus the schedule becomes the basis of social solidarity born out of resemblance. In this sense, Zerubavel argues, the calendar is a symbol of unity and those who are organized under a particular notation of time belong to one society.[3]

As a charter for action, the focus of the calendar lies in the use made of the commemorative liturgy. In this sense, time is truly qualitative because, rather than numerical segmentation, it is the arousal of certain moods and passions that the ritual calendar achieves.[4] It becomes a symbol of Christian life and identity, and communal celebration reaffirms Christian faith. It is for this reason that the *Moranaya Peryanaal* (the Lord's feasts) have a special place not accorded to the lesser festivals of saints and holy men. Through the commemoration of the life of Christ, believers are essentially integrated into one body.

The schisms in the Syrian Christian Church brought about by the ecclesiastical quarrel continue in such a way that the celebration of the Lord's feasts do not, in fact, bring about a conciliation between the two factions, which they would if the edicts of Christianity were practised in their fullest sense. However, there is a greater sense of the general unity of Christian brotherhood at Christmas and Easter than on any other day. The calendar may thus latently offer a model of separation. The Judaic, Islamic and Christian calendars, for example, are symbols of differing world-views. This is also very clearly evident in the manner that the commemoration days of holy men are celebrated among the Yakoba, where one party ignores events and festivals observed by the other.

The ritual calendar is also codified and printed, combining in this sense the qualitative and quantitative aspects of the calendar. Every Christian house has such a calendar which gives the dates of church festivals and other important days. Defined by the Western table of time and coterminous with the Malayalam Era and months, the calendar is also used for checking orally received information (the primary source) about when festivals will occur. Zemon Davis captures the essence of such calendars, speaking of early modern France: 'It may have jogged the peasant's memory. . . But it can hardly have brought them much new information or changed significantly their reliance on oral transmission'.[5]

The calendar in its codified and printed form is important, however, because it provides a tool both for recapturing explicitly the nature of the past and present as well as for anticipating the future. But this is usually for mundane reasons with ritual time being used as a marker for other social activities. People often say things like 'The children will be returning home for Christmas' or 'Our marriage took place after Easter'. Such notations of time would cancel out, for instance, the possibility of marriages occurring during Lent. The codified, printed calendar provides the important function of translating ritual time into chronologically accurate dates. However, the imminence of events such as Christmas and Easter are known not by reference to this calendar as much as through references made orally in conversations and sermons, and the onset of seasonal changes.

This superimposition of ritual time over mundane time (and vice versa) can be grasped more clearly if we look at the nature of the rites themselves. Mythemic time provides a framework for social life in the same way that it is the numerically coded time of the Western calendar that defines specifically when a rite should be celebrated. In the sacred calendar, caught within the grid of the quantitatively defined year, there is an oscillation between sacred and profane.[6] Time also oscillates within the sacred between fasts and feasts, these being the very signs by which sacred time is marked off as characteristically different from profane time. However, there exists a hierarchy within the sacred, and the calendar expresses an oscillation between the profane and sacred worlds in this sense. The sacred calendar becomes a map expressing the relations between man and the sacred.[7] As Bourdieu has most convincingly argued, technological classification ('practical taxonomies') are not very different from theoretical classifications. They are 'instruments of cognition and communication which are the precondition for the establishment of meaning and the consensus on meaning exert their structuring efficacy only to the extent that they are themselves structures'.[8] Thus the world-view of the Syrian Christian, codified and encapsulated in the calendar by the events of history, structures his perception of the present.

The Christian year is the condensation of a span of life, starting from Christmas, commemorating the birth of Christ, to the events of the Passion, which is the point of culmination in His life, ending in crucifixion and resurrection. Here, there is a substitution of 'a linear homogeneous continuous time for practical time which is made up of incommensural islands of duration'.[9] It was in this sense too that Warner described the 'holy seasons' of the Christian calendar, each with its separate dimensions of joy, sorrow and hope. These unique commemorative moments culturally bind the Christian into an apperception of time that also includes eschatological notions.

There is a second ritual calendar, rather like a subset of this dominant sacred cycle centring around the life of Christ, which is based on the festivals of the saints. As in kinship studies where ego can be understood only in terms of its relation to ancestors, descendants and collateral relatives, so also in the analysis of the Christ's biography it is necessary to look at the relation of Christ to those persons who are in close association with Him: Mary, the saints and the holy men. Here, closeness is defined in terms of 'spiritual' closeness rather than by blood ties or genealogy. The ritual calendar of the Syrian Christians is defined by two configurations of events around Christmas and the Passion.

Christmas (Janana Peryanaal)

The twenty-five days before Christmas are days of Lent but, unlike the Lenten period before Easter, this time is marked by an anticipation of joy. Lent here signifies the necessity for the Christian to prepare himself for the sacred.

The days before Christmas are days of hectic activity. The house is cleaned and made ready for guests. On Christmas Eve people begin to arrive. As the evening progresses, anticipation and excitement grow, especially among the children as all the cousins get together.

At the churches there are special services—*sandhya namaskaram* (evening prayers) at one, carol singing at another, the *tirumeni* (bishop) comes to a third to deliver the Christian message. On this day *sabha* or denominational differences are not given much importance. Yakoba families, for instance, may go to the nearby Church of South India (CSI) cathedral where carols are being sung. The roads are thronging with people. Women walk together keeping time with the elderly, who for once leave their homes to participate in the Christmas excitement.

On Christmas Eve all the churches are kept open, decorated, and festooned with streamers. People stop over at Kurisu Palli on their way back from other places. Children are given small coins to put in the *nerca petti* (offertory), and prayers are said standing in the chapel. The houses on the roadside are brightly lit up, and the streets are full of children. Each Christian house is marked by a big paper star symbolizing the 'Star in the East' heralding the birth of Christ.

Most homes have a Christmas tree. A tree in the garden is chosen, and on it streamers and coloured lights, tinsel baubles and balloons are hung: all the work of children. In some houses a bough of a tree is brought inside and placed in a copper vessel and decorated with brightly coloured objects. There is no traditional exchange of gifts in the Western sense, and even the sending of cards is not very frequent though letters of greeting are exchanged. The primary emphasis is on the elaborate preparation and eating of ceremonial food and on spending the day together. Those who are wealthy have their houses white-washed. Others clean, polish and wash their houses the week before Christmas so that everything gleams.

The first part of the Christmas *susrusha* or service begins on Christmas Eve, the main service taking place in the early hours of 25 December.

Sandhya namaskaram (evening prayers) in Kurisu Palli begin on the
24th evening at 6 p.m. with incantations to Mary. Prayers refer to the
birth of Christ to the Virgin Mary, which took place without violating
her virginity. (Popular interpretations speak of the birth of Christ
occurring without pollution, from the tearing of her thigh.) The
prayers speak of the wise men (the Magi) who gave gifts: gold,
symbolizing kingship, myrrh, which is the sign of the prophet, and
incense for priesthood; and of the shepherds who adored the child
born in Bethlehem, of the lineage of David. The priest reiterates the
lowly birth of the Christ, born to man in a manger, among animals,
and wrapped in rags.[10] He speaks of the fire in the womb of Mary, the
Dwija Agni (twice-born fire) which was the Christ, which left Mary
unharmed, untouched. There are references also to the bush engulfed
by fire which Moses saw and which was a manifestation of God; to
Isaiah and Jeremiah and to the Psalms of David where such a virgin
birth was foretold.[11]

The evening prayers juxtapose death with birth for without resurrection there is no meaning in Christ's birth and death.[12] Man's
death is to be understood in the same terms. The service closes with
prayers for the dead, after which people leave, anticipating the breaking
of the twenty-five day Lenten period after the *Qurbana* the next day.
However, the buying of ceremonial food will have already taken place
in most households.

At 3 a.m. on Christmas morning, the average Yakoba family will be
on its way to the neighbourhood church, carrying a cross made of
palm leaves. This cross is given to them in church on Hosanna Sunday
and preserved very carefully, not being allowed in the interim to be
polluted in any way. Wrapped carefully in newspaper, the cross is
brought to the church and given to the priest's assistant (*cemacen*)
along with oil, candles and incense as gifts to the church. The road,
though it is dark and early in the new day, is full of people coming
silently and quickly to the church.

In church, worship begins with the prayers of the night. The priest
wears brilliant robes, the candles are lit, and the church is filled with
the smell of incense. Mary is said to cry:

> The pain of labour comes upon me. Oh, Just One, take me to
> Jerusalem. I have neither bed nor mattress. He who will save the
> world must be born in a cave.[13]

The verses recall the joy of the divine birth, stopping to ask: how did Christ bear the manger, how did Mary bear the birth of He Who is responsible for creation? In these verses, an important place is given to Mary. She is *deva mata*, the mother of God, *rajamakal*, a princess, and *David putri*, a daughter of David.[14] At the close of this part of the service, the congregation moves towards the priest in an orderly queue and receives from him a spoonful of *kundrikam*, the perfumed resinous extract of a tree found locally, used as incense.

The priest carrying a silver cross and a candle leads the congregation out through the left door of the church. Behind him are two men holding large red silk ceremonial umbrellas followed by six men holding up a coloured canopy and, finally, attendants with candles. Everyone walks barefoot on the gravel to the space behind the church. It is barely 4 a.m. The priest faces the east in the stillness of the morning. He holds the candle by the light of which he reads the Bible, placed ceremoniously as always on a lectern. The people stand in a semicircle looking eastwards at the sky, where the morning star hangs like a bright symbol of Christ's birth.

There is a cross-shaped pit on the western side of the church in the courtyard, about three feet in length and a foot deep, filled with the dried palm leaf crosses of Hosanna Sunday. The priest lights the fire, and the people each put in their handful of incense, the perfumed smoke rising into the early morning sky. This ritual is called *thiarrakal*. The fire symbolizes both the bright light which the shepherds saw and the fire around which they kept themselves warm.[15] The Evangelion (the scripture) is read: Heb. 1: 1–12; Luke 2: 1–14. Everyone walks around the fire, the umbrellas, crosses and canopy in front, with the priest leading the prayers. The chanting, the flame in the darkness, the smoke heavy and perfumed, the rhythm of the people moving as one in communion, the ceremonial umbrellas, the heat of the fire—all these create an image of unusual beauty. After the fire has died out worshippers return to the church through the southern door singing 'When I went to Bethlehem, I saw a young girl carrying a child'.

The service is an enactment in verse of the events of Christ's birth, the Christian's hope for a life worthy of heaven, and the removal of the curse of Adam. The priest prays that the blessing of the cross be on all, pleads that the prayers of Mary and the power of the cross may keep believers safe from evil. Praying, the priest faces east, west, north and south, the cardinal directions symbolic of the universe.

Inside the church, the priest begins to conduct the service at the altar—the prayers of the morning or the *prabhata prarthna* which describe the Christ who is born to redeem man, who lived in the womb of Mary, took her flesh, and was born in a cave.[16] References are made to the debt of Adam, to Eve's sin, which is liberated by Mary. The human aspect of Christ's birth is celebrated through the image of the infant crying in the manger. Kadavil Paul Ramban describes the scene:

> Before they disperse after the Holy Mass, they all kiss the cross and put offerings as on Easter day. Here they kiss the cross as if they are coming and seeing the new born Babe in the manger and kissing him; and their offerings remind us of the wise men from the East coming and placing gifts before him.[17]

Dawn breaks as people begin to leave the church. The narrow roads and by-lanes are full of early morning worshippers greeting each other. There are no special Christmas greetings—everyone shares the event of the birth of Christ without much verbal exchange. No one is dressed in their newest or best, and people come to church in simple, everyday clothing, the older generation in stark and traditional white. The very fact that they have all woken up at 2.30 a.m. is an indication of the special nature of the day: greetings, gifts and new clothes are still part of an alien Western idiom.

Christmas lunch is the most important event of the day other than attending *Qurbana*. The children and the men eat first, being served by the women for whom this act of service is considered both an honour and an obligation. Attending on their families is not something that is left by the women for servants to do, particularly on festive occasions. Christmas lunch is a celebration because it breaks a long anticipatory lenten period of twenty-five days and also joyously marks the birth of Christ.

Denha Peryanaal

The next ritual of importance is *Denha* or the Epiphany, a feast day falling on the 6th of January, and connected with the baptism of Jesus in the River Jordan.[18]

The morning prayers begin at 7 a.m. at Kurisu Palli. After the *Tubdein* (which is the prayer asking for the blessing of saints, holy men and bishops, both alive and dead), the priest and deacons, wearing celebratory vestments, carry in procession a transparent jar of water with a small wooden cross placed at its mouth. The jar is covered with the *sosafa* which is otherwise used to keep the paten and chalice covered. Taking cross, Bible and candles, the priest, deacons and worshippers leave through the northern door, circle around the church once, and enter again through the southern door. Carrying the jar of water signifies the flowing of the River Jordan; that it is covered signifies the Old Testament period in which everything remained implicit and unrevealed. Hymns are sung which refer to John the Baptist, to the River Jordan and to the dove, the manifestation of the Holy Spirit. After the prayers and the blessings of the censer, the *sosafa* on the jar is lifted, the wooden cross taken out of its mouth and the water blessed by the priest. The lifting of the *sosafa* signifies that the Old Testament period is over with the arrival of Christ the Saviour.

In the last part of the service the cross is taken to the baptismal fount and the blessed water poured over it, signifying the baptism of Jesus Christ. The priest returns to the altar with the jar and, placing it there, celebrates the Holy *Qurbana*. After the Eucharist celebration, everyone drinks a few drops of this sacred liquid, starting with the celebrant. The water left over in the jar is kept in a chest in the sanctuary, to be used when someone in the parish is ill or in trouble. The prayers speak of Jordan as the mystical water, the water of joy;[19] references are made to John the Baptist, to the Baptism which is to come by fire and the Holy Spirit,[20] and to the destruction of Satan through drowning.

The blessing of the water is believed to give it curative properties which are used for healing the sick, for giving strength to the weak, for barren women, for sheltering homes, for safety from the devil, from lies, envy, murder, anger, revenge, sorcery, evil sprits, idol worship, for removing evil forces from the atmosphere, for growing seeds, sheltering crops, and for ripening fruit.[21]

The rituals of initiation represent a point in the biography of the Christ following his birth, symbolizing that his adult life and his work proceed from the event of baptism. The next most important set of rituals centring around the biography of Christ are those related to His Crucifixion and Resurrection.

Shubhakona susrusha

Shubhakona susrusha or the Service of Reconciliation marks the first day of Lent, where the priest prays for the people that they may observe Lent (*Noimba*) with piety and strength of purpose, and not waver or be distracted in the keeping of resolutions. The ritual takes place on the Monday before the beginning of the Great Lent at the time of *Ucca Namaskaram* (the noonday prayers). It is a brief service with much genuflection, with the head being made to touch the ground (*kumbhasaram*) each time. An old priest who was officiating spoke of the purpose of the rites:

> We gather here to ask God to give us the strength to keep *Noimba* with piety and strength of purpose, not to waver or be distracted in our resolutions. Fasting is an important way of expressing our love for God, our desire to see Him and to keep pure for Him. The prophets saw their visions and Moses received the commandments at such a time. We keep this Lenten period in remembrance of the forty days that Christ spent in the desert, keeping himself pure from the temptations of Satan.

An important element of this ritual is the giving and receiving by each individual of the *kaisthudhi* or kiss of peace achieved through the mutual clasping of hands, which are then lifted to the lips. This handclasp signifies that all enmities must be forgotten, and those who touch each other thus have to be mutually loving and helpful. Informants say proudly that they continue a tradition which is centuries old, it having been a part of the ceremonies of the early church. After prayers are said and the creed recited, people bow and touch the ground with their heads forty times. This, according to the prayer book, is a time of asking for forgiveness, for granting peace; the priest prays for himself and for the people, asking for reconciliation and forgiveness. Psalm 51 (Have mercy on me, O God...) is recited. The priest says the stain of sin is upon him: yet, just as Christ had mercy on the robber, the sinful woman, and the publican, may He have mercy upon all present; may those who are separated by anger and strife have their hearts filled with God's love.[22]

Several readings from the Bible follow. The first is from John 4, 11–21, where Jesus talks to an adulterous woman at the well, and speaks of that which is to come. A verse read from I Cor. 13, 4–10, asks that each individual examine himself, 'whether ye be in the faith; prove your own selves'. The call to forgive the sins of others and repentance is expressed in Mathew 18, 18–35. Where Peter asks of Christ: 'How oft shall my brother sin against me and I forgive him? Till seven times?' Jesus replies, 'I say not unto thee until seven times but until seventy times seven'. In conclusion the priest kneels thrice before the people, while the people do the same, asking God for forgiveness and mercy. The general trend of this service is penitential, and the prayers are essentially for peace (*samadhanam*), love (*sneham*), unity (*yojip*), oneness (*aikyma*) and devotion (*bhakti*).

Pakthi Noimba

Mid Lent or *Pakthi Noimba* is the next important ritual in the Syrian Christian calendar. The ceremony always falls on a Wednesday, being calculated 'according to the Paschal Moon'.[23] The service for *Pakthi Noimba* begins on the evening of the preceding Tuesday as the day is reckoned from the evening onwards in eastern churches.

The veneration of the cross is the central theme of *Pakthi Noimba*, celebrated on the twenty-fifth day of Lent. On this day Christ, represented by the cross, is seen as having come among the people. The cross is covered or dressed in a red 'robe' called the *ankhi* and placed in the centre of the nave till the evening of Hosanna Sunday to represent Christ in the temple at Jerusalem in the midst of believers. At this time, garlands of jasmine are hung around the cross and when people pass by, they lift the *ankhi* (representing the robe) to their lips. The cross is wooden, bigger than a handcross, but placed on a pedestal so that it stands above worshippers' heads. The robe has a large cross embroidered on it in gold thread. Two candles are lit on either side. Informants liken the cross to the *agniserapam* (the fire snake) which redeemed Moses from the tyranny of the Pharoahs.[24]

And the Lord said unto Moses, Make thee a fiery serpent, and set it upon a pole; and it shall come to pass that everyone that is bitten, when he looketh upon it, shall live.[25]

At the centre of this ritual is the theme of the victory over evil and an implicit homology between Moses and Jesus. The service is characterized by the exaltation of a handcross in the four cardinal directions.

Hosanna Sunday

The Sunday before Easter is called Hosanna Sunday and begins the Passion Week (*Kashtanubhavikunna nyyayarcha*) or 'the week that pain was experienced'. People believe that they experience with Christ the pain of trial, torture and death during this week. Hosanna Sunday is not merely an expression of joy at the triumphant entry of Christ into Jerusalem; it is also the beginning of the Passion.

On the evening before, small children bring strips of palm leaves to church to be made into crosses. Since their offerings are small, the young men who assist the priest spend the evening helping the children cut the leaves into strips.

Early the next morning people assemble in the church which is packed to overflowing so that many people have to stand outside, the women near the southern door, the men near the northern. The *kurusolla* (palm leaf crosses) are tied up in bundles, each with a reed cross placed at its centre, slightly longer than the rest of the bundle. During the *Qurbana*, the specific ritual for blessing these *kurusolla* begins. The priest gives one bunch to each child; preceded by those holding the silk umbrellas, silver crosses and ceremonial canopy, the procession exits through the northern side of the church.

In the *Anduthaksa* (*Book of Annual Feasts and Liturgies*), the procession is described as Christ, Son of God, riding on donkey—before Him go the prophets, the disciples, waving the branches of trees, singing Hosanna. The donkey is described as a *vahanam* (vehicle), and is therefore sacred.

The procession stops at the western door. The sexton brings the lectern from the *madabaha* and places it at the western door. The priest reads from Mark 11, 1–19 the passage relating to Jesus's entry into Jerusalem. Two altar boys throw flowers from a basket in front of the lectern so that the ground is strewn with flowers. The procession moves and this time enters the church through the southern door.

The *kurusolla* are collected from the children and again placed on the table in the sanctuary. The priest takes a bundle of these which have not yet been untied, with its cross clearly visible at the top, and begins the prayers of blessing. These include the recitation of the psalm of confession and reconciliation,[26] and the description of the entry into Jerusalem.[27] The verses speak of the Prophet Zachariah who described the coming of the king riding on a donkey. There are many readings, both Old Testament prophecy and New Testament fulfilment:

'Thy father's children shall bow down before thee.' (Gen. 49: 8–12)

'Behold, thy king cometh unto thee: he is just, and bearing

salvation; lowly and riding upon an ass...' (Zach. 9: 9–12)
'Therefore the redeemed of the Lord shall return and come
singing unto Zion...' (Isa. 51: 9–11)

The blessing of the palm leaves includes prayers that those who
receive the leaves may receive the gifts of firm faith, blessed homes, the
removal of bad thoughts, and the annihilation of wars. There are also
prayers for shelter and safe keeping. After elevating the bundle of
palm leaf crosses in the cardinal directions, the sheaf is placed on a
table, and the *Qurbana* service completed.

After the *Qurbana*, each member of the congregation goes forward
to receive a *kurusolla* which he takes home safely and places where
there is no chance of the cross becoming polluted (*asudham*). Should it
touch the ground or in any way be desecrated, people believe that
harm will come to the person, even death, though this extreme consequence is dismissed as superstition. However, like all holy objects, it
must be treated with respect. On the dawn of Christmas day, the
kurusolla is put into the holy fire around which the people circle. This
is the *thi-arrakkal* ceremony. The ashes of this fire have the power of
healing and are also thought to bestow fertility on plants and to cure
them of disease. People believe that receiving a clear unblemished
kurusolla presages good fortune for the year, while a damaged one
indicates a difficult year.

. During the Passion Week there are no prayers to Mary or the saints,
the veneration of the cross alone being of crucial significance. There is
also no *kaisthudhi* or the blessing by the priest with the handcross.
For, as one man said,

The cross symbolizes the most tragic and human period of
Christ's life on earth; his suffering and his pain which we share
during this week.

Since the Eucharistic liturgy is essentially joyous and life-giving, it is
not celebrated on any day except Saturdays or Sundays during Lent.
Parts of the usual liturgy are used on weekdays but not the significant
portions relating to the Eucharist itself. The prayers of the different
parts of the days are often grouped together. Readings from the Old
Testament and the Epistles are made by the deacon or servers (*susru-
sharkar*) while the New Testament is read by the priest. These readings
have a very important place during Lent in the rituals of the church

and are acts of celebration. The priest now moves from the chancel and climbs the steps from the south, kissing the pillar before entering the *madabaha*. He dons a coloured silk vestment, a beautiful strip of cloth that is slipped over the head. By this time the *kappiar* (sexton) has placed the lectern in the centre of the *madabaha*, and lit two candles symbolizing the light of the world on either side. The priest kisses the Bible, chants the prefatory Syriac and proceeds to read the Bible in the intonation of a chant. When he has finished, he removes the vestment and returns to the chancel.

Since the days and events in the life of Christ are closely followed, the readings for each day and commemoration are given. Thus, the forty-first day of Lent, for example, is the day when Lazarus was raised from the dead, and the people are reminded of the event by the day's lesson. One Sunday, I asked a neighbour where she was going and was told 'To attend the marriage at Cana'.

On the Wednesday of the Passion Week, *kumbhasaram* or confession is compulsory since on the next day, *Pesaga* (Passover), all Christians are expected to participate in the *Qurbana*. Confession consists of self-examination, repentance, meditation, the resolution to not sin again, penance and communion. Confession is made resting on one's knees and knuckles, with the head touching the ground. There is no veil between confessor and priest. Those who are in the habit of confessing frequently, develop black rings around the knuckles. One informant showed me the rings around his knuckles saying, 'I have them only because it is Lent now. Some monks have them permanently.' During Lent it is the custom to prostrate oneself frequently. Confession is compulsory on the Wednesday before *Pesaga*, but the believer is expected to confess during all the five long periods of Lent in the year, thereby fulfilling the precept that a dutiful Christian should confess every forty days or so.

The Passover

Pesaga or the Passover is generally celebrated in the early morning of the Thursday preceding Easter, at 2 a.m., but since in Puthenangadi the priest happened to be very old, it began at 4 a.m. The *Qurbana* is celebrated as usual except that there are references in the prayers to the Passover Meal, and its meaning for Christians. The songs are all Passover Songs, hymns of lament, and the text for the day is, of course, the reading of the account of the Last Supper. At the end of the church service, *aviyal* (a complex dish consisting of various vegetables) is given to the people attending the prayers, symbolizing the sharing of the Lord's supper.

A ritual connected with the Passover is the ceremony of the washing of feet, conducted on the afternoon of Passover Thursday. It is a dramatization of an incident found in the thirteenth chapter of St John's Gospel, where Jesus washes the feet of his disciples.

After the introductory prayers, the bishop gets up and, wrapping a towel around his middle, washes the feet of the twelve disciples seated on the stage. The disciples are either priests, deacons or choir boys, according to the availability in each place and occasion. They come with clean feet and sit on seats arranged for them on the platform. No one likes to be called Judas, so no one is named except Peter, who has a definite role to play in this drama.

Good Friday

On Good Friday (*Dukha Vellyarcha* or Sorrowful Friday), the cross is taken from the centre of the nave where it has stood for twenty-five days. The red cloth draped over it is replaced by a black one signifying death.

The service on Good Friday begins at 8 a.m. Since Kurisu Palli has its particular fame as a church where personal prayers are heard and where miracles occur, a great crowd assembles here on such ritual occasions. A shelter made of cadjan (*olla*) is constructed outside, adjacent to the north and south walls. Coir mats are spread on the gravel, and over this the *paaye* (reed mats). Inside the church too, reed mats are spread with spaces in between for people to kneel and prostrate themselves. This prostration (*kumbh iddikuga*) is a constantly repeated expression of humility and piety, and is central to the *Dukha Vellyarcha* service. The *trisheela* or veil is drawn and the altar hidden from view. Only the immense stone cross in the sanctuary can be seen over the top of the veil. Since all the lamps, candles and electric lights are put off in the *madabaha*, the nave and sanctuary are in semi-gloom. The cross with its black *ankhi* (robe) also shifts to the centre of the nave. Jasmine garlands and the cloth around the 'shoulders' of the cross are removed. Everything is plain black, the entire service expressing through songs of lament the nature of collective mourning.

The atmosphere created is in fact like that of a house in mourning. Songs describe the events in the life of Christ; there are frequent readings from the gospels regarding the period of trial so that, through the spoken word and its images, the people are brought close to the events of that distant day. The service lasts from nine in the morning till five in the evening, and for all that time except for a very short period of rest (*vishram*) the people remain standing, frequently kneeling and bowing so that their heads touch the ground.

The agony of Jesus on the day of his crucifixion is for Orthodox Christians the greatest indication of the nature of Christ, that He was as much a human being as He was God. It is this suffering which is remembered, and which the service seeks to recapture.

The veneration of the cross follows; it is removed from its support, draped in white linen, and the base tied with a *kurusolla*. The cross is then taken around in a procession or *rasa* outside the church, accompanied by a slow sad chanting of the prayers of death and mourning.

The priest takes the cross from the chancel, and places it on his right shoulder over which is draped a piece of white cloth. The procession moves from the southern door and enters the church through the northern. There are no celebratory objects such as umbrellas or brass gongs. All the worshippers are expected to follow the *rasa* but the women generally remain behind in the church, reminiscent of the funeral processions of ordinary people which are male-dominated. The procession symbolizes the taking of Christ to Golgotha (the place of skulls) to be crucified. The song sung during the procession describes how Christ leaves on his journey to Golgotha, with a woman following him. The song describes the tears of the mother who was plunged in sorrow, like a dove.

The worshippers return to their places as the priest begins the service. The meaning of Christ's suffering and death is here most expressively recalled. For the lay, the relationship between the Old and New Testament is felt to be extremely vivid. In their conversations about belief, as in their prayers and hymns, there is a constant interplay between the Judaic and Christian traditions. Thus they affirm that the death and resurrection of Christ symbolizes the re-entry of man into Paradise from where he had been exiled after the sin of Adam and Eve. Similarly, the idea is expressed that just as Abraham was ready to sacrifice his son Isaac, so too God sacrificed His only begotten Son. Isaac carried wood, Christ the cross, but Christ is both Isaac and the sacrificial lamb.

On either side of the table in the centre of the nave where the priests say their prayers, two mud pots are placed, and quantities of incense are burnt in these, soon filling the nave with fragrant fumes. The cross is taken in procession again, this time within the church by the priests and the *susrushakar* while the people stand aside to make place. Then the *trisheela* is drawn aside and the cross raised thrice while prayers are recited.

The cross is the symbol of peace, victory and salvation. The central place given to the veneration of the cross can be seen from its functions: to shelter and safeguard, to remove evil, war, quarrels, nullify punishment, make the angry loving, make humble the proud, keep enemies away, attack pride, destroy the power of evil. A powerful and central symbolic image that emerges is of Christ who was crucified on a tree.[28] Further, a correspondence is posited between Christ and Adam. The creation of Adam took place on the sixth day; similarly, the crucifixion of Christ is marked six days from Hosanna.[29]

The preparation of Christ's body for burial is described in a song. Joseph of Arimathaca and Nicodemus took Christ down from the cross, carried Him in their arms and, rubbing Him with *muron* (chrism) and wrapping Him in silk, they put Him in a new tomb shutting the grave with a rock.[30] Darkness immediately fell upon the earth, expressing the shame of the elements. When Christ was resurrected after death, Adam, who was fallen, was also raised and returned to the Eden from where he had been expelled.[31]

The cross is placed on a chair covered with a piece of black cloth. The people come one by one and, kneeling in front of it, kiss the cross. They chant 'We say with the robber, remember us, O Christ'. Offerings of money are made at this time. Interestingly, in Kurisu Palli only Christians may approach the cross representing Christ. Two Hindu women, recognizable by their attire, were pushed aside by the Syrian Christian women who said, 'Outcastes may not come near' (*Purajyadi-kale sammadikhilla*).

The cross is taken to the *madabaha* after all the worshippers in the church have made their obeisance. The *trisheela* is drawn, and nothing can be seen of the burial service except the rising smoke of the incense, which grows so thick that it obscures the magnificent cross from view. The altar is in darkness, and there is only the low lamenting sound of *Kyrie eleison*, so melancholic that the church resounds with this quality. While it is the victory of Christ over sin and death, it is also a time of sorrow and human lamentation over his mortal departure. The atmosphere created by collective mourning is so intense that the very young, who do not understand it, begin to cry in fear.

Behind the veil, in the sanctuary, two urns filled with incense are lit. The cross is washed in rose water and then wrapped in white; incense is placed on the cross under the shroud. The cross is placed on the altar with its head towards the south and its foot (base) to the north. (Even in procession this is the way the cross is always held.) Two candles are placed on the cross. They are unlit and placed cross-wise (X), and covered with the altar cloths. No' *Qurbana* may be celebrated on the altar till the day of the resurrection.

One of the servers emerges from behind the veil and upturns the candles and crosses on the two lower altars, on the northern and southern side of the chancel. The burial ceremony is over.

The worship ends with the giving of *kaipe vellam* (vinegar) to all the people. There are two reasons given for this: firstly, that this is done in remembrance of the sop of vinegar that was given to Christ; secondly, vinegar is considered good for tiredness, as all the people certainly are, after eight hours of standing and singing without break and in a state of fasting.

When the people emerge from the church the sombre notes are fewer. It is as if a cosmic act of catharsis has taken place.

The ceremonial meal that follows is typical of the rituals of mourning. The meal consists of rice, green pulses and pickles. In front of each person is placed a shallow bowl in which is put hot steaming gruel (rice, and the water in which it has been cooked, flavoured with salt). The most important element of the meal is called *aval*, made of pounded rice, coconut shreds and jaggery. The food is blessed and eaten in silence. It is called *kanji nercha* (an offering of rice greul) and is the responsibility of the eighteen dominant families who are the trustees of the church.

Dukha Shanyarcha

On the next day, *Dukha Shanyarcha* (the Saturday of Sorrow), Eucharist is held in the church at the time of the noonday prayers. The songs continue to be Passion songs, slow and soft. It is on Easter that there is an appreciable change in the music, a quickening and a joyousness. On *Dukha Shanyarcha* it is believed that Christ went to *sheol* or *padallam*, the land of the lost or the dead, to serve those who had not received the Word. On this day too, Christians remember their own dead; in the afternoon, trips are made to the cemetery and candles lit at family tombs. *Dukha Shanyarcha* is also marked by the anticipation of *noimba veedi* (freedom from Lent). It is the end of the Great Fast and a return to the world.[32] By the evening, relatives have begun to arrive and family reunions take place over the last vegetarian meal for some time. There is not much sleep that night, since at 2 a.m. the family will be walking towards the church as the bells peal.

On the evening of *Dukha Shanyarcha* the altar cloths are changed from black to red. The prayers for Easter also begin on this evening and from this time too the kiss of peace is given.

Uyerrp or Resurrection

The prayers for Easter begin on the previous evening as the day is reckoned according to the Old Testament phrase that 'the evening and the morning were one day'. At *sandhya namaskaram* there are gospel readings, as on the evening before all feast days and Sundays,[33] *kai sthudi* (the kiss of peace) as well as prayers for those in Lent, for the rich, the poor, the hungry, the sick, the weak, for orphans and widows, for sinners, for those who have left home and those who are near. Everyone is remembered in these joyous prayers.[34]

Three times the priest makes a proclamation: 'The Lord is risen.' To this the people respond three times 'We believe that He is risen'. Through the formulaic language of the liturgy, the people confirm their belief year after year in the resurrection. Without this voiced proclamation and the fullness of response, the Christian creed can have no meaning. The prayers emphasize Christ as the Prince of Peace: He is compared to Noah's ark, and to the passage created for Israel through the Red Sea; the prayers also refer to the manner in which Jesus calmed the sea when the apostles were afraid. The text has *samadhanam* (peace) as its key word.

The Easter service is also marked by a complete change in musical style. The resurrection is viewed with joyousness, and nothing expresses this shift from mourning to overwhelming joy better than the music. Once the *Qurbana* is over, worshippers kneel to kiss the cross which is now wrapped in a piece of bright pink cloth. When the people leave the church, it is 6 a.m.

The collective festivities end with the raising of the flag to mark the *Puthiya Nyyarcha* (New Sunday) festivities. The drummers (*chendakar* of the *Izhava* caste) arrive, the men gather around the flag-pole at the church while the women as usual stand in a group a little to the back. The priest climbs up the three steps to the base of the flag-pole and hoists the bright orange triangular flag distinguishable from temple flags by its cross. This done, the group follows the drummers and the priest to the shrine (*kurusunthotti*) down the road. Here there is always a candle lit, and a light burning. Walking down the road, the people are in a mood of revelry evident in the way the young men and the boys shout, push and jostle each other, all the time crying *Poyin Poyin* recalling earlier times when Syrian Christians, being of a higher caste, asked for the way to be cleared so that they could walk unpolluted.

Another flag is hoisted after which people return home to eat the ceremonial Easter breakfast consisting of pancakes and duck cooked in coconut milk. After the fifty days of fasting and vegetarianism, it is a relief to be able to eat meat again. As an altar boy said,

> It is on Easter morning that even the best of us makes mistakes while serving the priest. Half our minds will be on the *Qurbana* and the other half on what we are to eat.

Puthiya Nyayarcha

This festival commemorates the appearance of Christ among the Apostles and is celebrated on the Sunday after Easter. It is of particular significance to the residents of Puthenangadi because Thomas is their patron saint and, according to them, it is the doubting apostle who plays the most important role here, being given the opportunity to feel for himself the wounds in Christ's flesh and to admit that it was indeed his Lord and God.

In lay perception, *Puthiya Nyayarcha* centres around Thomas the Apostle, and the people's affection for him is intense. This is a day when Christ meets the disciples and through His Resurrection they too are reborn and filled with new spirit. On this occasion every house and every person in it is blessed by the priest.

Swarg Arhonam

Swarg Arhonam (The Ascension) is celebrated forty days after Easter. When I was in Puthenangadi in 1982, it took place on the 20th of May. The ten days between Ascension and Pentecost are marked by prayer and meditation and called *kath irrikunna divasangal*, days of watching and waiting. The coming of the Holy Ghost upon believers is a momentous event for which preparation is required. During these ten days there are no marriages or baptisms. Even though this is not a time of fasting, solemnity nevertheless prevails. Before Pentecost, houses must be washed clean and *veedu kudasha* (the ceremony of sacralizing the house) performed.

Pentecost

This festival is celebrated fifty days after Easter and is the day when the Holy Ghost is believed to have visited believers when they were gathered together at one place. Hymns relating to the arrival of the Holy Ghost are sung. The Pentecost service is of great length and there is much prostration. Between Easter and Pentecost there has been an absence of ritual prostration, perhaps because this is a period marked by true ritual joyousness. Prostration or *khumbasaram* is resumed at Pentecost signifying that the people have seen 'tongues of fire' representing the Holy Ghost and cannot endure this awesome sight.[35]

In the special service of the Pentecost day rituals, following the *Qurbana*, three clean vessels with holy water form part of the ritual, symbolizing the Father, the Son and the Holy Ghost respectively. The priest, assisted by the deacon, sprinkles holy water on all those present. The people stand respectfully; a few push forward so that some of the water representing the Holy Ghost may fall on them. In the first ceremony, water is sprinkled in the name of the Father, is the second in the name of the Son, and the third in the name of the Holy Spirit. Through this ritual, believers are rejuvenated and experience anew the presence of the Holy Spirit within them.

THE CATEGORY OF LENT

In Syrian Christian ritual, Lent is opposed to feasting, and celebration can in fact be understood only in terms of the fasts and abstinences of Lent. Lent as a period of ritual importance is liminality of the type that Van Gennep describes in his classic *Rites of Passage*. It marks the transitional phase in the movement from the profane to the sacred. This period of fasting may be of different lengths of time—as long as fifty days before Easter, or as short as three days in memory of Jonah and the Whale. (According to one informant, Jonah bears the same relation to Christ as the Whale to the tomb.) Other than the annual Lenten periods, three days of every week are characterized as lenten, beginning at 6 p.m. on Tuesday and ending at 6 p.m. on Wednesday, and similarly on Fridays and Saturdays. These Lents are in memory of Mary (on Wednesdays) and Jesus. On such days meat, eggs and milk are prohibited, fish too was once avoided but this restriction does not hold anymore. Those who are exempted are all those under the age of eighteen or over sixty, pregnant women, lactating mothers and the ill. The reason for vegetarianism during this period is related to the control of flesh as meat and eggs are thought to be 'heating foods' which heighten passions. Sexual intercourse and all forms of merry-making and festivity are also prohibited. Sexual abstinence implied that children born in December were a great embarrassment, and parents had to confess their sin and repent. As one of my informants said, 'I guarantee you that none of our children were conceived on Wednesdays or Fridays'.

Three days of Lent anticipate the Great Lent of fifty days. In between is an eighteen-day interval called *pathnettu ayya edda*, associated with merriment, luxurious living, eating, drinking and festivity. These are days for marriages and celebrations culminating on the Sunday before *Shubha Kona Susrusha*, the ritual which marks the beginning of Lent. After *Shubha Kona* begins the *Ambatha Noimba* or the fifty-day Lent. During lenten periods in general, and particularly during the Great Lent, Holy *Qurbana* is not celebrated except on Saturdays and Sundays. The Eucharist is conducted, though, on the day marking the passage of twenty-five days, the *Pakthi Noimba* or Half Lent. During the rest of the year, *Qurbana* can be celebrated at any time it is asked for, provided the *Qurbana pannam* or Eucharist fee is paid.

In the period of *noimba*, from 3 a.m. in the morning till 4 p.m., no food or water may be taken. Lent is a denial of the joys of even the ritual life: consequently, there are changes in the routine of worship. No kiss of peace is given, the priest does not bless each person with the cross as is the custom, no one may take holy oil from the hanging lamp and there is no customary general blessing from the priest, as at the close of every service ('Let there grow peace among all of you').

Lent is a time for prayer and fasting and for *dhyanam* or meditation. Each believer must feel the need to search for God more intensely and passionately than at any other time. Searching for God (*devathine anishikuga*) helps to discover oneself and one's brother (*sahodaran*). The cross in this context is an important symbol of pain, of victory over death, and of redemption from sin.

The period of Lent before the Resurrection is one marked by deep personal mourning objectified and enacted through the ritual processes of society. The homology between the life of Christ and the life of the individual is made vivid as the days of penance and prayer pass. Yet people understand that they may participate in the ritual of suffering and crucifixion only vicariously. It is a problematic relationship and one question remains central to the mourners. Who is the Christ? Clearly, while the Christians share the suffering of the Christ, they remain only observers; yet, they participate mimetically in the event of the crucifixion. They are crucified too, yet at the same time asking (like the thief who repented, and who asked to be seated on the right hand of Jesus) that they be taken along to heaven with the Christ. It is a delicate balance, then, for the Christians: to participate in this ritual, and yet to always remain aware of their own sinful mortal identity.

In earlier times, at the beginning of Lent, certain ritual precautions were taken, the most important of these being the use of new dishes for the lenten period. No vessel in which non-vegetarian food had been cooked could be used. Secondly, the earthen kitchen floor was laid over again with *channakam* (cow dung). Both practices have died out in Puthenangadi.

Lent is the epitome of the liminal period: a transition period between man's carnal nature and the life renewed in Christ. It is a time of separation from the profane life in anticipation of a sacred state that is arrived at through the ritual of the festival celebrated. *Qurbana*, the Eucharistic sacrifice, is the central ritual and is at once sacrifice and festival. Fasting is compulsory for the believer before he or she participates in the *Qurbana* but after the partaking of bread and wine, the fast must always be broken. Since *Qurbana* is festive, since it is joyful, it does not take place during Lent. There are also a further twenty-five days of Lent in anticipation of Christmas, fifteen days in the name of Mary (August 1–15), and fifteen days in September in the name of the twelve apostles and Paul. According to an informant, one-hundred-and fifty-six days of the year are lenten days. Dates of the lenten period are checked from the ritual calendar (*panchakam*), provided by the *Malayala Manorama*, a local newspaper.

Lent expresses essentially a 'marking off' of time as a liminal space whereby preparation for the celebratory events may take place. It is a time of spiritual rejuvenation and Syrian Christians are, for the most part, careful about keeping the rules by which they are bound for this period. Profane and sacred are closely in relation as the time approaches for the consummation of the sacred through the rituals of commemoration. After the day of celebration concludes, there is a noticeable lull in the activities of the neighbourhood, a diminishing of effervescence in the Durkheimian sense, and the profane aspects of social life once more predominate.

PRAYER

Another problem I shall briefly consider is the position of the liturgy among the Syrian Christians, since it is the type of prayer that seems most commonly in use. Hymns, prostrations, prayers and chants are all subsumed in the framework of the liturgy. Worship is Eucharist-centred, mass is celebrated daily, and believers fill the church every morning, particularly during festive periods. Prayer is thus collective, communal and institutionalized, beginning at 7 a.m. and concluding an hour later. *Sandhya namaskaram* or evening prayers are similarly collective, and it is customary for the women and children to attend these services as well. The category that is in fact absent here is personal extemporary prayer, the Orthodox Syrians preferring formulaic chants and circumscribed limits within which to express their mortal spiritual longings. Extemporary prayer as a type are associated with the Reformed Sect (the Mar Thoma) and express the markedly individualistic nature of worship, where communion is weekly, taking place only on Sundays, the place of the priest thus becoming more limited and diffuse.

The problem of prayer is one that most anthropologists have not dealt with in a direct way or at any great length. Evans-Pritchard's work on the Nuer is, of course, a classic on the nature and function of prayer but, inspite of his sensitivity to the problem of language in ritual, he too emphasized typically the acts of the rite rather than the words.[36] The unease that anthropologists felt about the nature of belief (which prayer attempts to verbalize) is captured most succinctly in Rodney Needham's work.[37] Victor Turner attempts to look at the language of the spell, chronicling the manner by which modes of thought represent themselves in terms of oppositions in the particular case of Ndembu healing rituals.[38] In his *Quest for God*, Heschel identifies the polarity that has made the study of prayer a difficult one for analysis.[39] It is a problem which he handles somewhat polemically as well as biographically, referring to the shortcomings of Jewish worship. The polarity of prayer, according to him, lies in the fact that there are laws: how to pray, when to pray, what to pray. There are fixed times, fixed ways, fixed texts. On the other hand, there is *kavanah* (inner devotion), where prayer is worship of the heart, the outpouring of the soul. A dilemma exists, then, which is at the heart of practical worship—loyalty to 'the order' on the one hand, and the requirements of *kavanah* on the other.

The requirements of *kavanah* made upon a devotee are extremely difficult for the anthropologist to describe. However, in Peirce's sense, 'the word or sign which man uses is the man himself'.[40] Language in this sense becomes an expression of the man himself, and *kavanah* becomes revealed to us through certain indexes which dynamically connect the sign and the object.[41] Thus, frequent attendance at church is almost mandatory for the individual as a participant in collective worship, and becomes a statement of his devotion. The quiet that he maintains, the vigour of his discipline, the stance of his posture, and the alertness of his demeanour are all objective, easily perceivable statements about *kavanah*. *Kavanah* does not take place in a void but exists within the context of socially meaningful behaviour.

Just as inner devotion is difficult to analyse without the help of indexes, so also the subject of worship which is God. I have attempted here an analysis primarily in terms of folk representations (as in the preceding chapter). Within the liturgical service, the notion of God's presence, to whom the prayers are addressed, is explicitly that of divinity as power, as *mysterium tremendum* rather than as anthropomorphic deity. This seeming duality is captured particularly in the ideas of God's presence which are at one level abstract, and at another level iconic. The presence of God as if He were everywhere goes beyond the purview of the symbol and this is what Heschel means when he says that, for the believer, symbolism is an empty language. On the other hand, God is represented in the cross, the altar, the celebrant; in these icons, as they are used in celebration, the likeness of God is played upon by language. As Peirce argues, it does not matter whether any such object actually exists or not.[42] The actual existence of God, of heaven, of a historical personage like Christ or an event such as His suffering is never questioned because for the Christian 'there really is such an object', and the icon resembles that object and is used as a sign for it. The substitutability of the icon for the object is most clear in the language of the rite where, by a process of substitution, the prayers become addressed to the cross. The veneration of the cross in the Passion Week is the clearest example of the subject of worship taking on iconic representation. It is the cross that is garlanded, clothed, placed in the sanctuary, and treated as if it were the Christ, laid to rest in its tomb. The keening and wailing that follow is the typified way in which mourning takes its form, where the icon is separated from the viewer, and Christ's presence for a ritual moment is terminated by His symbolic burial in the tomb. The absence of the icon demarcates the absence of God Himself from earth and this is symbolized by the fact that on Good Friday the altars are shrouded.

But the fact that Eucharist is actually celebrated on *Dukha Shanyarcha* (Holy Saturday) in honour of the dead whom Christ is supposed to have visited is a statement indeed that the liturgy (and therefore Christ) is alive. The liturgy, then, in my reading, becomes not merely a symbol in the Piercian sense[43] where the object and the sign are denoted by an association of general ideas which take on the name of a law, where Christianity affirms itself through the existence of a charter of ritual conduct, but also one where the liturgy itself becomes an icon of the life of Christ.

Through language, the life of Christ is replicated and relived. Between the event of replication (which involves the idea of a liturgical author), and reliving (which is the practical expression of religious life) lies the realm of interpretation. In this sense, language is like a mirror, reflecting the nature of man and his being; this is why interpretation is both collective as well as individual in its exercises. Collective interpretation of the liturgical text continues to dominate the Orthodox Syrian Christians and it is perhaps for this reason that they eschew informal, individualistic, and voluntary forms of prayer, preferring priests, ritual frames and liturgies. M A K Halliday[44] has prescribed a triadic formulation for the understanding of the contexts in which language is used, which I shall use as a frame for understanding why the Orthodox Syrian Christian prefers to use formal rather than informal language in his conversations with God. The first of these is the 'field of discourse'. Here we are concerned with the church as the institutional setting for the elaboration of discourse. The Syrian Christian is habituated to worshipping collectively and the walls of the church structure religious experience in a clearly demarcated way which he welcomes. There is hierarchy (priest/lay), difference (male/female, ecclesiasts/lay) and order (the rules are known and collectively followed). While the prayers meant for various times are said individually or with one's family at home using a prayer book, these do not constitute a religious celebration in the way that worshipping at church does. The language of discourse, then, is collective rather than individual or subjective. The person who chants out of turn, who kneels when others stand or who does not get up to receive the blessing of the priest's handcross, is singled out and stared at. Liturgical language affects the very nature of action, for everything is codified in terms of the dictates of the text, captured in formulae such as 'Now you may be seated' or the frequently uttered *Stomen Kalos* (stand well). The collective language of the rite demands attention and standardized behaviour.

The second term that Halliday propagates is 'tenor': the relationship that exists between participants, the variations in formality, and questions such as the permanence or otherwise of the relationship defined here. The ambiguous relation between priest and laity is one of great complexity. The priest is the embodiment of the liturgy, substituting for Christ Himself. The lay are in awe of the priest primarily because he is a keeper of sacred tradition and knowledge, because he is the one most proximate to the sacred. Their relation to him is defined primarily in terms of this power. As an informant said, 'The priest may be a good or a bad man, but he is the keeper of the liturgy'. The language of prayer becomes, in terms of this unequal relationship, a language of mimesis. The whole text is in the hands of the priest, while the people may own a fragmentary portion consisting mainly of responses, instructions and the closing phrases (symbolizing cueing, where respondents must speak) used by the priest.

Clearly, knowledge is the basis of division, difference and inequality, and the people are severed from the text. Interpretation for the lay then becomes an act which is based on the heard rather than the read text. Just as the *trisheela* serves to separate the worshipper from the entirety of the rite, so also the withheld liturgical text serves to keep apart the priest from the lay. There is a secret language and a secret rite which hierarchizes the men of knowledge over the lay. The secret language of prayer operates at two levels: first, it may be inaudible, being said behind the *trisheela*; second, it may be audible but in Syriac, which is largely unknown to the people. Knowledge, secrecy and power combine to create a formal monolithic ecclesiastical structure against which the individual is pitted, with the latter's identity and function only to be understood in terms of the relation of the part to the whole.

The third term that Halliday uses is that of 'mode' or the channel of communication which is adopted. The complexity of the liturgical rite can only be understood with analogy to drama as Warner has done, and which I have attempted to capture.[45] Even though the enactment of the text takes various forms in song, chant, invocation, lamentation and mime, all of which I subsume under prayer as a general dialogic relation between Man–God, the text of the liturgy in the Syrian Christian case remains the corner-stone of the Syrian canonical rites.

In an essay called *The Death of the Author*, Barthes argues that writing entails the destruction of every voice, of every point of origin; where the subject slips away, where spaces which are neutral, composite and oblique are constructed 'the voice loses its origin.'[46] This is the very essence of the St James Liturgy as used by the Syrian Christians. Legend has it that it was instituted by Mary and the apostles and transcribed by St James.

Who is the author? This question becomes pertinent particularly when we are looking at sacred texts, which by their very nature seem to be revealed and inspired by God. Here more than anywhere else, the text becomes open to interpretation every time it is enunciated. While all Christians are united by the text in moments of collective worship, the text speaks to every individual Christian, at each rendering, in the manner that he requires. The voice of the author in this sense becomes separated from the text and unites with the listener to become his own voice. Thus, every text is both the collective voice of the Christian association and also an interpretation by each listener in the multi-dimensionality of his own personal and subjective experience.

Following Barthes, this time through the essay *Work to Text*, I wish to argue that unlike the 'work' which is a fragment, the 'text' is a methodological field. The liturgy, then, in this interpretation, is at once codified and formal and yet capable of multiple interpretations at the very moment of its enaction. Barthes writes that the text is not a coexistence of meanings but a passage, an overcrossing, it answers not an interpretation—even a liberal one—but an explosion, a dissemination. For the Christian, participation in the collective prayers of the liturgy symbolizes just such an explosion of meaning. It is a carving out through language a model of the universe. The images that are used by the text, while encoded and fixed through writing, are nevertheless polysemic.

Barthes captures the radical symbolicity of the text which like language is structured but without closure. It is in this sense that prayer is able to weave the collective and the individual through its mode of discourse, because while there is a collective frame within which a metaphor of the religious universe is constructed, it is the individual who, through his participation and subjective identity, gives this frame substance. Part of the power that liturgical prayer has upon the individual Christian is in terms of its function as a performative of ritual language. Here we are not so much concerned with the truth or falsehood of statements made in the liturgy as with the fact that through language, gesture or invocation, performance utterences are used to perform an action.[47] Ritual language is performative to the extent that here the speech act in some senses becomes an end in itself.

The performativeness of ritual language lies in its ability to construct a world where history and myth, past and present and future, mortal and immortal interpenetrate. As in the Anamnesis or Sacrificial Memorial, the people pray: 'We commemorate Thy death, O Lord, and Confess Thy Resurrection and await Thy Second Coming: May Thy blessings be—upon—us all.' The truth conditions of this semantic domain need not correspond to empirical reality. Cresswell offers the criterion that the truth of a sentence has to be understood with reference to the existence of 'a possible world' where such a truth may hold.[48] The prayers of the Public Celebration begin with an invocation which illustrates this idea:

Mary who brought Thee forth, and John who baptized Thee shall be suppliants unto Thee on our behalf. Have mercy unto us.

Scripture and its resource are called upon by this very enunciation. The Christian knows which Mary and which John are being referred to, and the images that are created take into account both the linearity of historical time and the closure of mythological space. By closure here I refer to the invariant roles that Mary as Mother and John as harbinger must play till the end of time.

Similarly, in the prayers of exit the deacons sing:

The Lord whom the seraphs and cherubs are afraid to behold, in wine and bread, is made manifest to the faithful on the altar.

Here language creates meanings through utterance which binds the listeners as ·one body, creating in Durkheimian terms a collective effervescence by which men believe themselves transported into an entirely different world.[49] It is in appreciation of this state that a Syrian Christian said: 'When the *trisheela* is parted, heaven is revealed to us.'

Therefore, liturgical prayer while being formal, rule-bound, structured and closed is in its subjective dimension plural, polysemic and open to interpretation. However, this subjective dimension is always rigorously defined by the dictates of the clergy who are keepers of the text, and deviance in interpretation is ecclesiastically defined as heresy. Subjective perceptions and religious experience are thus socially constructed and modelled upon the activities of the community.

Notes

1. Emile Durkheim and Marcel Mauss, *Primitive Classification* (London: Cohen and West, 1970), p. 81.
2. Ibid., p. 5.
3. Eviatar Zerubavel, *Hidden Rythms* (Chicago: University of Chicago Press, 1981).
4. Warner, *Family of God*.
5. Zemon Davis, *Society and Culture in Early Modern France*.
6. Edmund Leach, *Genesis as Myth and Other Essays* (London: Jonathan Cape, 1979).
7. See for e.g. Evans-Pritchard, *The Nuer*; Claude Larre, 'The Empirical Perception of Time and the Conception of History in Chinese Thought' in Louis Gardet (ed.), *Cultures and Time* (Paris: Unesco Press, 1976).
8. Pierre Bourdieu, *Outline of a Theory of Practice* (Cambridge: Cambridge University Press, 1979).
9. Ibid., p. 105.
10. *Anduthaksa* (Kottayam: CMS Press, 1982), p. 22.
11. Ibid., p. 5.
12. Ibid., p. 2.
13. Ibid., p. 13.
14. Ibid., p. 14.
15. Kadavil Paul, *The Orthodox Syrian Church*, p. 74.
16. *Anduthaksa*, p. 23.
17. Kadavil Paul, op. cit., p. 74.
18. Kadavil Paul, op. cit., p. 74–5.
19. Ibid., p. 52.
20. Ibid., p. 63.
21. Ibid., p. 63.
22. Ibid., pp. 71–4.
23. Kadavil Paul, op. cit., p. 58.
24. Exod. 7:9; Kadavil Paul, op. cit., p. 158.
25. Num. 21:8.
26. Psalm 51.
27. *Anduthaksa*, p. 91.

28. Ibid., p. 138.
29. Ibid., p. 147.
30. Ibid., p. 156.
31. Ibid., p. 157.
32. Ibid., p. 176.
33. Kadavil Paul, op. cit., p. 67.
34. *Anduthaksa*, p. 180.
35. Kadavil Paul, op. cit., p. 71.
36. E.E. Evans-Pritchard, op. cit.
37. Rodney Needham, *Belief, Language and Expeience* (Chicago: University of Chicago Press, 1972).
38. Victor Turner, *The Ritual Process: Structure and Anti-structure* (London: Routledge and Kegan Paul, 1969).
39. Abraham Joshua Heschel, *Quest for God* (New York: Cross-road, 1982).
40. Kaja Silverman, *The Subject of Semiotics* (Oxford: Oxford University Press, 1983), p. 18.
41. Charles Sanders Peirce, *Principles of Philosophy*, Vol. I. Collected papers. (Cambridge: The Beknap Press of Harvard University Press, 1974), pp. 143, 170.
42. Ibid., p. 143.
43. Ibid., p. 143.
44. M.A.K. Halliday, 'The Users and Uses of Language', in Joshua A Fishman (ed.), *The Sociology of Language* (The Hague: Mouton, 1968).
45. Warner, op. cit.
46. Roland Barthes, *Image-Music-Text* (Glasgow: Fontana Collins, 1977), p. 142.
47. J L Austin, 'Performative-Constative' in J R Searle (ed.), *The Philosophy of Language* (Oxford: Oxford University Press, 1974), p. 16.
48. M J Cresswell, 'Semantic Competence' in F Guenther and M Guenther-Reutter (eds.), *Meaning and Translation* (London: Duckworth, 1978), pp. 7–27.
49. Emile Durkheim, *The Elementary Forms of the Religious Life* (New York: Free Press, 1969), p. 258.

7

The Festivals of the Saints

The festivals of certain saints occupy a position of importance in the Syrian Christian canonical ritual calendar. These are ceremonies associated with Mary, the mother of Jesus, with St Thomas, His apostle, and with holy men who are deeply revered by the community, even if they are uncanonized. All such ritual events are categorized by Syrian Christians as commemorations, (*Orma divasam*) or festivals (*peryanaal*), and have certain features in common—the breaking of the fast, the advent of the pilgrimage, the conducting of a fair (*bazaar*) and, of course, the festivity. Their differences lie in the myths surrounding the saints associated with such feasts. In this context, Mary, St Thomas and the *bawa*s (Holy Fathers) have separate historical identities and distinctive personalities.

Several different kinds of problems arise in the analysis of these three kinds of festivals. In the festivals relating to St Mary, the key themes are the opposition between the official canonical church and the unofficial realms which surround it at the time of ritual and, on another level, the nature of female possession. The analysis of the festival of St Thomas raises questions relating to the place of the patron saint in the neighbourhood. A third set of problems centres around the cult of the holy men, including the position of the present Patriarch, and the respect accorded to him. Here, the nature of pilgrimage as an act of veneration and reflexivity is discussed, where the journey is as important as the arrival.

ST MARY'S FESTIVAL

The festival as fair becomes the meeting place between the official and the unofficial.[1] While the official world centres around the activities and events of the church: worship, prayers, hymn singing, oblations, penances, ritual bathing, works of charity and devotion, and the celebration of the Eucharist, the unofficial relates to the existence of a market based primarily on the motives of profit, social encounters between pilgrims, the buying and eating of food, and the purchase of odds and ends such as bangles, beads, pots and pans. These events are not related to the sacred in any primary sense. They are, nevertheless, manifestations of what we may term the fair, which acts as a celebratory circumference around the central official ecclesiastical code.

Space is a key symbol in the analysis of such temporary social relations. It demarcates the area of interaction between individuals and defines the nature of these relationships—casual, official or intimate—in terms of the meanings inherent in symbolic space. At the fair, the organized ecclesiastical world of Christianity comes into direct contact with popular and local effervescences of religious life as experienced by common people.

In terms of space and architecture, the interior becomes a symbol of the official, the exterior that of the unofficial. These categories are architecturally and hierarchically represented, and for purposes of description we may use certain representations: the interior of the church versus the courtyards, the inner versus the outer courtyards. The inner courtyard of the church, separated from the outer yards by a wall, consists of shops offering for sale those goods considered 'sacred' and 'sold' by the church to devotees: oil for lighting the sacred lamps, calendars and holy pictures, and what Febvre has called the literature of the colportege.[2] In the outer courtyards are sold everyday articles necessary for the pilgrims, who spend days in the open as they pray and fast, waiting for a miracle to unfold.

Bakhtin, in a pathbreaking interpretation of Rabelais's work, has shown how the carnivals of medieval Europe built a second world and a second life outside officialdom. For a time, people entered the Utopian realm of community, freedom, equality and abundance.[3] While the carnival in the Western sense is absent among Syrian Christians, the festival nevertheless provides these very images of unstructuring. This is explicit in the congregation of crowds, where 50,000 or more people may be found at any one moment on a festival day at a pilgrim spot dedicated to Mary. In the overflowing canopies constructed to shelter pilgrims, those who are in need of miracles and spiritual succour come into close, yet socially peripheral contact. The human body, at such moments, is unbound from the traditional strictures of convention. In the life of the tents, unmindful of the proximity of others, the private and the personal are rendered public and collective. Individuals are bound together by the social bond of pilgrimage which transcends community, neighbourhood and locality.

In the festival dedicated to St Mary, celebrated after eight days of fasting, the act of pilgrimage itself—of 'getting there'—is not as important as the manner in which the Christian conducts herself at the pilgrim spot. The route is of little significance but, at the church, activity is of a clearly intense ritual nature, marked by fasting, prayer, eucharistic celebration and ritual bathing.

Mary is venerated here as the Mother of Jesus; as one who is in a close biographical and spiritual relation to Christ. The first miracle that Jesus brought about occurred at Cana, through her intervention. Nothing is too trivial to take to her; she is primarily a woman and a mother. I was told:

A man does not understand when food or drink runs short at a wedding. These are the matters of the kitchen. Yet so many small things make up our life which are ordinary and of no importance to anyone other than ourselves—these we take to the Mother.

It is to the mediators (Mary and the saints) that the people take their temporal concerns—birth, disease, marriage, money, lost property, litigation and employment. In some sense, then, there is a division of labour between the mediators and Christ, for while the spiritual life is almost entirely in the hands of Christ (penance, repentance, fasting, abstinence, prayer and the Eucharist), the mundane is relegated to the saints and holy men. The accusation that Christ is forgotten in this process may be levelled against miracle-seekers, but it has its own rhetorical counter-argument that because human beings are sinners, they approach the saints, who are holy, to mediate with God on their behalf.

The festivals dedicated to St Mary also show how such events may provide avenues for individual and social transformation.[4] However, it must be noted that these festivals, compared with the *Moranaya Peryanaal* (Feasts of the Lord), are celebrated with less rigour and here canonical dictates are fewer. In this context, the 'second life' of the people emerges. Here, as opposed to the purity and the clear demarcations of the liturgical form as expressed through the central symbol of eucharistic worship, we have the expressions of the temporal, the material, even the grotesque. In the festivals of the mediators man expresses his corporeal self. The humiliations of the body, the expression of physical and mental torment, are explicitly made possible and socially condoned. There is ecclesiastical laxity here as opposed to canonical rigour. This is why the saints' festivals express the potentially open nature of a belief system, bringing about the possibilities of change and transformation, for in the very slackening of the canonical imperative lies the possibility of changes in forms of faith and beliefs. The festival is a celebratory but liminal phase, lying between the profane life as anticipating transformation and the profane life as transformed. It then corresponds to what Turner expresses as a scene and time for the emergence of a society's deepest values in the form of sacred dramas and objects; but it *may* also be the venue and occasion for the most radical scepticism about cherished values and rules.[5] The self-reflexivity brought about by liminality and impending communitas is the central dynamic of the festival.

In this context, the grotesque becomes an important element for analysis. According to Bakhtin, the grotesque image reflects a phenomenon in transformation of which death, birth, growth and becoming are the unfinished stages of metamorphosis.[6] Further, he argues that the theme of madness is used in the grotesque to escape the false 'truth of this world' in order to look at the world with eyes free from this 'truth'. The importance to us of such an analysis becomes clear when we look at cases of possession which are particularly frequent at the festival associated with Mary at Mannarkadu Church, near Kottayam.

In line with the data, states of possession may be viewed as expressions of individual anxieties or neuroses, but in the dramaturgical and liminal frame of the festival, they are articulated in codes which are mystical, and become legitimate avenues for certain forms of social expression. These may be anti-ecclesiastical and subversive but being, ostensibly, expressions of the Holy Spirit, are accepted not always as mental disturbance but often as prophetic and revelatory. In all these cases the grotesque is not opposed to the sacred. By rebelling against a given order, possession in fact re-establishes and confirms the legitimacy of the given order.[7]

Ettu Noimbu: The Festival of St Mary (The Eight-Day Lent)

The festivals devoted to the cult of Mary express the close relation of mortal beings to the Christ through the person of Mary. The most important festival in Mary's honour is one which culminates the eight days of Lent called the *Ettu Noimbu*. In its very largeness of dimension, it takes on the nature of a festival, typifying an overabundance of prayer and piety. This festival of Mary is, however, non-canonical—it is not present in the official calendar of festivals and is in some measure suppressed by the Church. Informants say that this period of Lent grew spontaneously from the hearts of women; it is celebrated by all those who have faith and are in need. The eucharistic services offered at this time are attended mainly by women. I wish to show that this non-canonical yet ostentatiously celebrated fast is in fact an avenue for emotional catharsis, particularly for women. Women speak to the priests at this time with a freedom born out of a role-identity with Mary, and in this freedom from restraint, they allow for the possibility of transformation of given ecclesiastical structures. However, such occasions for the liberation of speech are not frequent, and are guarded against by the priests.

In a more canonically positive sense, Mary is the ideal image of the Mother, and in the folk imagination she becomes the symbol of fertility. The importance that Mary has for barren or expectant women is explicit in the following account:

> Before the birth of Christ there was knowledge of His coming, through prophecy and the placement of stars. Many of the women of the land fasted and prayed that the Messiah be born in their womb, that they be the one chosen by God to carry the Saviour.

Mary, as the chosen one, becomes an object of veneration for the expectant mother or for childless women seeking a miracle. Further, Mary is described as being someone who has experienced sorrow and is therefore most easily approached by supplicants:

> She was always fleeing enemies in the early years; it could not, then, have been easy bringing up a young boy who by the time he was twelve years old was already in the quest of his Father. Which mother can see her son tortured and crucified, watch his pain in death? If she could suffer so much in her life how well she must understand our human pains and sorrows.

The life of Mary, though known to the people through apocrypha, is recapitulated through the discourses of priests on festival days. At these times, *dhyana prasangam* ('meditative discourses') occur. Notably, along with sermons, scriptural plays and songs, oration is closely related to the culture of the festival. It is an ecclesiastical art that bases itself on the text of the Bible and using it as a springboard elaborates threads of emotion that may not be found in the Bible itself. In the Orthodox Syrian Church, it clearly draws from apocryphal traditions. Oration is an art whereby the mythological imagination of people is given rein and with the bare structure of a story, the priests produce a tale which novelistically brings the people close to an event that occurred almost two thousand years ago.

All the various aspects of Mary as she emerges in the accounts of people cannot be discussed within the scope of this book. What is important is that she is revered as a symbol of maternity. In her goodness, Mary serves to bring the people into a closer relationship with Jesus Christ, who is, in fact, more feared than loved by Syrian Christians. The face that they visualize most often is perhaps that of the angry Jesus, who will separate the sheep from the goats on Judgement Day. One reason why the Church wishes to de-emphasize the cult of Mary is perhaps because of the greater affective feeling that Orthodox Syrians have for her, in contrast to their awe of Jesus. Mary serves as a very important model for the women who are in many ways the heart of the Church, for it is they who sustain it through their loyalty and devotion. Informants say that if the women are steadfast, and bring up their children as Mary would, the moral code would remain strong.

The *Ettu Noimba* feast of Mary commemorates her Immaculate Conception.[8] It is most ostentatiously celebrated in a town called Mannarkadu which lies some miles away from Puthenangadi. Many people come from far-off places and spend the week there, sheltered from the sun and wind by just a palm-thatched canopy erected outside the church. Most pilgrims are accompanied by their families, including infants. They cook their own food, and sleep on reed mats spread out on the gravel. Fortunately, at this time there is no rain at all, it being a break between the monsoons. In the morning, rows of wood fires are started on the side of the shelter. Abstinence and ritual purity being associated with *noimba* or Lent, *Ettu Noimba* involves vegetarianism, fasting, ritual ablutions, and the wearing of clean white clothes. The churchyard turns into a large domestic area, with food cooking on small fires and clothes drying on the gravel.

The food cooked in the morning is usually boiled tapioca. People who genuinely observe Lent do not eat meat, fish or eggs, or partake of milk, curds, butter or buttermilk. Women are often heard criticizing those who break this norm for such people are, in effect, refusing to make a sacrifice in honour of Mary. Women, more than men, observe the Feast of Mary, and rigidly observe the rules of prayer at the expected hour, and maintain the required abstentions in diet.

Between the church and the public thoroughfares lies the market-place. Here congregate the sellers and buyers of religious goods, ornaments, pots, pans and refreshments. This is a market typical of its kind, with beggars weaving through the crowds. Water and lime juice are sold out of buckets by men walking around in the sun and calling out to people. Children selling candles in packets with bright crudely-etched pictures of the Holy Family run through the crowds. Candles are an important element in worship, since all those who say a prayer to Mary light a candle in her name.

Three types of market-places are seen to coalesce here: the market organized by the church authorities, the market that springs up temporarily around the church as a result of the congregation of itinerant pedlars on land auctioned for rent during festival time by the church, and thirdly, the market of Mannarkadu hamlet which has organized itself on the main streets near the church, and is a permanent fixture catering to the interests of devotees during the whole year.[9] Bargaining is an accepted form of interaction between sellers and buyers, and is conducted in loud voices, with threats of departure made by customers being counteracted by sellers making the motion of putting away items under consideration. Underlying this is what Geertz has called 'the shadow price of time' which takes into account that one needs to know not only how to bargain, but for how long.[10]

This market with its beggars and festival merchants ends at the gate leading to the inner courtyards of the church. But within the inner courtyard exists and flourishes a different kind of market—the one run by the church. As in Sefrou, the religious institution here does not merely sanction trade, it engages in it.[11]

Here are stalls where coupons are sold for the saying of *Qurbana*, a custom which has existed for centuries, and was in fact one of those elements of Eastern Christianity that the sixteenth century Portuguese ritual colonists were most offended by. Here economic considerations predominate over ritual ones. Members of the church sit as cashiers collecting money (fifty paise for each person for whom *Qurbana* is said), and writing out receipts. This custom has to be seen in the light of the institution of church and priesthood as it traditionally existed, where the income of the church came from such daily offerings of devotees. One part of the *Qurbana pannam* or money goes to the priest, a smaller fraction to his deacon, and the largest part to the church for its maintenance, and the buying of incense, candles, bread and wine. The amount of money that comes into the coffers of the churches associated with miracles and divine healing is popularly thought to be phenomenal. An informant said, 'The priests slip on the oil and silver that devotees bring to the church' (*Achenmaar ennaem vellilu thennunu*). This is not a metaphorical remark about possibly venal priests and overflowing coffers; it is a literal statement.

Stalls with banners proclaiming what is being sold can be seen all around the church. In one shop *Qurbana*s may be paid for; in another, children are dedicated to the church (*adima kodukuga*). This act entails the gifting of a rupee to the church and receiving in return a receipt showing that a child has been accepted and dedicated to Mary. There are shops where one may buy candles, others where religious tracts and pictures are sold, still others where *prasadam* (divine offerings which are edible) is given in exchange for money. The most interesting of these transactions is one where deacons sell tiny silver replicas of various parts of the human body. These are bought and dedicated to the saint by people in the hope that there will be a regeneration or restoration of diseased or amputated limbs or organs.

These days, though, things are done differently. A devotee comes to the deacon in charge of the stall and, offering some money, says, 'Please give me an eye'. The man at the counter says, as he has said to countless others:

> Just put whatever money you like in the box, and take the whole pile in your hands, and pray to the *Matav* (Mother) for whatever you need. There is everything in the pile.

After having done this, the woman relinquishes the replicas. The next person in the line asking for a 'leg' or 'hand' is delivered the same quick staccato speech. This changes the practice whereby, formerly, a devotee bought himself a silver replica which he offered personally to Mary, by putting it into the offertory box near the sanctuary. By telescoping sequences as the church has done in this case, there is distortion. The commercial aspect dominates, with the devotee reduced to a figure in a queue, conscious of other 'customers' pushing him from behind yet believing, nevertheless, in the magical powers of the silver models which he holds for a moment in the palm of his hand. The church keeps both money and talisman, renting the latter out by the moment where, earlier, it had to go through the trouble of collecting the silver dropped in the offertory and translating it back to currency. In some senses, the gift relationship turns itself into a contractual one.[12]

Three spaces have thus been marked: the outer courtyard, the inner courtyard, and the church. The church has an open verandah called the *nadashala* which mediates the western entry and the inner courtyard. The church expresses a closed space for the enactment of the liturgy; it is holy, closed, an official space. It is also a male bastion in the ecclesiastical sense that the priests and servers who are the controllers of the ceremony are male. However, this situation is challenged by the transformative functions of the festival through the role of women in the paranormal situation of possession. In fact, cases of possession present themselves in the guise of prophetic transformative gestures and statements.

Cases of *bhadam* or possession are often recorded at Mannarkadu but they rarely occur inside the church at the time of *susrusa* or service. Here, in the interior of the church, in the midst of spiritual discourses, priests often taken the opportunity of cautioning devotees of spiritual danger. A prelate said:

> There are some among you who believe that Mary speaks through the mouths of certain people here—that is wrong. The blessedness of Mary cannot be expressed in the tone and manner of those who swear they speak in her name—that is some other experience. Some say that I have the power to heal given to me by Mary—that is also wrong. And among you there is a man who blows on water that you bring him saying that Mary has given him *shakti* (power) which he infuses into the water—he merely pollutes the water with his breath, there is no effect on it, and none of your sick will be healed.

Yet again, these are the occasions for elaborating the myth of the Virgin. The priests legitimize the place of the relic in Christian belief, for instance, through the telling of such tales:

> When Mary died, she was an old woman of seventy. By her bedside the apostles were gathered, except for Thomas who was

at that moment in India. Christ appeared and asked her what
boon she would like to leave to the world. She answered that
whoever should pray to her should receive whatever was asked,
and this was granted to her.

For Thomas, who was again absent, having set out on apostolic
missions, she threw down her sash as she ascended to heaven—a
sign of her death and *swarg arhonam* (ascension). This he took to
the Apostles on his return, showing that he knew the time of her
ascension, for she had given him proof of it.

A fragment of this sash (*arra kettu*) was brought to Mannarkadu by
the Patriarch of Antioch and installed at St Mary's Church in 1982,
immediately becoming the subject of intense ritual veneration. While
it represents spiritual power, it expresses also the continuity of the
historical episode. Bones of saints, fragments of their clothing, are
statements of mortality that evoke the temporal or material aspects of
the divine or holy. In this context, the exhibition of the relic is of great
ritual importance.

On the second day of the fast, the relic, which till then been
concealed from the public gaze, was taken around the church in a
ceremonial procession. While going in procession around the church,
the prelate and priests wore the celebratory vestments made of brocade
normally worn during the *Qurbana*. Multi-coloured canopies were
held above them, the believers following with lighted candles. The
relic was on view for a very few days. As a result, it was always
obscured from general view by the great numbers of people milling
around it. Those who prostrated themselves or spent too much time
rapt in devotion before the relic were prodded on by volunteers. The
order that is to be maintained in the queue thus becomes of greater
significance than the actual experience of veneration before a relic,
which cannot ideally be measured in moments of time.

Outside the church, in the inner courtyard, stands a large stone
cross. Here, sacred oil is distributed by retainers and assistants of the
priests. Tempers are constantly fraying for the sun is hot, and the
devout fight each other for access to the oil. When the *Vishudha
Qurbana* (Holy Sacrifice) is being celebrated, there are long periods of
meditative stillness in the middle of which one can hear clearly the din
of holy-oil seekers and the infuriated cries of the man who seeks to
bring order among them, screaming 'Edda, podda!' (You, get going!)
as he boxes the ears of the bolder ones.

Around this central granite cross on the western courtyard of the church one may see various symbolic forms of penance. There are those who dripping from a bath in the holy tank, appear wet and bedraggled, to crawl several times on all fours around the cross on the rough gravel. At the end of this penitential exercise, their knees and hands are grazed, and they weep with exhaustion. They stop each time they approach the church to lift their arms and pray.

The most abandoned in expression and devout in manner are the Hindu women, usually of lower caste, who can be marked out as different both by their apparel as well as by their stance, which exhibits an unease not found on Christian faces or body postures. They call out loud prayers to the cross, addressed to the *Matav* (Mother), asking for blessings, for forgiveness, for prayers to be answered. With candles lit and held in uplifted hands, tears stream down the faces of these devotees as they pray loudly, crying out their woes to Mary, unconscious of the hot wax falling on their fingers. The poor come with large bottles instead of the small plastic containers sold by the church stalls to collect oil. This infuriates Korah, the man in charge, who is perpetually angry, bare-chested and betel chewing, and ready to fell the pilgrims 'like so many hogs'. From his perspective, the poor whom he blatantly abuses take away more than they give. The balance of exchange must be maintained: people must make an offering of oil as well as take away some, and it is Korah who sees to the pouring out and the taking away, to make sure that the latter does not exceed the former.

States of possession are most frequently encountered among pilgrims around this stone cross. The other arena for transformative vision is the sacred tank where, according to legend, a sacred serpent resides, which bites the feet of the arrogant, causing them to lose control of themselves and behave peculiarly. These states have to be defined as *bhadam* by onlookers to have legitimacy, otherwise the crowds dismiss it as '*thallael sukham illa*' (not well in the head). This distinction between spirit manifestation (whether good or malefic) and psychological imbalance is one made by the people themselves.

In September 1982, I saw three cases of *bhadam* or *thullal* (leaping, or religious frenzy). The first of these took place at the western entrance of the church. Here there is a large sheltered porch of considerable length and breadth. Covered by a roof, it is open on three sides, the fourth being the western wall of the church, with its main door. Standing here, it is possible to see the beautiful painting of Mary and the Christ child, an object of particular veneration exposed to public view only on the seventh and eighth day of the fast. All week, this porch or *nadashala* is full of people struggling to enter the church or gain a glimpse of the portrait of the Mother and Child.

On the eighth day, the porch was illuminated by a large traditional bronze lamp called *nilla villuka*. It was about four feet in height, its head carved in the shape of a cross. People kept pouring coconut oil into the lamp's large shallow oil container. Small cotton wicks were lit by devotees who crossed themselves with fingers dipped in the holy oil. The flames rose higher and brighter as more wicks were added.

Around this lamp the *cendakar* (drummers) ranged themselves. With consummate skill they began their drumming, the rhythm growing faster and more urgent till it reached a crescendo, ending only to start all over again. To the surprise and excitement of the people watching, a woman appeared and began going around the lamp in a strange, stylized, self-conscious series of movements. With fractured twists of the body, she grimaced at the fire, shook her fist at it, reached towards the flame, withdrew, and then repeated these movements. The crowd cried, '*Thullal aa! thullal aa!*' (What is implied here is that someone is in a state of frenzy.) The crowd at once swelled. Old women in the crowd crossed themselves because *bhada* and *thullal* both imply that a devil or an evil spirit has, in the presence of holiness, been forced to state its presence.

The possessed woman said nothing at that time, seemingly unaware of her audience, and continued her frantic posturing and gesturing. At times she knelt and with exaggerated piety looked at the picture of the *Matav* and the Christ child hanging in the sanctuary. Then, rising again, she began her contortions. Women in the front lines of the semicircle that had formed around her cried, 'Cover your head!' every time she made a gesture of obedience to the Mother, but she lost their sympathy by refusing to do so.

That she was not a true case of 'possession' was expressed by some onlookers, who described her as *kirki* (cracked) and not well in the head. Nevertheless, it being a spectacle, they continued to crowd around her. For half an hour she moved in the same stylized manner to the beating of drums, with no change of movement other than the three or four basic steps, saying nothing. Then the *cendakar* stopped, and one of them came to her angrily and said, 'What are you doing here? This is a sacred place.' She replied in a high cracked voice, 'I am waiting for my Mother who is in the crowd.' A man in the crowd interpreted this to mean: 'She is waiting for the *Matav*.'

Exactly at that moment, a woman ran into the centre of the crowd, her husband following, and attempting to restrain her. She screamed and prostrated herself before the lamp. Attention was at once diverted from the first to the second 'possessed' woman. The facial expressions and gestures of the first 'possessed' woman pronounced very clearly that she disliked having attention diverted from her. She looked angry and stopped her contortions. She tied her loose hair into a tight knot, adjusted the folds of her sari (like an actor with a moment's reprieve from the audience setting his costume in place) and with an irritated expression on her face, sat down with her palms folded together in an attitude of meditation in front of the lamp.

The second woman, being possessed by a far wilder spirit, was up in one sudden movement, and with her body half-bent and hands outstretched cried, *'mareen, mareen'* (move, move). That segment of the crowd to which this was addressed hastily made space. With incredible speed, half-doubled over still, she rushed out, followed by her husband. She fell into a stupor in the front of the large granite cross, where she lay in the sun for many hours, before being taken away by her husband.

As the second woman lay quiet, the first one arose and began what now seemed to people her repetitive actions and, finding these monotonous, the crowd melted away. The drummers having fulfilled their traditional obligation to the *Matav* went out of the porch. People began gathering in orderly queues for the *Ucca Namaskaram* (noonday prayers) and the 'possessed' woman disappeared into the crowds outside.

Both cases of possession were viewed with interest and some distaste by the Syrian Christians for one clear reason: both were lower-caste Hindu women. Syrian Christians believe that it is mainly those individuals who are not prepared to meet the holy who are thus broken down and beaten and shamed by supernatural forces. There is a certain lack of clarity in the manner in which they view such individuals. At one level there is empathic concern, at another, disquiet. They are, in any case, never sure what sort of spirit it is that grips such a person and view these events as reminders that they must keep the rules of the fast, pray, and be virtuous, so that they too are not reduced to dust. An informant said to me,

My brother's wife was overcome once at Mannarkadu. She screamed and cried and prayed in a loud voice. We were all so ashamed, and when we went home, my brother gave her a shouting.

Such attitudes toward *bhadam* underline the restraint which the Syrian Christian believes is essential to the form that worship must take. The cult of Mary is in fact continuously de-emphasized by the church in some measure because it offers an avenue for protest which cuts into the rigour of ecclesiastical covention. Only in a situation like Mannarkadu can a woman shake her fist at a priest (under the influence of 'a spirit') and say,

I will write to *bawa* (Patriarch) and tell him what exactly goes on here, how you priests behave.

The priest replied:

Go and state the case instead to the *Matav*. She will listen to you and correct your grievances. Go to her with tears and prayers.

Mary is viewed as the symbol of purity, of innocence and grace (as opposed to anger and rebelliousness) and by his tone, the priest strongly conveyed this belief. Informants constantly reiterate that those who are possessed are people who are conscious of their own importance and so God makes them come to realize their own insignificance. Secondly, usually, people who are possessed have not prepared themselves to meet the holy. Divine revelation makes them mad. Thirdly, it is believed that Hindus, who think Mary to be a manifestation of Meenakshi, become possessed because they, as a community, have greater ability to worship without restraint, unlike Christians who cannot go beyond a certain level of religious experience, and are ashamed if they exceed their limits. For these reasons Syrian Christians sometimes prepare for *Ettu Noimba* with great stringency, for their dread of being made to prostrate forcefully before the Divine is very great. However, it must be underlined that this is seen, for the most part, as a woman's fast, and often the men laugh and say, '*Penangle andakiye noimba aa*' (A fast which the women have made). One woman said to a neighbour,

My husband wouldn't mind eating meat and fish, but out of fear of his mother, who keeps the fast stringently, we don't cook or buy any fish or meat.

Certainly, the number of women who visit Mannarkadu far outnumbers the men, particularly, women who have come with their children. This is pointed out as being an expression of the fact that Mary is the *Matav* associated therefore with motherhood and all its joys and cares. In their sermons, however, the priests constantly reiterate that *Ettu Noimba* is often an expression of selfish and individualistic desires. A young priest sermonized:

> What is it that you pray for? Is it for the orphans in Vietnam? Is it for the Palestinians who are being wiped out by the Israelis, for those in your country who are flooded out of their homes? No, it is for yourselves, your children. You ask for jobs, for bridegrooms, for health. I am not saying that you should not do this, but rather that you must pray for a fuller life, for stronger spiritual conviction, for the grace of God. When you sit here in church, fasting and praying and lighting candles, remember to examine your hearts—ask why you are here, what you are praying for, and what God's answer to you should be.

There are often in these sermons words of caution and injunction. A visiting prelate said:

> It is clear that there are among our people those who lay more importance to this fast in honour of Mary than they do to the lenten period before Easter in remembrance of the Passion. If you put Mary before Christ, if you pray to Mary while forgetting Christ, it is a grave error. Remember that Mary is nothing without the grace of God, that she is nothing without Christ. She, as the Mother, never pushed herself forward for attention. She always said, 'Do as He commands,' pointing to the Christ. So those of you who do not have the freedom to go straight to Christ to ask for that which you seek, you will receive nothing by going to Mary.

In all these sermons, the priests constantly cry out that the hierarchy of Jesus over Mary, and, implicitly, male versus female, as well as the official versus the unofficial, the canonical versus the non-canonical, must be maintained.

The third case of 'possession' I have recorded shows that while such a state of being may be clothed in the symbols of religion, it may nevertheless be conflicts of other social ties that are thus expressed, such as the natal versus the conjugal. This time, the woman was a

Syrian Christian but again of lower class status. Her husband constantly tried to restrain her but she would shake his arm off and scream to those listening,

> He is Satan. If it were my father or my brothers, they would have let me stand here to ·pray. For some time here, I was happy calling out to the *Matav*, but see, the devil pulls at my arm.

Shaking off his hand, she raised her head to look at the noonday sun, and with sweat and tears pouring down her face began calling out again to Mary. Part of her long speech included admonitions to the crowd, moral injunctions to lead a good life coupled with statements such as,

> All of you must take home with you a bowl of *pachor* [here, the *prasadam* of the *Matav*, to be bought in church stalls]. It is the gift of the *Matav*. It will heal you of all sickness if you eat of it. Remember your dead too, because they are always with you.

The people responded to her with nods and statements like,

> She speaks the truth. We forget the dead but to do that is wrong.

Some people stayed on to listen as if she were a seer whose words were of importance. However, to many it seemed evident that the woman was highly disturbed mentally, and they moved away casting sympathetic glances at her husband, who was holding the woman's wrists and not looking at the faces in the crowd. At times, the woman jeered and mocked Mary saying, 'Do you not know that those who come here seek their ends alone?'

At this, the crowd would quickly disperse, but new faces, attracted by her screams, congregated. A woman said to me, 'She is being troubled by evil spirits, but she is fighting them.'

The woman who was possessed believed, however, that she was moved by a wise spirit, and constantly exhorted the people to listen to her, believe in God, and go in faith. She said that those who understood the importance of what she was saying would be blessed. Her speech was heavily laced with religious imagery; looking at the sky, she spoke of Mary travelling on the clouds in all her beauty. She sang in a high, parched voice familiar songs about the grace of Mary but the crowd did not join her, afraid to lend her voice legitimacy, and believing her to be either mad or possessed by evil spirits.

At this, she grew angry and spoke of Christ on the cross. She described in detail the thirst He had suffered, the heat, the pain, the people staring at Him, both believers and unbelievers; she spoke even of the flies and the blood drying on His head. The women surrounding her were visibly moved by her description. She turned on them in sudden rage:

> No one to give water to Him then, and no one now to quench my thirst. Look on these people, Lord, who come as if to a market-place to stare at the tormented and the beggars.

Then she turned her anger on the skies, to Mary, and laughed so wildly that her husband became anxious and begged her to come into the shade, to drink some water, to come into the church with him and pray. However, the woman began screaming again that the man clutching at her arm was indeed Satan. An onlooker said to me:

> The *bhadam* is strong now. It will leave her only when she has expressed all her fear. She was all right when she came, she did not even know she had these devils in her fighting for control. It happened to her when she was attending the *Qurbana*. They will surely leave her because she prays.

The woman's husband finally managed to take her away, but on parting she said to the crowd:

> Satan is always like this. Just as I have reached a state of happiness he pulls my arm, and I must go. But Satan is my husband and I must leave with him. If it had been my father or my brothers they would have let me stay.

On the day in question, all three cases I observed were those of women, viewed for the main part by the Syrian Christian crowd as if they were pathological. No one joined the possessed women or imitated their actions, even in hymn singing, because that would entail too close an identification with them, and who knows the nature of such possession?

Informants admit that it is mostly women who are thus moved but are not clear what induces such a state. *Thullal* is associated with the 'recognition' of the Holy Spirit, its existence, its power: one sees God and is reduced to nothing, one goes into a state of exhilaration and near-madness. *Bhadam* is associated with evil spirits, and in earlier times such people were exorcized by priests; present-day priests prefer to dissociate themselves from these happenings. In fact, informants said that cases of *bhadam* were fewer that year because the official prelate had spoken strongly against it:

> There are many who speak, pretending to be the voice of the saints but it is a sin to believe them. If the Holy Spirit enters any one, his faculties are made finer, his knowledge more pure. Believing in the prophecies of men and women who desecrate the sacred places of God is a sin.

If *bhadam*—malefic possession—enters more women than men, it is thought to be because women are more readily frightened than men. Where there is fear and lack of hope, there is place for evil spirits. Fear implies for Christians lack of confidence in God. However, what such disturbed people say is often taken to be true, and even interpreted by a few as expressions of the angry Holy Spirit. One woman screaming near the stone cross was heard to say, 'God, tell these priests not to step on the child.' No child was in evidence but people interpreted this to mean the suppression of the innocence of the Christ child by ecclesiasts, saying to each other, 'She speaks correctly'. In Bakhtinian terms, this is the mode whereby, through the second language of the fair, rebirth occurs. The grotesque is the passage mediating between classic, official, hierarchic, pure forms, and the possibility of an entirely new ecclesiastical event or form. The rejection of the *Ettu Noimba* by church officials can be understood only in these terms.

By force of circumstance, the relationship of the people to their priests is basically weak. Priests, as a class, are often thought to exploit the church for their own material gains. Informants reiterate that their spiritual needs are not adequately met, that priests are more concerned with the collection of *Qurbana pannam* and with 'going over' from one ecclesiastical persuasion to the other with the blowing of each litigational wind. Allegations made about the inefficiency of the clergy have to be understood in relation to the long history of crises and feuds in this church. Yet, without priests, the *Qurbana* cannot be experienced; they are the axis on which corporate worship—so important to the Syrian Christian—rests.

On another level, official feasts (the best examples of which are those which celebrate the life of Christ) exemplify the male as opposed to the non-canonical feast of the Mother, which expresses the female and the non-official. These festivals are dominated by the sanctury as theatre space where the eucharistic drama of the Christ is enacted, the players or celebrants again being male. The *madabaha* becomes a stage, the devotees being the audience—passive worshippers who are yet respondents to the main themes articulated by the celebrants. In the non-canonical feast of Mary, the priests are less important than the devotees, who are mainly female. More important than the Eucharist is the veneration of an image of St Mary, and her relic. Nevertheless, some coincidences between Passion Week and *Ettu Noimba* exist as the same number of days are spent at church. However, the Passion Week liturgy celebrates death and resurrection while the Feast of Mary celebrates temporal life. Both are in some ways reversals of the other:

Mother	vs.	Son
Birth	vs.	Death and Resurrection
Female	vs.	Male
Temporal	vs.	Spiritual
Material	vs.	Incorporeal
Life	vs.	Death and Afterlife

Further, the closed nature of the eucharist-oriented, liturgical feasts associated with the Christ allow for fewer cultural interpretations. They are canonically defined as opposed to the festivals of the saints, which are more open to cultural influences from the outside. Saints' festivals are open to the second language of the fair and market-place, and to the effects of communitas and anti-structure.

ST THOMAS THE APOSTLE: KURUSAOOPEN

The Christians of Puthenangadi have various kinds of places of worship: first, there are significant pilgrim spots whose churches may be associated with a monastery, for instance, Devalokam or Pazhe Seminary; second, parish churches with their stable congregations such as St Mary's Church, Pazheangadi, commonly known to the residents of Puthenangadi as Cherya Palli; third, the miracle churches with their own parishes but whose importance lies in the large floating population of devotees, such as St Mary's Church, Mannarkadu. Fourthly, there are chapels where Eucharist may be celebrated but not the life-cycle rituals as in Kurisu Palli, Puthenangadi. Finally, there are the *Kurusunthotti*, the wayside shrines or granite crosses to which people make ritual obeisance, and which are found everywhere.

Miracle churches have a significant floating population attached to them which, in the main, comprises pilgrims visiting from afar. The strength of the miracle church is reflected in the income or *varumannam* that the church receives, this being a concrete expression of the piety of devotees, translated into architecturally ornate churches as well as the building of colleges, schools and hospitals. Parish priests of lesser-known churches where miracles have not taken place tend to view miracle churches askance:

What does a church mean when there is no sense of congregation together? They come there and pray, each for his own, and their attachment is to the church as a building, and to the fact that it is known for its miracles. To worship God one must see further than one's own personal and often petty needs.

A miracle church can be understood only in terms of the beneficience of the presiding saint. The presence of a saint in a church is conceived of by the people as something intangible, inexplicable and powerful—the holy as *mysterium tremendum*.[13] But the saint is someone who can be 'sent' away by falseness and betrayal. An informant told me that,

Due to quarrels among the parishioners of my natal village church, St Paul, the keeper of the church, left it. Since then it is empty (*shoonya*), there is no power (*shakti*).

The church then becomes a shell holding the accoutrements of worship, but the believer knows that it is empty, a profaned place lacking in grace.

People often state that the importance of the miracle church lies in the miraculous acts thought to be performed by saintly mediators. Consequently, it is they who are approached most often, and not Jesus

Christ. This is clearly a symbolic reflection of the distance between Man and God, evoked in this comment:

> Sometimes we are too poor in spirit to approach God ourselves. If it were not for the saints, sometimes we may feel hesitant to ask God for the things we need. It is not that we worship the saints, but that we ask them to help us, mediate for us.

St Thomas is the patron saint of Kurisu Palli, and indeed of all Puthenangadi. He is called *Kurisaoopen* or old man of the cross, loved and revered by all the residents of Puthenangadi even though the church quarrel has served to escalate his position *vis-a-vis* one group (the Catholicos's party), and undermine it in relation to the other (the Patriarch's party). The notion of the patron saint is a common one in Kerala, and every locality has its own church, associated with a particular patron to whom the residents owe an affectual loyalty. St Thomas is without doubt the patron of Puthenangadi—so much so that expostulations of surprise and fear are often prefaced with '*Ende* (My) *Kurusaoopa*'. Pictures of St Thomas are found in many houses: in these he is depicted as a small-statured man. Many homes also have pictures of Malayatur, a beautiful hill where Thomas is believed to have often retreated to pray and be in meditative solitude. For Christians in Puthenangadi, a pilgrimage to Malayatur is something to be desired, specially since it is a place associated with miracles, and where one may actually see a small footprint in the rock, believed to be that of St Thomas. At one level, informants admit that there is no proof by which the legends of conversion by St Thomas may be validated, but they also say that 'there are too many stories about Thomas and these must have some base in truth'. The miracles that Thomas performed are often recollected and form part of a coherent oral tradition.

St Thomas continues to perform miracles even today and Kurisu Palli is frequently and vehemently described as having St Thomas's *shakti* or power. Acharya Chovati, an old, low-caste Hindu woman has lived in the shadow of the church all her life, her family having been associated with Puthenangadi and Kurisu Palli in the function of a serving caste for seven generations. Every Friday it was her custom to light a lamp in honour of *Kurusaoopen*. In 1981 she was eighty years old; her story represents the compelling influence that St Thomas has on all the residents of Puthenangadi.

I never pass the church without saying a prayer to *Kurusaoopen*. He has helped me whenever I have needed help and sometimes when I thought that there was no way, he has shown miracles to me. My husband died, my son was an alcoholic. I could not live with my brothers for the shame that my son's ways brought on us. I went to Jacob Saar one day and told him, 'Even a crow has a nest and I have nothing.' He was off somewhere and had no time for me. Hopeless and despairing, I went to Kurisu Palli and there I prayed for a long time. I looked at *Kurusaoopen* (referring to a portrait), and I saw him then, not as a person, but as *shakti*. I said, '*Kurusaoopen*, help me. First, I need a house, a small house on a small piece of land, so that I can take my son and his wife away from my brothers' house without bringing any more shame to them.' I prayed that my son would drink no more. 'I am old, *Kurusaoopen* must help me so that I can have somewhere to live. I prayed for many days, wept and prayed again.

Then, one day, Jacob Saar stopped me and said, 'What were you saying that day?' I told him, I wanted to build a house, but first I must have a piece of land. He said, 'Today is the right day. I heard only this morning that Thomas of Cherayil is selling his land cheap before it is taken from him. So if you ask him he will give you five cents[14] for almost nothing. Tell him I sent you.' So I went there, and right away, his son measured out five cents for me and even marked out a road from the remaining land for me. And he said, 'You give us thousand rupees now, and pay the rest slowly.' Was that not a miracle and only after the fourth Sunday of my praying! So I had my land. Then I went to Jacob Saar again and told him that I had the land but I needed the materials. He gave these to me. John Saar heard I was building a house, and he gave me two hundred rupees. In the same way, without my asking them, the Malayil family gave me hundred rupees, and Tamaravellil family gave me fifty. Slowly I got everything I needed. This is how *Kurusaoopen* helped me when I prayed to him. I had my own house, and I lit candles to him in gratitude for forty days. *Kurusaoopen* doesn't want from us gold, money or elephants—he wants only one candle lit. I prayed for seven years after that before he cured my son of drunkenness, seven years I prayed without ceasing, and one day it just passed. The anger, the beatings, the shoutings all stopped and once in a while, even if he did drink, he came home quietly and slept without disturbing any of us. Was that not a miracle?

This evocative account expresses at one level the affectual relations in existence between Syrian Christians and the people who work for them. At another level, the account of the miracle could have been from any devotee describing the manner in which miracles are wrought.

Kurisu Palli

Kurisu Palli, the church of St Thomas in Puthenangadi, gets its name from a giant stone cross that stands on the altar. The cross, in fact, has become representative of Thomas, who brought Christianity to Kerala, and the term *Kurusaoopen* affirms this.

The Kurisu Palli cross is of unusual height, and the power that devotees believe it radiates is clearly evident in the belief of some people that it increases in height ('grows') every year. The cross is made of three pieces of granite carved in the last century by a *kalasari* (stone mason) brought from Chengannur. Ninety years ago, a Syrian Christian family called Cherakadayil, by profession gold merchants, are said to have donated the gold-leaf work that adorns the cross and makes it an object of unusual splendour and beauty. There are two other religious objects of great distinction in Kurisu Palli: the wall paintings behind the *thronos* (altar), and the *thodu vellaku* or hanging lamps, which are constantly alight. The paintings depict the risen Christ in translucent colours; below Him is a representation of Thomas the Apostle, in rich dark colours. Informants say these paintings are the work, in the last century, of a Goan caste called *manjumel* who had been taught the art by the Portuguese, and whose paints were made of a secret recipe which included vegetable dyes and white of egg.

The silver-coated bronze lamps that hang from the rafters in Kurisu Palli were a gift in the last century from someone who wanted to make an offering to the church to stave off an epidemic of smallpox. As soon as one steps into the nave, these lamps draw attention by their many wicks, aflame in the oil-filled base. A larger copper canister at the bottom traps all the excess oil that falls from the basin since devotees continue to pour oil as an offering or *nercha* into the lamp even when it overflows. The oil is not just to keep the small wicks alight, it serves to comfort and heal those who are ill and believe in its power, for it is holy oil. Lighting these oil wicks (or candles) is an important part of the evening for most women and children in Puthenangadi. Every candle that burns in the long metal trays symbolizes a prayer of appeal or thanksgiving. The reputation of Kurisu Palli has been built up over time through word of mouth as people describe how their prayers have been answered. On Fridays and Saturdays, particularly, there is a steady stream of pilgrims, both Christian and Hindu, who bring their offerings of coconut oil in bottles wrapped in newspaper. One sort of offering is to light all of·the hundred small lamps around the walls of the church, small black metal cups encased in low, narrow, concrete stands. Often one can see women going to each lamp, pouring in oil, and lighting a lamp. The oil in the lamps of Kurisu Palli is thought to have miraculous powers and is certainly one reason why people tend to take away as well as bring oil.

The notion of *shakti* pervades the descriptions of the character of this church and it is common to hear statements such as

I never pass the church without saying a prayer to *Kurusaoopen*. He has helped me whenever I have needed help, and sometimes when I thought there was no way, he has shown miracles to me.

Or, as in another case,

It is a habit with me to go to Kurisu Palli every evening holding candles which I light in memory of *Kurusaoopen*. If I don't do this, I feel frightened and feel as if I have missed something of great importance to me.

A number of such believers in the power of Kurisu Palli are Hindu women, distinctive in their traditional garments, hair washed and loosely tied as when they go to the temple. Their eyes are lined with *kohl*, the *pottu* (a circular red mark) adorns the brow. In appearance they are utterly different from Syrian Christian women who, by tradition and sacred custom, may not wear the *pottu*, considered to symbolize Shiva's third eye, or ornament their face in any other way. Many of these Hindu women are brought by Christian friends, and tend to be outsiders who have heard of Kurisu Palli's miracles. The reaction of the neighbourhood to Hindus coming to worship at Kurisu Palli is usually adverse. In the beginning, whenever the Christian women expressed their annoyance, the parish priest refused to take an antagonistic stand on the matter saying, 'Their faith is strong and cannot be denied'. The Christians of Kurisu Palli are first *Syrianigal* (Syrian people) and then 'Christians', and this tends to colour their ability to share their church with low-caste believers. As for 'converts', as newly baptized people are called, there is no place for them either. By colour, feature, and apparel, they stand marked, and even when they take on Christian names, the Syrian Christians of Puthenangadi still insist on calling them (Jagadan) Thoma and (Sridevi) Maria. For Syrian Christians these people, though Christians, are still *Izhavas*. Besides their inability to incorporate Hindu worshippers and Christian converts of 'lower caste', devotees of Kurisu Palli also tend to exclude those who belong to the Patriarch's party.

Kurisu Palli *Peryanaal* is one of the most important festivals celebrated in Puthenangadi, and cuts across denominational difference, in honouring St Thomas. It concludes the ritually most crowded ritual fortnight of the year which begins with Hosanna Sunday and ends with *Puthiya Nyyayarcha*. The New Sunday is of particular importance to Puthenangadi residents because of the event that proved Christ's resurrection most completely: Thomas being given the opportunity to feel for himself the wounds in Christ's flesh, and admit that it was indeed his Lord and God. The resurrection is continually emphasized as the most important happening to be remembered in the Messiah's life. The Christian concept of everlasting life is a gift to believers, for death is not the end, and the body and soul will be resurrected to find new life in heaven. The victory over death thus forms one of the chief motifs in the Christian religion, and Thomas's role in providing proof is, therefore, crucial to the Syrian Christian imagination.

The festival, which goes on for three days, begins with the *sandhya namaskaram*, with everyone gathering at dusk, the drummers before the service begins. The drummers are of the *Izhava* caste, and have been given this privilege for generations, performing as a *nercha* to Kurisu Palli.

The streets are festooned with palm leaves, strips of which are twisted into decorative patterns. There are no paper streamers; instead, rows and rows of light green leaves are strung on coir rope. In the backyard of the church, a *nella villaku* (bronze lamp) about five feet high, has been filled with oil, the lone flame burning brightly. Around this, in a semicircle, the drummers stand in white *mundu* (sarongs), bare-chested, their *chendas* (drums) tied obliquely across their shoulders and chest with a sash, so that they rest at the level of the navel. The drummers use two sticks, slim and ivory coloured, slightly bent at the corners to beat their drums. When the church bells ring, the *chendakar* stop, and everyone enters the church to say the prayers of the evening. Outside, shops selling bangles, ribbons and rings have magically sprung up. There is an air of festivity around the church.

When the evening prayer is over on the first day (which is a Friday), there is a *rasa* or procession to all the houses in the *angadi*. *Puthiya Nyyayarcha* commemorates the moment when Christ meets his disciples, who, at his resurrection, are reborn too, and filled with new spirit. On this occasion, every Christian house and every person in it is blessed by the priest. As the procession weaves down the *angadi* with its old Persian crosses, its candles, torches, sequinned umbrellas and the large ceremonial canopy, supported by four men, under which the priests walk, every house is seen to be decorated with lighted candles. Outside each door, a family stands waiting for the priests' blessings, the children in their parents' arms, the older ones standing alert and expectant in front of the adults. Every window-sill and verandah is illuminated by candle light, so that the whole dark street (lamp posts are few and far between) is caught up in points of light, and looks cheerful and festive. In front of every house, reed mats (cream-coloured woven *paaye*) are spread out; on each stands a small table covered with a spotless white table-cloth. The old household *nella villaku* (brass lamp) has been taken out and polished for the occasion. This is lit to signify that the household is a Christian one, desiring the blessings of the church. Not surprisingly, the Hindu household in the street also puts forward a lamp. A priest holds out a collection plate into which money is put by every individual who has been touched by the priest's small handcross. The offering is never much, perhaps a rupee or two, because Orthodox Syrians frequently tell me that it is not how much money one gives that is important, it is the gesture, the intention of expressing Christian love. The priest is ceremonially clothed in a cream and gold silk *kappa* (cope) or robe; on his head he wears an unusual three-coned cap called the *vettu thoppi* or *rasa thoppi*. It too is of silk, stiff and mitre-like, and very different from the usual black flat cap worn on ordinary occasions by priests. Such a cap is worn by them also at the time of their own deaths, suggesting perhaps that death is always accompanied by resurrection for the Christian.

The *rasa* completes one circle which is in fact commemorative of the route that St Thomas is supposed to take as guardian of Puthenangadi; it does not stop at every house in Puthenangadi. Those who live in by-lanes must bring their lamps to the main route or link up with a neighbouring family. The procession stops at the *kurusunthotti* where the *susrusakar* light the censer, and the priest says a prayer. Then the *rasa* returns to the church where the bells are ringing as a signal for the people to gather. It is very late, almost midnight, and prayers are said before worshippers finally disperse.

Saturday, the second day, is one on which *Qurbana* is said in the morning. It being a special occasion, *Qurbana* is served at three altars. This is called the *Munnamel Qurbana*. The chief celebrant uses the main inner sanctum—the *madabaha* of the church—while two other priests conduct the service simultaneously on the side altars in the chancel. Some informants were against the system of the three-altar *Qurbana*, saying it is only ostentation, a legacy of the sixteenth century Portuguese in Malabar. In fact, it goes against what some informants believe the true rites ought to be. The two priests at the side altars celebrate *Qurbana* silently so that these services are reduced to mere mimicry. Those who dislike the pomp of the three-altar *Qurbana* say, 'Christ spoke; it is in the words that He said to His disciples as much as the action of the ritual that there is significance'. To leave out the words of the liturgy is therefore completely unacceptable to them.

Two events, the *Qurbana* and the procession, mark the event of *Puthiya Nyyayarcha* associated with St Thomas. The *rasa* again takes the route that Thomas is supposed to take according to the legends when he rides on a white steed at night as protector of Puthenangadi, keeping vigil over the neighbourhood. The procession consists of all the residents of Puthenangadi, regardless of ecclesiastical affiliation, because St Thomas is a well-loved figure even if claims vary as to his control over the Christians. In that sense, he unites the neighbourhood, if only in a ceremonially superficial way. This is the one occasion when followers of the Patriarch enter the chapel, forget their differences, and are able to pray there. I saw expressions of intense piety on the faces of some Patriarch's party women, for whom praying in Kurisu Palli is a rare event. This is also the only time when all the priests of several local churches walk together, and share the financial privileges of *rasa*, regardless of ecclesiastical division.

The first Sunday after Easter is celebrated with great enthusiasm in Puthenangadi because it commemorates the day on which Christ appeared in person to the apostles, and filled them with the Holy Spirit. It particularly commemorates the memory of Thomas who on this day slipped his fingers into the wounds of Christ. One man said,

Here is the proof that Christ was perfect man and perfect God, and that He was resurrected in the flesh, and appeared in the flesh to His disciples.

Eucharist is celebrated in the normal way, but one can sense a difference, a jubiliation that is to culminate in the events of the festival. Several sorts of entertainment are organized during the three-day festival. That particular year, a troupe of artists were called all the way from Kumarakam (some miles away from Kottayam) to perform the *Margam kalli*, an art form that is fast disappearing. The performers were all men, dressed in everyday clothes. Ten dancers stood around the brass lamp which was five feet high and lit by a single flame, at the western door of the church. They folded their hands in an attitude of prayer and, with eyes shut, intoned a prayer for safe keeping, and in praise of Jesus Christ.

The performance consists of songs which are descriptions of events described in the Bible, some in microscopic detail. One of them, for instance, is a song of Mary, the Mother of Christ, who says, 'Have you seen my son? They took him this way. His face was covered with blood'. Another song is about John the Baptist, with lines from the Bible which speak of his unworthiness in untying the latchet of His shoe. There are songs about pilgrimages: one describes the legend of Malayatur where St Thomas's footprint is seen in the rock, and where a golden cross was discovered; another speaks of the sights that may be seen at pilgrim places—the wealth of the church, its people and the shops. This song is a list of the places in Kerala where there are important churches; names are reeled off by the performers in a tongue-twister style, faster and faster without pausing for breath. A similar sort of song is one called *Angadi Marannu* which refers to the 'green medicines' of Ayurveda, the herbs of healing. This is really a song meant to evoke laughter, having no sentence structure, and being only a rapid naming of the hundreds of items that are used in the making of *ayurvedic* oils.

The *katha prasangam* is another traditional art form where events are recalled from the Bible. It consists of a story enacted through mime, prose and song, being a lengthy memorized piece describing an event, punctuated by songs recited in dramatic style. The audience's appreciation is shown by the giving of garlands of paper money to the artists.

The festival of the patron saint, in fact, tends to unite the neighbourhood in a way that even the canonical festivals celebrating the life of Jesus do not. *Puthiya Nyayarcha* truly integrates the neighbourhood at all planes of social life, for the church quarrel and ecclesiastical differences are forgotten for once. All the residents of the neighbourhood join in the festivities—the prayers, the procession, the dramatic enactment and the fireworks. For three days there is a sense of communitas and exhilaration, for *Puthiya Nyayarcha* celebrates the concern for the empirical validation of Christ's resurrection that the Eastern Christians rejoice in, since it was proved to the world in a way that faith alone could not. The resurrection is of central concern to Syrian Christians, for by this act the divinity of Jesus was revealed to the world. Secondly, as the one who brought the Christian faith to the people of Kerala, St Thomas is given a significant place in the hearts of believers even though they may today be divided by ecclesiastical differences.

COMMEMORATION OF HOLY MEN

Through the festivals of 'holy men', I wish to show how commemoration and pilgrimage can in fact be symbols of cleavage. Being the most blessed and virtuous of mortals, the role of holy men is primarily understood in terms of curing the fatally ill or helping the victims of circumstance. In this context, it is not surprising that Parimala Tirumeni, the only prelate of the Orthodox and Jacobite Syrian Churches to have been canonized as a saint, was referred to by informants as a *yogi* (a person capable of expressing great supernatural powers). The miracle cure is a major aspect of the cult of the holy men: because they were ascetic, holy and spiritually powerful when alive, they continue even after their death to influence the lives of ordinary men. Their spirits do not die but mediate with God for lesser men. Prayers to the holy men express the hierarchies in which men place themselves and others in terms of closeness and distance to God. The act of pilgrimage to invoke the blessings of these holy men expresses humility, suffering and hope. It is a *nercha* or offering, wherein it is hoped that there will be a reciprocal return of blessings.

The pain of pilgrimage—hunger (in ritual abstention from food), tedium, long hours of standing, waiting and walking—is the manner by which the Christian reduces the physical self so that a miracle of some kind, whether material or spiritual, may be wrought. William Lafleur has looked at pilgrimage in terms of the correspondence between social locations and spatial movements. He reviews Turner's work on pilgrimage as an analysis of a phenomenon where society's rules and roles are in abeyance, perhaps even inverted. More importantly, he suggests that pilgrimage must be considered not only in terms of where individuals are going, but what they have left behind, emphasizing therefore the 'road' of the pilgrimage.[15] Pilgrimage implies a dislocation which becomes an act of reflexivity in itself. For many festivals, then, the route is more important than 'getting there'. This is most typical in the pilgrimages to the tombstones of dead prelates.

The pilgrimage to Mar Elias's tomb at Omaloor incorporates three planes—neighbourhood, route and pilgrim church. That distinctions of affiliation divide the neighbourhood is what I wish to prove. While geographical space may remain intact, the social space of the neighbourhood becomes distinguished and demarcated; one group may mourn, the other remains silent. While one group is immersed in the activities of celebration or commemoration, the other remains a passive witness or angry vilifier, depending upon how great the emotional breach between one party and another may be at any given time.

For the Patriarch's party, a great saint lies at Omaloor where a deceased Patriarch of Antioch had died fifty years earlier. The event of his death, and the attendant circumstances are vividly remembered: the heat of the summer, the sense of defeat that was all pervasive, for this patriarch too had come with the hope of affecting a reconciliation. The prelate had premonitions of his death and, as he travelled over many miles of rough country trying to integrate the quarrelling parishes, he said, 'The priests want my skeleton (*asthikoodam*)'. Further, he asked his deacons, 'Do you know the songs that are sung at the time of death of a high Metropolitan?' He taught them the songs and the next day he 'passed his time'.[16]

Puthenangadi is one stop on the pilgrim's route to Omaloor, and those of the neighbourhood who wish to make the pilgrimage may join the travellers here. The pilgrims arrive, tired and hungry, walking slowly, in a single, dishevelled, straggly line. They have been walking over many miles of tarmac in the hottest time of the year, each carrying his little bundle or bag of belongings. Many of them are barefoot, some hanging on to the shoulders of the one in front. They hold up bright yellow banners, and those who can, tiredly chant praises of the *Bawa*.

The pilgrims speak of miracles they have known either experientially or vicariously, and in this way disseminate the power of the holy man. It is this aspect which helps Christians affirm relationships across ecclesiastical or denominational cleavages. But again such relations are tenuous and individualistic. Those who belong to a particular denomination or party may think twice about visiting a pilgrim spot in the hands of the opposite party. Those who have done so, and have experienced miracles, are the most vociferous about the need for the quarrels in the church to end. An informant said:

> I know the woman to whom this miracle happened so you can say it is my personal experience. She was afflicted by increasing blindness. She returned from her husband's home as the disease progressed. She lay in her father's house thinking, 'How can I go back to my husband's people?' Her brother was a priest, and he prayed along with relatives who were gathered in the house. Then her brother said, 'Let us all pray at the *kabar* (grave) of the *Bawa*. Let us go to him and tell him our trouble.' As they went, the woman sadly thought that it was not her *bhagyam* (good fortune) to see the grave of the *Bawa* and to pray there. As she lay in the darkness, suddenly there appeared before her a man in black robes, and a skull cap, with a beard and a gold cross on a chain around his neck. She could not see his face clearly, but he stood over her, and with his hands he made the sign of the cross over her eyes. She felt a cool comfortable sensation, then the vision disappeared. Again, he appeared before her and motioned towards her with his hands, and the coolness radiated into her eyes. The third time he appeared, he pressed hard so hard into the eyeballs that she screamed in pain. Her relatives came running into the room, and it seemed to her that she could see them clearly. She told her brother what she had dreamed or thought she had seen, and then said she could see everyone clearly. Everyone knelt in praise of God, the Bible was brought to her, and she read to them from it. Tears streamed down their faces as they heard and saw her read and they understood the miracle. Since then she and her family have visited Omaloor every year to give thanks to the *Bawa*.

Another informant said:

My husband's family belongs to the *metran*'s party. Of course, I
was not allowed to go to Omaloor and pray at the tomb there.
But two or three times I did go there, from my own home. The
second time that I went, I was carrying my son who was just
three years old. While I was praying, he loosened my hold on
him and wandered away. I searched everywhere for him. I
realized then the pain that the Mother (*Matav*) must have felt
when the Christ child was lost when they returned from the
temple in Jerusalem. Finally, we found him. Even though this
happened forty years ago, even today, every year without fail I
say a prayer and have a *Qurbana* said in thanksgiving to Elias
Baba.

In Puthenangadi there is hectic activity in the households of those
who belong to the Patriarch's party. The Orthodox Syrians, while they
accommodate the incoming pilgrims, are courteous but at the same
time uncommunicative. This is, after all, a holy man belonging to the
'other side'. For many of the pilgrims who have been walking for days,
their arrival in Puthenangadi marks the last phase of their journey.
Walking, Omaloor lies only two days away. The priest of the Patriarch's
church comes to greet them with members of his *palli* (parish); in a
ceremonial procession complete with lighted candles, silk and beaded
umbrellas (*muth kodda*) and silver crosses, they are taken into the
church where evening prayers are said after which all the pilgrims are
fed. In earlier years, reed mats were spread out in the yard surrounding
the church, banana leaves were set out, and food served to the
travellers.

On such occasions, a communal kitchen is set up, and the residents
volunteer to cook and serve the standard vegetarian food of mourning:
rice, green bananas cooked with pulses and coconut, and buttermilk
which has been cooked to a golden colour with oil, onions and
turmeric. This is their *nercha* to the *Bawa* and his pilgrims.

Feeding the pilgrims becomes an important co-operative event for
the Jacobite Syrians in Puthenangadi. Everyone belonging to the
Patriarch's party brings to the church what they can—rice, stacks of
raw bananas, green pulses, firewood, curds, mustard seed, oil, condi-
ments, pickles, spices, banana leaves, newspapers, rubber bands—
everything is a gift from the people of the parish. The banana leaves
are cut into the required size, the surface wiped clean with a damp

cloth, then singed over the fire so that the leaf takes on a pliable parchment-like quality, suitable for folding and wrapping. That year, one thousand five hundred bundles of food were distributed. A woman said:

> When we saw the crowds we were worried about how to feed them, but then it is like the fish and *appam* (bread) that Christ blessed. There are always baskets of food left over even though one may have thought 'How can so many be fed?

At night the pilgrims sleep in the courtyards of houses in the neighbourhood or in the fields outside the church. Quarrels between denominations are forgotten in this respect, since the pilgrim as fellow Christian must be accommodated. Yet there is some tension between the category of stranger and fellow Christian:

> No one in Puthenangadi sleeps that night. Inside, each one of us feels a little fear; who can trust the times?

Despite this feeling of insecurity, curious friendships often result. One household has given shelter for forty-nine years to a man who walks to Omaloor every year from the Nilgiris.

> No one may deny hospitality. *Athithi satkaram* (hospitality) is a distinctive trait of our Syrian Christian culture. Now hospitality costs money, times are difficult, but two generations ago, many families were still agricultural families in the fullest sense, so it was not difficult to feed a family or two of pilgrims who stayed the night. Now rice costs money.

Pilgrims who meet each other once a year greet each other with affection.

> When they see me they hug me, for even though we meet for one evening of the year we have made friends among them. With the sweat and the dust all over, they hold me close. For them, our house is a safe resting place for the night and we are believers like them.

The route to the church is lined with streamers and flags. In

February 1982, the Patriarch of Antioch was to celebrate the Eucharist, so the number of pilgrims was perhaps higher than in other years. The Patriarch is treated like a saint since he stands in the place of Peter and carries apostolic grace by virtue of his office.

At the pilgrim spot in Omaloor, the fields were full of people, resting where they could in the shade of the trees outside the church. As at every festival, a market-place had sprung up with the delightful trivia that vendors bring—bangles, plastic toys, eatables, kitchen paraphernelia, candles, oil, pictures of the present *Bawa* as also of the one who is described by custom euphemistically as 'he who had passed his time'. There are calendar and clay models depicting the Holy Family, miniature representations of the saints, Jesus, Mary and Joseph, depicted on medallions and beaded on black thread. Beggars, too, wait and watch for pilgrims, calling on the *Bawa*'s name for alms.

In the church the crowds moved slowly around the tomb. Money was put in collection bowls as offerings to the church. So much oil was poured into the lamps that the floor was slippery. People touched the tomb with their foreheads and prayed, then circled around it. Women stood with their heads covered, and looked with reverence at the picture of the *Bawa*, represented in the portrait as an imposing figure with the symbols of his status: beard, ceremonial robes, crozier. The *Bawa* has, for believers, the power to cure, heal and comfort, a power which continues beyond his death.

Often, the walk to Omaloor is a fulfilment of a vow taken many years ago, in thanks for favours received; but most often the first pilgrimage is to pray that blessings (*anugraham*) may be received, and a promise to the saint that further pilgrimages may consequently be undertaken. The route, which links the points of origin and culmination, is of particular significance because the journey is homologous to life where suffering, reflection, the joy of sharing and meeting have the function of anticipating and preparing the Christian for ultimate resolution and celebration. It is the supreme period of liminality. Underlying the event of the pilgrimage, however, are the tensions born of ecclesiastical fission. For the Syrian Christians of Puthenangadi, pilgrimage expresses the manner by which the actor is caught in the grids of choice whereby, to follow the path of a particular pilgrimage is to make a choice of ecclesiastical allegiance. Exception are the saints' festivals; yet, even so, a particular church may be monopolized by one ecclesiastical party or another. On such occasions, the pilgrim, if he finds the power of the saint greater than his official sympathies, may choose to go on a pilgrimage which acts against the loyalties of allegiance.

But again, the festival is a period where liminality maturing into the culmination of celebration offers the most complex of situations, becoming the time when a society questions its own structure; the communitas of the festival lies, as Turner has shown, in its anti-structure.

But the festival expresses not merely the nature of social drama in the sense that Turner meant, whose style is explicated in the notion of characters roles and platforms for performance; it incorporates also as a central motif the drama of the liturgy. The notion of liturgy as drama is evident to the Christian himself, who distinguishes between *koodasha* (sacrament) and *natakam* (play or drama), to which the eucharistic service may descend if profane, spectacle-creating interests predominate over spiritual concerns. But that the metaphor of the drama has often been used in an analogical non-derogatory sense is evident in both lay perceptions and anthropological literature. Lloyd Warner used it for the purpose of analysis in his Yankee City study, classifying the drama as consisting of characters, actions of the hero, plot, the several scenes and the emotional involvements, identifications and evocations.[17]

It is in this sense that I wish to look at the role of the Patriarch, both as a potential saint as well as the representative of Christ, the head of a section of the people under whose hands the Eucharist service takes on a significance far removed from the normal vein of events. The Patriarch is *parishuddhan* (saintly). He is the expression of Christ's presence, the perfect symbol of the Church. An informant said, having openly wept on seeing the Patriarch:

> It is given to some to become as angels on earth and in doing so they are closer to God than we ever could be. So we approach them as sinners would and pray that they mediate for us.

The present Patriarch's visit to Kerala was seen as a pilgrimage on his part, honouring the Christians of Kerala. The churches were filled beyond capacity, and the streets lined with people, for to 'see' the Patriarch is a pilgrimage in itself. *Qurbana* in this context takes on a special meaning, and people followed him from one church to the next, eager to see him, hear his voice and perhaps be touched by him in blessing.

Old people said, 'This is a pilgrimage' (*a teertha yatra*). Everyone, even small children, had arranged to wear white. At Kodimatha, where the Patriarch was to appear, the crowds had already gathered when the pilgrims from Puthenangadi arrived. Banners with symbols of the Syrian Church were up (the Keys of Peter and the dome-shaped turban of the eastern prelate), and pedestrians had taken over the roads. Loudspeakers blared songs of praise of the *Bawa*, the shepherd who took care of his flock in the pasture of life. People picked up the chorus: with the *Bawa*'s coming the *Suriyani* (Syrian) *Sabha* had awoken, and thousands of joyous people had gathered to see the golden face of the holy lord. One of the songs described the Patriarch as the head of the ancestral *taravat* from which the *Suriyani Sabha* of Kerala had sprung and the people here were descendants of the *Antiocha Simhasanam* (throne). Another song said that the Patriarch was *athipathi* or the ruler of all Syrian Christians, at the sound of whose voice the whole world trembled. His throne was a war horse that pushed ahead to the front lines of battle, his flag fluttered over heaven and earth.

The old tunes are slow and lilting, having been imported from the Syrian Church along with the words. New tunes now popular are met with disapproval by elders: 'This is exactly like the Hindus, all that is lacking is the temple elephant'. One song had actually been tacked on to the tune of a traditional boat race song with its characteristic chorus call: *Oh thithithara thithithai*. Women nostalgically recalled the old tunes they had known from childhood.

The sun went down, and the *Bawa*, who was supposed to have arrived at 4.30 p.m., showed no signs of arriving. Some of the younger women got restless but the older ones said, 'If you want to see a holy man, it is not so easily done. You have to wait in patience'.

Meanwhile, excited organizers were walking busily among the people, giving instructions and words of encouragement, for the crowds had been waiting almost three hours. At 7:30 p.m., when it was dark, the first siren of the jeep could be heard, and the crowd was alert at once. Under the dim light of the street bulbs, suddenly thousands of yellow flags held by the devotees began to be waved. One woman said sadly, 'It's dark now, we won't be able to see him'.

However, the coming of the Patriarch changed the nature of the crowd. The sudden sight of the head of their church turned the quiet, orderly crowd into a turbulent mass without any centre. Slogans were shouted against the Catholicos at Devalokam, antagonist of the Patriarch. It was no longer a *teertha yatra* but a *jyatha*, a procession with political connotations.

The residents of Puthenangadi were forced to move out. They stood at the edge of the crowd, on the pavement, angry and disappointed at being mere spectators, unable to participate, for the nature of the event had changed. Forced to return without having heard the Patriarch speak, the pilgrims passed through Tirunnakkara Maidan at the centre of Kottayam. There the Christians stopped, for they could here the voice of the Patriarch, distant but distinct, through a megaphone. They sat under a peepul tree outside the temple and heard his speech. For these people there was nothing paradoxical about sitting in a Hindu temple courtyard in order to listen to the voice of the Patriarch. The next morning they were again to leave early to be at the church where the Patriarch was to celebrate *Qurbana*.

On one particular day, the Puthenangadi people followed him to three separate places, after which one of them said, 'Now we will never see him again from so close that we could reach out and touch him. It is an honour given rarely in a lifetime'. At the end of the day, the neighbourhood had already begun losing its festive look—banners welcoming the Patriarch were being taken down, and the yellow streamers were rolled up carefully for future use. Only the streamers made from dry palm leaves knotted together hung from electricity wires. The young banana trees which had been set up near the gates of the church were already wilting in the sun.

The Patriarch's visit to the followers of the *Antiocha Simhasanam* signifies his temporal power, to be read in terms of the politics of ecclesiastical control. His visit was heralded by certain forms of violence, verbal abuse and angry silences as well as physical violence. Expressions of these are to be seen in the reactions of certain newspapers, the Orthodox followers' hope for 'stay orders' to the visiting prelates by the courts, the denial of entry to West Syrian prelates into certain churches in the neighbourhood, the theme of autonomy versus 'foreign power', and the sudden upsurge of violence in the crowds waiting for the Patriarch to arrive, directed at the autonomous position taken by the Catholicos. On another level, we have the theme of the spiritual power of the Patriarch which is the transmission of grace through office. The attitudes expressed by the pilgrims towards the Patriarch are those of veneration and awe because he comes from the 'same place' as Christ. There is constant tension between the two roles. The first indicates the subjectivity of time and history where each Patriarch is an individual who succeeds another, biographically distinct and memorable by his actions. The second indicates that every Patriarch is an objective symbol of ecclesiastical control.

The death of a Patriarch, if it were to have occurred in Malabar, becomes at once an event of great importance. Death transforms the holy man as representative of Peter (i.e., an ecclesiastical office) to a holy mediator between man and God. No expectations of miracles were ever expressed by the pilgrims of the mortal holder of the spiritual office but at the death of a 'good and saintly' Patriarch, the soul is liberated and freed from mortality; it would seem that the closeness to God is further established through death. Emanation of power is thus more evident after death. As one man said to the present Patriarch:

> Fifty years ago, we heard of the death of Patriarch Mar Elias at Omaloor, and we went there to ask that the body be buried in our church. But they refused to give it to us.

This kind of statement may cause discomfiture to the present Patriarch and attendant prelates, who are reminded of their mortality, but the spirit of the statement implies the importance of the relic. The relic expresses both emanation of power and the mortality of the saint. This unity of soul and body continues in the folk imagination after death, and hence the importance of the mausoleum of the saint. Spiritual grace is thus the latent attribute of the Patriarch by virtue of his office. If miracles become associated with him, this is not because of office, role or function merely but in terms of such power as is arrived at through prayer, fasting, penance and service. The seal of the holy man thus lies in the life that he leads.

The Priests and the People

The problematic relation of priests to the people is evident when one looks, for instance, at women's experience of transformative visions and their impact on ecclesiastical codes, as well as the relations of people to ecclesiasts vis-à-vis the church quarrel. The premise so far has been that Syrian Christians are dependent on their priests, for it is they who perform the sacred rituals necessary for the maintenance of Christian life. Nevertheless, believers are critical of the priests as individuals, who are divided by ecclesiastical allegiances and loyalties, and among whom, frequently, there is a sense of apathy in relation to their parish duties. When the priest celebrates the *Qurbana*, he is revered by everyone present in church in his role as one who keeps alight the *kedatha villaku* (the eternal lamp). On the other hand, people's personal relations with parish priests are far from satisfactory, and often the most unrestrained and abusive of language is used to describe them. There is a collapse of the traditional structures of the church not only because of the effects of the church quarrel but also because of the effects of secularization. I attempt here to discuss the tenuous relation between priests and people in terms of three sets of problems. In this sense, what is offered here is clearly the people's representation of priesthood and its responsibilities.

The first problem relates to the traditional organization of the church, the second shows how the priests reflect the anomie within the church, the third is based on how people react to the disintegration of what they conceive to be moral ecclesiastical codes.

An informant, referring to the church quarrel and the consequent disintegration, described the old order:

> In the traditional system, every church was basically autonomous. Ecclesiastical organization was still at a minimum, for the church consisted of the patron saint and the people. The priest was always someone known to the people, literally a *pujari* (one who celebrates ritual ceremonies) who inherited his rights and duties in the church from his father before him. The death of the priestly vocation in these families has led to the emergence of a new kind of priest who is chosen because of academic merit and his desire to join the priesthood—one who is taught at the seminary. In the traditional system, *vallyachen* (elder priest) taught *kochuachen* (younger priest)—no systematic theology there—and yet that seemed to have been a time when saints were born.

The existence of priestly lines has been well documented. Thomas the Apostle landed in Kodungaloor in AD 52 according to tradition, converted high-caste Hindu families, consecrated priests and built churches. Hereditary priesthood was an accepted fact in the Christian tradition of Malabar, and contributed, in fact, to prelatial lines of succession also. The autonomy of the Syrian churches is perhaps to be understood in the context of the weak ecclesiastical links established with the eastern churches before the sixteenth century. It is with Portuguese ritual colonization, culminating in 1599, that there emerges a true hierarchical organization of Syrian Christian churches. However, its repudiation by those who longed for the allegiance with the Eastern Church reasserted the partial autonomy of the former. The nineteenth century which saw the organizational dilemmas of Syrian Christians and their problems with the Anglican and West Syrian churches, has been described in the second chapter. The church quarrel is explicitly about the problems of allegiance and autonomy. From an anthropological perspective, it would seem that ecclesiastical affiliation with the Patriarch of Antioch in fact implies the autonomy of each parish and its vicar. The network of ecclesiastical organization and of hierarchy is here comparatively weak. On the other hand, the indigenous Catholicos who stands for the autonomy of the Indian Church expresses a centralized authority which in time will reflect to a greater extent the Western (Protestant or Catholic) interpretation of ecclesiastical order.

According to an informant, one of the complaints of the reformer Abraham Malpan in the early decades of the nineteenth century had been that deacons were accepted into the church at a very early age, often when they were barely eight or nine years old. The establishment of the seminary in 1813 by the CMS was, in fact, for the purpose of educating Syrian Christian priests. The missionary Joseph Fenn reported in December 1827:

> Colonel Munro, the British Resident in Travancore found it (the Syrian Church) in a state of great degradation—the priests and the people alike, illiterate, poor and oppressed.
>
> When the missionaries first arrived, there were thirty or forty subdeacons, youths between the ages of fourteen and twenty-two, intended for the order of the Priesthood: these were brought to the college by the Metropolitan. Some of them could not read their own language, and but few were desirous of any knowledge beyond that which was absolutely necessary to enable them to obtain admission to the Priesthood.[18]

Of course, the missionaries who believed that the Syrian deacons should be taught 'Virgil and Horace in Latin, St John and Xenophon in Greek, Syriac, English, Euclid and History'[19] would have found the traditional system of education for a boy destined to become a priest startling. A biographer of Parimala Tirumeni (the well-loved mystic and saint of the Malankara church) described the latter's education under his uncle Chathuruthy Malpan Gevarghese. The saint had been ordained a deacon at the age of ten by the Metropolitan of the Malankara Church, Palakunnath Mathew Mar Athanasius. His paternal uncle, who was his teacher, was not only a renowned Syriac scholar of his time but also had interests in occult 'sciences such as astrology, palmistry and *ghoula shastram* or foretelling events by the movements of lizards.[20]

Deacons were ordained at a very young age because they came from families where priesthood was demarcated as a vocation. Informants constantly affirmed that, traditionally, priests always came from the 'best families' that is, those which had 'both status and money'. Another important criterion was physical beauty—the child was to be both strong and well-featured. Some children are marked by a startling grace, a difference that separates them from other children. Physical beauty or *yogya* was often considered a sign of spiritual grace.

Even today, boys of ten and twelve are chosen to serve at the altar, and learn at an early age its rituals and secrets, and participate in the rigours of fasting. A boy who has the inclination for it can be easily encouraged to adopt priesthood as a vocation. Further, there still exists the practice of taking children to the *aramana* or *dairya* (Bishop's Palace and Monastery respectively) to be blessed by the *metran*s, particularly on examination days, birthdays or ritual events. People even now say that the *metran*s have the ability to see and recognize a child with 'the priestly quality'. It was on the basis of this recognition that, in the old days, the best priests were chosen. The *metran* would say 'I will take this child with me' and though 'there was sorrow in parental hearts at being parted from such a beautiful child, there was the sense of being honoured and the acceptance of destiny'. Such a child lived with the *metran*, served him, and acquired religious training.

An eighty-year-old woman described how her grandfather was taken into priesthood. The child was only nine years old when he was noticed by the *tirumeni*. When the latter had come to the church, the boy's maternal uncle had prepared a letter of praise and thanks to the bishop, and an account of the parish's affairs. He was so nervous that he could not read. So evident was his distress that his sister's son said, 'Give it to me, I shall read it', and proceeded to do so in a strong and clear voice.

At the end of the ceremonies, the *tirumeni* said, 'Whose son is he?' On hearing the name of the partilineage, he said, 'It can be understood, then, for the family has priesthood in their blood'. He asked that the boy be given to the church. The custom then was that the child should appear before the *edavaga* or the parish for three consecutive Sundays, and only after having been seen and examined by the *edavagakar* or parishioners, could he be allowed to proceed to attain a religious education.

The priest described in the narrative had two sons. When they were of age, the younger one, who was clever, quick, and aesthetically pleasing to the eye, was asked to take *pattom* (ordainment); though only nine years old, he said he needed three days to think about it. At the end of it, he refused, saying his elder brother had greater aptitude and a disposition more suited to the calling. My informant said:

> It is true that this was so, for many people have told me that my father from a very young age knew all the prayers by heart. He would make from the shells of the coconut and some strings a *dhoop-petti* (censer) which he would fill with burning coals from the kitchen fire and walk near the river swinging it and saying his prayers. He wanted to be a priest and he was born to be one.

Another problem is the autonomy of the priest in terms of his influential status in the community. It is a known and often confirmed fact that Syrian Christian priests often were, and are, very wealthy. There may be two reasons for this: priests were traditionally drawn from the best households. A priest was a man of power and influence and being a member of a particular kind of family granted him that privilege, and the laity followed his leadership not only because of his place in the spiritual hierarchy but also because of his social status. Even now, on all social and ritual occasions, the priest is someone who is marked off as important. He is always given the most honoured place—at the centre, the head or at other times, a place apart.

The second source of wealth is from the payments of devotees for ritual services. One of the charges made by the Reformer Abraham Malpan against the Jacobite churches was about the payment of money to priests for the Eucharist celebrated. Priests who are affiliated to wealthy churches particularly profit from *Qurbana pannam*; Kurisu Palli, for instance, is known to be extremely prosperous because it is associated with miracles, and many hundreds of people come there to have *Qurbana* 'said' in their name. The 'price' of a *Qurbana* is often only fifty paise, though ideally, since it is a gift, the person may give as much as he pleases. Of this the priest is said to get one-fifth, though usually people say *orru bhagam* or 'one part'. The important function of this payment was that it provided for the priest's material needs. Since he was not traditionally salaried, this money formed the main part of his income. This income, necessarily, could have no fixed character and could be either 'enough to live on' (*Achenna Jeevi-kande?*) or contribute to the image of the priest as belonging to a group who is money-making. Those who make their money from *Qurbana pannam* are looked down upon. Priests are also critically viewed when they show an exaggerated tendency to attend weddings, baptisms and funerals, since for all these services they are given a gift of money called *kaimuth* (literally, kissing the hand). Such eagerness to attend life crises ceremonies is opposed to their apathy, according to some informants, to come to the spiritual aid of their parishioners when they are in trouble or under emotional strain. The priest's duty is to visit the people often and provide spiritual succour.

One reason why Syrian Christian priests traditionally may not have given full attention to their flock is perhaps because many of them wei. engaged in secondary occupations like agriculture. The oldest priest of Puthenangadi owned both rubber plantations and rice fields. Not surprisingly, an informant told me, 'Our priests are landlords'. They were also, in many cases, family men. Allowed to marry before being ordained, the priest assumed all the responsibilities of the householder.

The problems of the priests in their relation to the people is most clearly understood in the light of the church quarrel. While Orthodox Syrian priests were being paid fixed salaries in 1981, Jacobite Syrian priests were still dependent on gifts to the church. However, for Orthodox priests too, the hold over *palli varumanam* (church income) continues to be steadfast. As the old priest of Cherya Palli said:

It is the rule now of the Catholicos (*Catholica bharanam*). I acknowledge his temporal power over the church, for I would not like to lose my rights there. Our family has been in possession over them for many generations. But in my heart I acknowledge the ecclesiastical authority of the Patriarch. They are two different matters.

The notion of 'claim' by some priests to certain churches is clear in his reminiscences:

When in 1086 (1910) Cherya Palli was first locked, Joseph Cattanar, my uncle, built a chapel for his use where he celebrated *Vishudha Qurbana*. But the remaining *Kattanar*s (priests) from the families of Poonathra, Erthakkel, Mekkat, Oopotil and Venkadath were left looking for new churches since Joseph Cattanar treated the chapel he had built as his own property and it was his rule there. . . Simhasana Palli was built and was ready for occupation in 1094 or 1095 (1919 or 1920). Venkadath Joseph Cattanar, who had been one of the priests serving in Cherya Palli (but had claims on Mannarkadu Palli where he went), returned to the *angadi* and became priest for Simhasana Palli. By 1118 (1943), I had completed my studies and received ordination and served with Venkadath *achen* at Simhasana Palli.

In 1958, I returned to Cherya Palli with the Peace (*Samadhanam*), choosing to believe with some others that by the Peace we were still under the Patriarch. There were some who refused to leave Simhasana Palli saying that the 'Peace' was nothing but a compromise of principles. Thekkaethallakal was one such family. It is difficult to name any one with any great certainty because over the years there were many who travelled from one side to the other. As for me, I remain of the Patriarch's party, but I stand with the Cherya Palli which is my heritage.

It is in the context of such divided loyalties (inheritance of a parish church, loyalty to the Patriarch versus obligations to the 'rule' of the Catholicos) that the indifference to pastoral duties can be understood. But the people find this difficult to accept or forgive, saying that *Qurbana pannam* corrupts. On the way to Cherya Palli, some Orthodox Syrian residents of Puthenangadi met a priest who officiated in their church. 'Where are you going?,' he asked. My companions were visibly startled by the question since the answer was obvious, specially to a priest of their church: it was the commemoration day of an important prelate of the church. One of them answered, 'To Cherya Palli, and from there to Pazhe seminary in a *rasa* (procession) in memory of Gevarghese Dionysius. Aren't you coming?' The priest laughed, and saying nothing, went his way. An informant said bitterly,

'There goes a man who stands in the church for the money he can get from it'. Latecomers to Cherya Palli asked their fellow processionists, 'How is it that we saw *Achen* (Father) going in the opposite direction?' The rest shrugged their shoulders and said nothing.

There is constant reiteration by informants that the clergy is unconcerned and uninvolved with parish life, that the priests do not participate in the life of the laity other than by holding the *Qurbana*. The people complain of the lack of sermons and compare their ecclesiastical situation with the Mar Thoma Church, a prosperous and sedate church. Informants said that the priests of the Orthodox Church were unable to speak without going into polemical details regarding the quarrel. Believers love sermons and even visit Mar Thoma churches to listen to them if a reputed speaker visits such a church. Prelates, more than priests of the Orthodox Syrian churches, tend to speak on special occasions, but these are rare events.

The prelates of the church are treated with immense respect and are usually inaccessible to common people, only visible to believers when they make public appearances at festivals and on other occasions of ritual importance. At a church festival, a priest was sitting in the prelate's presence, and this was noted with surprise and seen to be an indication of changing times. One Orthodox Syrian informant described the reverential distance that women particularly maintain in the presence of a bishop:

> Pakkomous *tirumeni* had come to my house. He called my mother-in-law and asked her to sit beside him. He is a fairly young man, but our old mother refused saying, 'How is it possible that I can sit with a *tirumeni?*' He insisted, saying, 'Let us see if the sky will break open'.

Face-to-face interaction is possible with prelates only if people are of a high status, linked with the life of the church in some close way or related to the *tirumeni* through blood or marriage. Encounters with prelates are recounted with great pride. When the *tirumeni* comes to celebrate the Eucharist, the church is filled beyond capacity. At the end of the service, everyone swarms forward to have their head touched in blessing by him. This is despite the fact that many informants say that prelates are powerful men in the worldly sense. They are described as men of academic standing and administrative capability, temporal qualities which often outrank their spiritual functions.

To have a priest in the family is an honour and, of course, the greatest of all honours is to be related or connected to the *tirumeni*. Informants have made statements (following the most preliminary enquiries on my part) such as 'My wife died three years ago. Her maternal uncle was so and so bishop'. Again, I was told, 'You know the *tirumeni* whose speech you heard yesterday. He is from our family'.

The bishop and the family from which he comes sustain each other in terms of social status. In fact, a criterion for being nominated bishop is certainly the 'quality' of the lineage, which must be impeccable. As one priest told me:

> If his sister ran off to get married, his chances of becoming a bishop would be negligible however saintly he himself is; similarly, an alcoholic in the family would be a negative point. These are not canonically laid down, but they exist.

Consequently, the *tirumeni* must be, and is always of a 'good' and well-known family. The rare occasion when some 'negative' attribute of the family is known, people either suppress it or, if they are detractors, they publicize the incident or trait in scandalous, vituperative detail.

Bishops are the leaders of the community in both temporal and spiritual terms, the names under which people of that denomination unite, for whom everyone prays in the common worship on Sundays and days of celebration. Everyone knows them by sight and by name. They are splendid in costume and in their bearing. To say therefore that you are the sister of such a one, or the niece of one, or that you studied with him, or live near his parents' house (and the family is therefore well known to you) is a great honour. The very sight of the *tirumeni* (literally, Lord) causes a change in the posture, expression and gestures of people. Conversations amongst them cease, everyone stands in an attitude of humility or at attention. Even if he is much younger than themselves, the most elderly members of the church express respect, almost awe. The decorated yet sombre mitre, the long beard, the ceremonial robes are all indicative of the highest authority. When the *tirumeni* speaks to them, it is like the head of the house putting his children to order. Those who know the *tirumeni* personally are committed to introducing friends and members of the family to him and he is always referred to in the third person titular and not by a pronoun even in direct speech. Those who come to him must bow their heads and receive blessing (*kaimuth*) which entails being touched on the brow with the handcross. To have a *tirumeni* officiate at the time of baptism, marriage or funeral is the greatest honour to a family. In any casual conversation in Puthenangadi, when the name of some *tirumeni* happens to be mentioned, one person or another will say to what degree they know him, or are related to him, or who they know who knows the *tirumeni*.

While there is a tendency to revile priests, there is not such marked antagonism to the prelates because Syrian Christians venerate the latter as monks who are ascetic, celibate, intellectual, and spiritual. They are insulting about the prelates of the 'other side' but towards their own prelates, there is only tremendous awe and admiration, and unquestioning loyalty. As one speaker at the celebrations commemorating the Catholicos's birthday said, *Catholicos Dinam* was to the Orthodox Syrian Church what Republic Day was to India.

Finally, I wish to discuss the ambiguous status of the priest. It is clear that in a eucharist-centred ritual life, the priest is of fundamental importance. To that extent, role and person are kept meticulously separate. Informants have told me the most harrowing stories of the greed of their parish priests, unverified by me, and therefore not recounted. Nevertheless, even after witnessing quarrels between two priests over how money from the procession should be distributed, Syrian Christians present themselves as willing subjects to a *Qurbana* celebrated by the same, so-called venal priests, seeing no paradox. The Yakoba cannot visualize the concept of the priesthood of every individual, and so the priest remains an important, often remote figure. When saintly, he is adored and treated with reverence; when not, he is thought to have fallen short of the role expected of him, and is a dishonourable human being. Even if there is a sense of loss over their priests' inadequacy, the church and its rituals are in no way discredited. As a prelate of this church said to me, 'Unlike the Mar Thoma, we may not have our individual interpretations of the faith. We may have only the faith of the church'. In this sense, there is no ambiguity about the priest and his functions.

The first level of ambiguity lies in the cleavage that exists so markedly between the ecclesiastical and ethical worlds. But as a staunch supporter of the Catholicos said:

It's not as if quarrels in the church are unusual or unique to us. The Apostles of Christ fought between themselves as to who was to sit next to him. St Paul framed a constitution about what to do when quarrels arose.

The second kind of ambiguity arises from the perceptions of the people toward the sacred, and the priest as a repository of the sacred: he is one who is kept apart.

The centrality of the function and role of the priest is evident in the Eucharist liturgy and the enactment of the life-cycle rituals of the Christ. He is questioned most when he acts contrary to the moral dictates of his vocation, when this role is fragmented by the church quarrel. Thus there is an innate tension in the role of priests, both as custodians of the faith—as safe-keepers of the liturgical texts—and as men constrained by the conflicts in the church to behave in a particular manner, sometimes unacceptable to their parishioners. People's representations express disenchantment with the temporal preoccupations of their priests.

Notes

1. Mikhail Bakhtin, *Rabelais and His World* (Boston: MIT Press, 1969).
2. Febvre and Martin. *The Coming of the Book*.
3. Bakhtin, op. cit., p. 9.
4. Turner, *The Ritual Process: Structure and Antistructure*.
5. Turner, 'Liminality and the Performative' in John S. MacAloon (ed.), *Rite, Drama, Festival, Spectacle* (Philadelphia: ISHI, 1984), pp. 19–43.
6. Bakhtin, op. cit., p. 165.
7. This kind of position has been taken by Joan M. Lewis, *Ecstactic Religion* (Harmondsworth: Penguin, 1978) and Gananath Obeyesekere, *Medusa's Hair* (Chicago: University of Chicago Press, 1981).
8. See, for an elaboration of myths around Mary, the Mother of Jesus, Maria Warner, *Alone of all Her Sex: The Myth of the Virgin Mary*. (London: Picador, 1985).
9. Geertz has defined the bazaar in Sefrou as the integration of physically separated market-places into a continuous system. Clifford Geertz, 'Suq: The Bazaar Economy in Sefrou' in C. Geertz, H. Geertz, L. Rosen, *Meaning and Order in Moroccan Society* (Cambridge: Cambridge University Press: 1979).
10. Ibid., p. 229.
11. Ibid., p. 152.
12. Mauss, *The Gift*.
13. Rudolf Otto, *The Idea of The Holy* (New York: Oxford University Press, 1981).
14. 100 cents = 1 acre.
15. William Lafleur, 'Points of Departure', *Journal of Asian Studies*, vol. xxxviii Feb. 1979, pp. 271–81.
16. *Kalam cheyithu*: the word 'died' is never used in such cases.
17. Warner, *Family of God*.
18. *Missionary Register* (London: CMS Press, 1827), p. 600.
19. Ibid., p. 602.
20. Sunny Thomas, *Behold a Saint* (New Delhi: Printaid, 1977), p. 5.

8

Conclusion

This study has centred around the relation between history, belief and ritual·among the Syrian Christians in a neighbourhood in the town of Kottayam in Kerala. It began with an attempt to map the nature of pluralism in traditional Kerala society, and the manner in which Christianity entrenched itself in the dominant environment of regional Hinduism. Time, space and number become manifestations of this conversation between Christianity and Hinduism, typified in both calendar and architecture.

When trying to examine the nature of the past which the Syrian Christians uniquely experience because of the legendary work of the apostle St Thomas, I was struck immediately by the plural interpretations of their historical tradition. Myth, history and legend interwove in complex ways, there was a blend of objective and subjective versions, of official and popular strands. The past took on different nuances depending upon the viewpoint of the exegetes and the side they took regarding the church quarrel. This quarrel between two ecclesiastical dynasties, one Indian and the other West Syrian in origin, was the fulcrum on which the narratives interlocked. The recording of the past and its complexities became an exercise in understanding levels of narrativization—individual, family, neighbourhood and community histories. It led me to rethink what truth meant and how people represented it, the polemics of neighbourhood life, and the severely strained loyalties of a people to their priests.

Yet the rhythm of neighbourhood life and the experience of Christian belief and ritual continue inspite of threatened schism and the contradictions inherent in a divided church. Syrian Christians recall the past not only in terms of various forms of ecclesiastical intervention—Syrian, Portuguese, Dutch and British—but also in terms of the presence of Christ's teachings among them. It is difficult to analyse experience: the web of emotions and feelings have a myriad strands, differing from one member of a faith to another. How, then, may we hope to understand faith and experience? I sought to locate what Durkheim called 'indexes' by which the analyses of faith could be rendered objective. Belief systems—myths, legends, sacred narratives—manifest interior states. Rituals become an even more elaborate codified account of such states. 'Believing' becomes an organized collective symbolic system and is no longer the abstract state of undefined individual experience.

I chose four sets of collective experience to work upon. One of these was the Eucharist as the central ritual of the Syrian Christians, with its twin aspects of being both gift and sacrifice. Another was the life-cycle rituals of marriage, birth and death, which expressed not only the Christian experience of the passage of life but also the intrinsic correspondence between the life of Jesus and the life of every Christian. Marriage rites express the belief that the bond between Christ and the Church will be replayed in the duty and love that a man feels for his wife, and the loyalty and devotion with which she must respond. The essentially patriarchal symbols of Christianity are symbolically well articulated here. Birth and death ceremonies similarly express the manner in which Syrian Christians view their existence in relation to Christ's biography. Death ceremonies clearly mark out a dualism between the regional cultures of Hinduism and Christianity, which interact so vividly in the life-affirming rituals of marriage and birth. Here, there is a barrier to the interpenetration of Hindu customs. The Syrian Christians seem to assert that their faith underlines the separateness of their destiny after death. In birth and marriage ceremonies, the two communities—Hindu and Christian—may be in dialogue, so food, rites for fertility or good health, or auspiciousness may be shared—but at the time of death, the Christian stands apart in his vision of the life after.

The ritual calendar too is an expression of the uniqueness of Christian experience. Christ's life is relived in this small hamlet year after year, and the people traverse the anniversaries of his works and days with the rhythm and stability of unendangered seasonal cycles.

The year ritually begins with Christmas, and the passing of time is associated with a particular kind of ritual anticipation as Christians move from one event to another in the life of Jesus. Time is therefore calendrically notated both in the secular, solar sense as well as in the mytho-historical manner of remembering Christ's life. Time is both linear and cyclic, and the Syrian Christians are enriched by this dual experience of temporality.

There is another coterminus calendar based on the life of saints whose biographies are spiritually associated with the life and work of Jesus. These festivals of commemoration are important primarily because they often contribute to the emergence of parallel structures and voices within the church. Canonical rigour is replaced by the potential for transformation and anti-structure. The ceremonies around the life of saints are associated with miracles, with fasts and penances and, concomitantly, with the great wealth of the 'miracle churches' where devotees offer money as alms. The patronage of the saints is sometimes seen to be threatening by the priests for sometimes the people seem more attached to their patron saints than to Jesus Christ. This is most evident in the attitude of the people to Mary who has many devotees among the women and is associated with the granting of desires, specially for the birth of children. The clarity of ecclesiastical structures provided by the eucharist liturgy becomes somewhat blurred in the festivals of the saints where emotion often overreaches itself and catharsis is almost routine. All the festivals commemorating the life of the saints are not the same, though the strand of the miracle does run through them. The Apostle St Thomas has great importance for these Syrian Christians not only because he is their spiritual ancestor but because he put to test Christ's resurrection, and proved to the world Jesus's ultimate divinity. In this sense, the generally negatively perceived doubting Thomas is for the Syrian Christians a powerful rational figure, and his act of doubt an act to be celebrated. Thomas, given the context of the church quarrel, becomes an ambiguous figure. For purposes of defining the origin of Christianity in Kerala he is important, but since the church quarrel contests his place *vis-à-vis* the power of the throne of Peter, he is relegated to a merely mythic status. In some senses, then, the myth of St Thomas in Kerala is sacred history that is not to be questioned; at other levels it is merely myth as illusionary narrative and not history at all.

While St Thomas is not yet the symbol of division, the holy men of the church often are. Their death anniversaries are commemorated by one church faction and not the other, their life histories represent one moment of the quarrel, beatified by some and vilified by others.

The church quarrel is clearly the axis on which neighbourhood life rotates, and the pain of impending schism has been evident now for close on a century. Fission however has not yet taken place, for debate about temporal proprietorship continues in the law courts. There are still two 'parties' and not two separate churches, which share the same preoccupations with liturgical life and social custom, but differing ecclesiastical allegiances often divide them and make enemies where once existed neighbours and friends. People are clear that until litigation ceases there can be no hope for the church.

I have tried to make people's voices and people's history the base for the writing of this book. I believe that the mirror they hold up to themselves and the priests of their church images identities and identifications that require the attention and concern of theologians, anthropologists and historians, for these are voices of protest which echo through almost two thousand years of the Christian era. What does it mean to be a Christian, what does it mean to survive as a Christian? How much of one's identity does one have to give up? What are the restrictions, the restraints and the camouflages by which one's identity could be maintained in a society dominantly Hindu in its composition?

In a sequel to this book I hope to raise many of the questions that the Syrian Christians of Kerala have left muted in their need to remain a community of survivors. What, for instance, is a missionary attitude? Is it implicit in Christianity? The Syrian Christians certainly did not think so, for they were non-missionizing in their work and world-view. There are other questions: can Christianity engage in dialogue with other religions? The umbrella of pluralism that Christianity in Kerala sheltered under was implicitly hierarchical; what becomes of pluralism in secular India, and what contributions does Christianity make towards a notion of nation and community? These questions can be answered only by moving away from regional history to the more general level of British colonialism, missionary movements in the nineteenth century, indigenous Christian response to colonialism and mission, the dialogic nature of the Indian National Movement, and the experiments and encounters that were to follow among theologians and others as a response to nationalism. Thus, I would argue that a people's view of history and religion must be placed in conjunction with a history of the contribution of Christian theology to the debates on pluralism and dialogue. Taken together, a more complete picture of Indian Christianity may emerge.

Bibliography

AGUR, C. M. *Church History of Travancore*, SPS press, Madras, 1901.

Anduthaksa, CMS Press, Kottayam, 1982.

ARCHER, Margaret S. 'The Myth of Cultural Integration', *British Journal of Sociology*, vol. 36, no. 3, 1985, 333–53.

ATIYA, Aziz S. *History of Eastern Christianity*, University of Notre Dame Press, Indiana, 1968.

ATTFIELD, Robin. 'Christian Attitudes to Nature', *Journal of the History of Ideas*, vol. 44, 1963.

AUDET, Jean Paul. 'Marriage', *Sacraments in Scripture: A Symposium,* Geoffrey Chapman, London, 1966.

AUSTIN, J L. 'Performative-Constative', in J R. Searle (ed.), *The Philosophy of Language*, Oxford University Press, Oxford, 1974.

AYYAR, L K. Ananta Krishna. *Anthropology of the Syrian Christians*, Cochin Government Press, Ernakulam, 1926.

BAKHTIN, Mikhail. *Rabelais and His World*, MIT Press, Boston, 1969.

BARTH, Fredrik. 'Descent and Marriage Considered', in Jack Goody (ed.), *The Character of Kinship*, Cambridge University Press, Cambridge, 1973.

BARTHES, Roland. *Elements of Semiology*, Cape Editions, London, 1967.

——, *Image—Music—Text*, Fontana Collins, Glasgow, 1977.

BASHAM, A L. 'The Practice of Medicine in Ancient and Medieval India', in Charles Leslie (ed.), *Asian Medical Systems*, University of California Press, Berkeley, 1977.

BENVENISTE, Emile. *Problems in General Linguistics*, University of Miami Press, Coral Gables, 1971.

——, *Indo-European Language and Society*, Faber & Faber, London, 1973.

BLOCH, Marc. *The Historian's Craft*, Manchester University Press, Manchester, 1954.

BLOCH, Maurice & PARRY, Jonathan (eds.) *Death and the Regeneration of Life*, Cambridge University Press, Cambridge, 1982.

BOHAC, Rodney D. 'Peasant Inheritance Strategies in Russia', *Journal of Interdisciplinary History*, no. 16, 1, 1985, 23–42.

BORSAY, Peter. 'All the Town's a Stage—Urban Ritual and Ceremony 1660–1800', in Peter Clark (ed.), *The Transformation of English Provincial Towns 1600–1800*, Hutchinson, 1984.

BOURDIEU, Pierre. 'The Berber House', in Mary Douglas (ed.), *Rules and Meanings*, Penguin, Harmondsworth, 1973.

——, *Outline of a Theory of Practice*, Cambridge University Press, Cambridge, 1977.

BOURDILLON, M F C. & FORTES, Meyer. *Sacrifice*, Academic Press, London, 1980.

BROWN, Colin. (ed.) *The New International Dictionary of New Testament Theology*, The Paternoster Press, Exeter, 1976.

BROWN, L W. *The Indian Christians of St Thomas*, Cambridge University Press, Cambridge, 1956.

BULTMAN, Rudolf, VON RAD, G. & BERTRAM, G. *Life and Death*, Pelican, London, 1965.

CHADWICK, Henry. *The Early Church*, Pelican, London, 1969.

CHAITANYA, Krishna. *Kerala*, National Book Trust, New Delhi, 1972.

CHERIAN, P. *The Malabar Christians and the Church Missionary Society 1816–1840*, Madras, CMS Press, 1935.

CHILDS, B S. 'Orientation', in *The Interpreter's Dictionary of the Bible*, Abingdon Press, New York, 1962.

Christian Missionary Society Register 1819, 427–9; 1819–20, 170; 1821, 515–19; 1826, 478–81.

Christian Missionary Society Record, 1836, 55.

Christian Missionary Society Report, 1839–40, 81.

Christian Mission Record, 1841, 120.

Christian Mission Intelligence, 1856, 220.

CHUMMAR, T M. 'Printing and Printing Presses', in George Menacherry (ed.), *The St Thomas Christian Encyclopaedia of India*, BNK Press, Madras, 1973.

CLANCHY, M T. *From Memory to Written Record*, Edward Arnold, 1979.

COHN, Bernard S. 'African Models and Indian Histories', in Fox (ed.), *Realm and Region in Traditional India*, Vikas, Delhi, 1977, 90–113.

———, 'Anthropology and History', in Theodore K. Rabb & Robert I. Rotberg (eds.), *The New History*, Princeton University Press, 1982, 227–52.

COLLINGWOOD, R G. *The Idea of History*, Oxford University Press, Oxford, 1980.

COCKBURN, J S. 'Early Modern Assize Records as Historical Evidence', *Journal of the Society of Archivists*, vol. 5, no. 4, 1975, 215–31.

CRESSWELL, M J. 'Semantic Competence', in F. Guenther & M. Guenther-Reutter (eds.), *Meaning and Translation*, Duckworth, London, 1978, 9–27.

DALY, Robert J. *Christian Sacrifice*, Catholic University of America Press, Washington, 1978.

DANIEL, K N. *A Critical Study of Primitive Liturgies especially that of St James*, TAM Press, Tiruvalla, 1949.

DANIEL, David. *The Orthodox Church of India*, Print Aid, New Delhi, 1972.

DANIEL, Valentine E. *Fluid Signs*, University of California Press, Berkeley, 1984.

DAS, Veena. 'Masks and Faces', in *Contributions to Indian Sociology*, n.s., vol. 10, no. 1, 1976.

———, *Structure and Cognition*, Oxford University Press, Delhi, 1977.

———, 'The Language of Sacrifice', *Man*, 18, 3, 1983, 445–6.

———, 'Paradigms of Body Symbolism: An Analysis of Selected Themes in Hindu Culture', in Richard Burghart & Audrey Cantlie (eds.), *Indian Religions*, Curzon Press, London, 1985.

DAS, Veena & NICHOLAS, Ralph W. 'Family and "Household" ', *Difference and Division in South Asian Domestic Life* (mimeo), SAPE Project II, ACLS-SSRC Joint Committee on South Asia, 1982.

DAVIES, J G. *The Early Christian Church*, Baker Book House, Michigan, 1980.

DAVIS, Natalie Zemon. *Society and Culture in Early Modern France*, Duckworth, London, 1975.

———, 'The Sacred and the Body Social in Sixteenth Century Lyon', *Past and Present*, no. 90, Feb. 1981, 40–7.

DELORME, J. 'The Practice of Baptism in Judaism at the Beginning of the Christian Era', *A Symposium: Baptism in the New Testament*, Geoffrey Chapman, London, 1964.

DERRET, J D M. *Law in the New Testament*, Darton, Longman & Todd, London, 1970.

Divine Liturgy of St James, The. Published by Metropolitan Athanasius Yeshue Samuel, Archbishop of the Syrian Orthodox Church in the USA and Canada.

DIX, Gregory. *The Shape of the Liturgy*, Westminster, London, 1954.

DOUGLAS, Mary. *Purity and Danger*, Penguin, Harmondsworth, 1970.

———, *Natural Symbols*, Penguin, Harmondsworth, 1973.

———, *Rules and Meanings*, Penguin, Harmondsworth, 1973.

———, (ed.) *Essays in the Sociology of Perception*, Routledge and Kegan Paul, London, 1982.

Diocesan Gazette, vol. 1, Kottayam, 1981.

DUMONT, Louis. *Hierarchy and Marriage Alliance in South Indian Kinship*. Occasional papers of the Royal Anthropological Institute of Great Britain and Ireland, London, 1957.

———, *Homo Hierarchicus*, University of Chicago Press, Chicago, 1980.

DUMONT, Louis & POCOCK, David. 'Pure and Impure', *Contributions to Indian Sociology*, vol. 3, 1959, 9–39.

DUNN, Frederick L. 'Traditional Asian Medicine and Cosmopolitan Medicine as Adaptive System', in Charles Leslie (ed.), *Asian Medical Systems: A Comparative Study*, University of California Press, Berkeley, 1977.

DURKHEIM, Emile. *The Division of Labour*, Free Press, New York, 1964.

———, *The Rules of Sociological Method*, Free Press, New York, 1966.

———, *The Elementary Forms of Religious Life*, Free Press, New York, 1969.

———, *Sociology and Philosophy*, Routledge and Kegan Paul, New York, 1974.

DURKHEIM, Emile & MAUSS, Marcel. *Primitive Classification*, Cohen & West, London, 1970.

ELIADE, Mircea. *Myths, Dreams and Mysteries*, Harper, New York, 1975.

EVANS-PRITCHARD, E E. *Essays in Social Anthropology*, Faber, London, 1962.

———, *Nuer Religion*, Oxford University Press, Oxford, 1974.

———, *The Nuer*, Oxford University Press, New York, 1979.

FEBVRE, Lucien & MARTIN, Henri Jean. *The Coming of the Book: The Impact of Printing 1450–1800*, New Left Books, London, 1979.

FENN, Richard K. *Liturgies and Trials*, Basil Blackwell, Oxford, 1982.

FIRTH, Raymond. 'Postures and gestures of respect', in Ted Polhemus (ed.), *Social Aspects of the Human Body*, Penguin, Harmondsworth, 1978.

FISHMAN, Joshua A. *Readings in the Sociology of Language*, Mouton, The Hague, 1963.

FLOUD, Roderick. 'Quantitative History and People's History', *History Workshop*, Issue 17, Spring 1984, 114–24.

FORTES, Meyer. *Kinship and the Social Order*, Routledge and Kegan Paul, London, 1970.

———, *Time and Social Structure and Other Essays*, Athlone Press, London, 1970.

FOX, Richard. *Realm and Region in Traditional India*, Vikas, Delhi, 1977.

FRUZETTI, L., OSTOR, A & BARNETT, S. 'The Cultural Construction of the Person in Bengal and Tamil Nadu', in Ostor, Fruzetti & Barnett (eds.), *Concepts of Person*, Oxford University Press, Delhi, 1983.

FULLER, C J. 'Kerala Christians and the Caste System', *Man*, n.s., vol. 2, 1976, 53–70.

GARDET, L., *et al. Cultures and Time*, The UNESCO Press, Paris, 1976.

GEERTZ, Clifford. 'Religion as a Cultural System', in Michael Banton (ed.), *Anthropological Approaches to the Study of Religion*, Tavistock, London, 1966.

———, *Interpretations of Culture*, Basic Books, New York, 1973.

————, 'Suq: The Bazaar Economy in Sefrou', in C Geertz, H Geertz & L Rosen (eds.), *Meaning and Order in Moroccan Society*, Cambridge University Press, Cambridge, 1979.

GEORGE, A. 'A Literary Catalogue of New Testament Passages on Baptism', *A Symposium: Baptism in the New Testament*, Geoffrey Chapman, London, 1964.

GEORGE, Pokail John. *The St Thomas Christians and Their Eucharistic Liturgy*. Thesis presented to the Faculty of the Perkins School of Theology, 1966.

GIBLET, Jean. 'Baptism: The Sacrament of Incorporation into the Church According to St Paul', *A Symposium: Baptism in the New Testament*, Geoffrey Chapman, London, 1964.

GINZBERG, Carlo. *The Cheese and the Worms*, Johns Hopkins University, Baltimore, 1980.

GIRARD, Rene. *Violence and the Sacred*, Johns Hopkins University, Baltimore, 1977.

GOODENOUGH, Ward H. *Property Kin and Community on Tonk*, Archon Books, Connecticut, 1966.

GOODY, Esther N. *Contexts of Kinship*, Cambridge University Press, Cambridge, 1973.

GOODY, Jack (ed.), *The Developmental Cycle in Domestic Groups*, Cambridge University Press, Cambridge, 1958.

————, *The Character of Kinship*, Cambridge University Press, Cambridge, 1975.

————, *Production and Reproduction*, Cambridge University Press, London, 1976.

————, *The Development of the Family and Marriage in Europe*, Cambridge University Press, Cambridge, 1983.

GOODY, Jack & TAMBIAH, S J. (eds.), *Bridewealth and Dowry*, Cambridge University Press, Cambridge, 1973.

GOODY, Jack, THIRSK, Joan & THOMPSON, E P. *Family and Inheritance: Rural Society in Western Europe 1200–1800*, Cambridge University Press, Cambridge, 1976.

GREGORIOS, Mar Paulos. *The Indian Orthodox Church*, Sophia Publications, Delhi, 1982.

GUHA, Ranajit. 'The Prose of Counter Insurgency', in Ranajit Guha (ed.), *Subaltern Studies II*, Oxford University Press, Delhi, 1983.

GUILLET, J. 'Baptism and the Spirit' *A Symposium: Baptism in the New Testament*, Geoffrey Chapman, London, 1964.

GUNDERT, Hermann. *A Malayalam and English Dictionary*, Nava Sahiti Publications, Trivandrum, 1982.

HALLIDAY, M A K. *Language as Social Semiotic*, Edward Arnold, London, 1978.

————, 'The Users and Uses of Language' in Joshua A Fishman (ed.), *The Sociology of Language*, Mouton, The Hague, 1968.

HÁNDELMAN, Don. 'Reflexivity in Festival and Other Cultural Events', in Mary Douglas (ed.), *Essays in the Sociology of Perception*, Routledge and Kegan Paul, London, 1982.

HARNIK, Gillian Feeley. *The Lord's Table*, University of Pennsylvania Press, Philadelphia, 1981.

HARRIS, Grace. *Casting Out Anger*, Cambridge University Press, Cambridge, 1978.

HAWKES, Terence. *Structuralism and Semiotics*, Methuen, London, 1978.

HELLER, Agnes. *A Theory of History*, Routledge & Kegan Paul, London, 1982.

HERNADI, Paul. 'Representing the Past', *History and Theory*, vol. 15, 1976, 45–51.

HERRENSCHMIDT, Oliver. 'Sacrifice, Symbolic or Effective', in Michael Izard & Pierre Smith (eds.), *Between Belief and Transgression*, University of Chicago Press, Chicago, 1982.

HERTZ, Robert. *Death and the Right Hand*, Cohen & West, Aberdeen, 1960.

HESCHEL, Abraham Joshua. *Quest for God*, Crossroad, New York, 1982.

HILLIER, Bill & HANSON, Julienne. *The Social Logic of Space*, Cambridge University Press, Cambridge, 1984.

HOCART, A M. *The Life-Giving Myth and Other Essays*, Methuen, London, 1952.

History Workshop Journal, editorial. vol. 12, Autumn 1979, 1–6.

HOSTEN, H. (SJ), *Antiquities From San Thome and Mylapore*, Baptist Mission Press, Calcutta, 1936.

HUBERT, Henri & MAUSS, Marcel. *Sacrifice*, University of Chicago Press, Chicago, 1973.

HUNT, W S. *The Anglican Church in Travancore and Cochin 1816–1916*, vol. 2, CMS Press, Kottayam, 1916.

HUTTON, J M. *Caste in India*, Oxford University Press, Bombay, 1961.

INDEN, Ronald B. *Marriage and Rank in Bengali Culture*, Vikas, New Delhi, 1976.

INDEN, Ronald B. & NICHOLAS, Ralph W. *Kinship in Bengali Culture*, University of Chicago Press, Chicago, 1977.

JAIN, Ravinder K. *Text and Context*, ISHI, Philadelphia, 1977.

JAKOBSON, Roman & POMORSKA, Krystyna. *Dialogues*, Cambridge University Press, Cambridge, 1983.

JAMES, Mervyn. 'Ritual Drama and Social Body in the Late Medieval English Town', *Past and Present*, no. 98, Feb. 1983, 3–29.

JOHNSON, Paul. *A History of Christianity*, Penguin, Harmondsworth, 1980.

JOHNSON, Richard., *et al.* 'Popular Memory: Theory, Politics and Method', in *Making Histories*, Hutchinson, 1982.

JOHNSTON, L. *Sacraments in Scripture: A Symposium*, Geoffrey Chapman, London, 1966.

JOSEPH, T K. 'St Thomas in South India', *Young Men of India*, July 1926.

————, 'Was St Thomas in South India?', *Young Men of India*, July 1927.

Judgement of The Supreme Court of India, KLT 721, 1958, Nalathira Printers, Kottayam.

KAUSHIK, Meena. 'The Symbolic Representation on Death', in *Contributions to Indian Sociology*, n.s., 10, 1976, 265–92.

KAUTSKY, Karl. *Foundations of Christianity*, Russel & Russel, New York, 1953.

KELLER, Suzanne. *The Urban Neighbourhood*, Random House, New York, 1968.

KERTZER, David. 'Anthropology and Family History', *Journal of Family History*, vol. 9, no. 3, Fall 1984, 201–3.

KLIJN, A F J. (ed.), *Acts of St Thomas*, E J Brill, Leiden, 1962.

KOODAPUZHA, Xavier. 'The History of the Church in Kerala in the Pre-Portuguese Period', in G. Menacherry (ed.), *St Thomas Christian Encyclopaedia*, vol. 2, BNK Press, Trichur, 1973.

KURUVILLA, K K. *A History of the Mar Thoma Church and Its Doctrines*. Published by the Christian Literature Society for India, 1951.

LADOURIE, Emmanuel Le Roy. *Montaillou*, Penguin, Harmondsworth, 1980.

LAFLEUR, William. 'Points of Departure', *Journal of Asian Studies*, vol. 38, Feb. 1979, 271–81.

LARRE, Claude. 'The Empirical Perception of Time and the Conception of History in Chinese Thought', in Louis Gardet (ed.), *Cultures and Time*, The UNESCO Press, Paris, 1976.

LEACH, Edmund. *Genesis as Myth and Other Essays*, Jonathan Cape, London, 1979.

Leslie, Charles (ed.), *Asian Medical Systems*, University of California Press, Berkeley, 1977.
———, *Social Research and Health Care Planning in South Asia*, (mimeo), SAPE Project II, New Delhi, 1983.
Lévi-Strauss, Claude. *The Elementary Structures of Kinship*, Beacon Press, Boston, 1969.
———, *From Honey to Ashes*, Harper & Row, New York, 1974.
———, *The Raw and the Cooked*, Harper & Row, 1975.
———, 'The Story of Asdiwal', in Edmund Leach (ed.), *The Structural Study of Myth and Totemism*, Tavistock, London, 1976.
———, *The Savage Mind*, Weidenfeld & Nicholson, 1976.
———, *Structural Anthropology*, Penguin, Harmondsworth, 1977.
———, *The Origin of Table Manners*, Harper & Row, New York, 1978.
Lewis, Joan M. (ed.), *Ecstatic Religion*, Penguin, Harmondsworth, 1978.
———, (ed.), *History and Social Anthropology*, Tavistock, London, 1968.
Logan, W. *Malabar* (1887), Government Press, Madras, 1951.
Lord, Albert B. *The Singer of Tales*, Harvard University Press, Cambridge, 1981.
Lukose, K L. *Kurisupalliyum Puthenangadiyum*, Ancheril Printers, Kottayam, 1983.
MacAloon, John (ed.), *Rite, Drama, Festival, Spectacle*, ISHI, Philadelphia, 1984.
MacMormac, Carol & Strathern, Marilyn. (eds.), *Nature, Culture and Gender*, Cambridge University Press, Cambridge, 1980.
Madan, T N. *Family and Kinship; A Study of the Pandits of Rural Kashmir*, Asia Publishing House, Bombay, 1966.
———, 'The Ideology of the Householder Among the Kashmir Pandits', *Contributions to Indian Sociology*, n.s., vol. 15, June-Dec. 1981.
Madras Church Missionary Record: no. 11, vol. 1, 1834; no. 12, vol. 3, Dec. 1836; no. 7, vol. 6, July 1839; no. 11, vol. 8, no. Nov. 1841; no. 6, vol. 9, June 1841; no. 10, vol. 9, Oct. 1842.
Malinowski, Bronislaw. *Magic Science and Religion*, Free Press, London, 1974.
Mar Julius Press, Pampakuda, 1979. Publication.
Marel, Pierre. *The Biblical Doctrine of Infant Baptism*, James Clark & Co., London, 1957.
Marriot, McKim. 'Interactional and Attributional Theories of Caste Ranking', *Man in India*, 39, 1959, 92–107.
Marsh, H G. *The Origin and Significance of the New Testament Baptism*, Manchester University Press, Manchester, 1941.
Mateer, Samuel. *The Land of Charity: A Descriptive Account of Travancore and Its People, with Special Reference to Missionary Labour*, John Snow, 1870.
Matta, Roberto da. 'Carnival in Multiple Planes' in John S. MacAloon (ed.). *Rite, Drama, Festival, Spectacle*, ISHI, Philadelphia, 1984, 208–40.
Mauss, Marcel. *A General Theory of Magic*, Routledge & Kegan Paul, London, 1972.
———, *The Gift*, Routledge & Kegan Paul, London, 1974.
———, *Sociology and Psychology*, Routledge & Kegan Paul, London, 1979.
Medlycott, A E. *India and the Apostle St Thomas*, David Nutt, London, 1905.
Menacherry, G. (ed.). *St Thomas Christian Encyclopaedia of India*, vol. 2, BNK Press, Madras, 1973.
Menon, T. Chandrashekhar. *Copy of Judgement in Original Suits* 1, 2, 3, 4, 5, 6, 7 & 8/79, dated 6 June 1980, High Court of Kerala, Ernakulam-Cochin, 1980.

MENON, Padmanabha K. P. *History of Kerala*, vol. I, Cochin Government Press, Erna-kulam, 1924.

Missionary Register, Christian Missionary Society, London, 1816; 1822; 1823; 1824; 1827; 1829; 1847.

MOLIAT, D. (SJ). 'Baptism Symbolism in St Paul', *A Symposium: Baptism in the New Testament*, Geoffrey Chapman, London, 1964.

MORAES, G M. *A History of Christianity in India*, Manaktalas, Bombay, 1964.

MUNDADAN, A M. *The Arrival of the Portuguese in'India and the Thomas Christians Under Mar Jacob 1498–1522*, Dharmaraj Press, Bangalore, 1967.

——, *Sixteenth Century Traditions of the Christians*, Dharmaraj Press, Bangalore, 1970.

MUNDAKUZHY, Rev. Thomas P. *Our Church, Malankara St Thomas Oriental Orthodox Church of India*, St Paul's Mission Press, Mavelikara, 1982.

MYERHOFF, Barbara G. 'A Death in Due Time', in John S. MacAloon, *Rite, Drama, Festival, Spectacle*, ISHI, Philadelphia, 1984, 149–78.

NEEDHAM, Rodney. *Belief, Language and Experience*, University of Chicago Press, Chicago, 1972.

NEILL, Stephen. *A History of Christianity in India*, Cambridge University Press, Cambridge, 1984.

NEWENS, Stan. 'Family History Societies', *History Workshop*, issue 11, Spring 1981, 154–9.

NICHOLAS, Ralph. 'Sraddha, Impurity and Relations Between the Living and the Dead', *Contributions to Indian Sociology*, n.s., vol. 5, 1 & 2, 1981.

OBEYESEKERE, Gananath. 'The Impact of Ayurvedic Ideas on the Culture and the Individual in Sri Lanka', in Charles Leslie (ed.), *Asian Medical Systems*, University of California Press, Berkeley, 1977.

——, *Medusa's Hair*, University of Chicago Press, Chicago, 1981.

ONG, Walter J. *Orality and Literacy: The Technologizing of the Word*, Methuen, London, 1982.

OTTO, Rudolf. *The Idea of the Holy*, Oxford University Press, New York, 1981.

PALLISSERY, John. 'Thomas Christians and Journalism', in George Menacherry (ed.), *The St Thomas Christian Encyclopaedia of India*, BNK Press, Madras, 1973.

PANIKKAR, K M. *Asia and Western Dominance*, Asia Publishing House, Bombay, 1959.

PARRY, Jonathan. 'Death and Cosmology in Kashi', *Contributions to Indian Sociology*, n.s., 15, 1 & 2, 1981, 337–65.

PASSERINI, Luisa. 'Work Ideology and Consensus Under Italian Fascism', *History Workshop*, Issue 8, Autumn 1979, 82–108.

PATTARO, Germano. 'The Christian Conception of Time', in L Gardet *et al*, *Cultures and Time*, The UNESCO Press, Paris, 1976.

PAUL, Kadavil. *The Orthodox Syrian Church, Its Religion and Philosophy*, K V. Pathrose, Puthencruz, 1973.

PEARSON, Hugh. *Memoirs of the Life and Writings of the Rev. Claudius Buchanan*, vol. I & II, Stahan & Spottiswoode, London, 1819.

PEIRCE, Charles Sanders. *Principles of Philosophy*, vol. I, Collected Papers, The Belknap Press of Harvard University Press, Cambridge, 1974.

PERUMALLIL, H C. & HAMBYE, E R. (eds.), *Christianity in India*, Prakasam, Alleppey, 1972.

PIERRSENS, Michael. 'Market, Fair, Festival', *Diogenes*, 1972, 181–7.

PITKIN, Donald S. *The House that Giacomo Built, History of an Italian Family 1898–1978*, Cambridge University Press, Cambridge, 1985.

PITT RIVERS, Julian. 'The Kith and the Kin', in Jack Goody (ed.), *The Character of Kinship*, Cambridge University Press, 1973.

PLAKANS, Andrejs. 'Identifying Kinfolk Beyond the Household', *Journal of Family History*, 2, 1977, 3–27.

POCOCK, David. 'Inclusion and Exclusion', *South-Western Journal of Anthropology*, vol. 13, no. 1, 1957, 19–31.

——, *Kanbi and Patidar: A Study of the Patidar Community of Gujarat*, Oxford University Press, London, 1972.

——, *Mind, Body and Wealth*, Basil Blackwell, Oxford, 1973.

PODIPARA, P J. *The St Thomas Christians*, Darton, Longman & Todd, Bombay, 1970.

——, *The Rise and Decline of the Indian Church of the Thomas Christians*, CMS Press, Kottayam, 1979.

POPE, M H. 'Numbers', *The Interpreter's Dictionary of the Bible*, Abingdon Press, New York, 1962.

PORTELLI, Allessandro. 'The Peculiarities of Oral History', *History Workshop*, Issue 12, Autumn 1981.

Proceedings, Christian Missionary Society, London, 1822–3; 1823–4; 1825–6; 1838–9; 1839–40; 1846–7.

Proceedings of The Church Missionary Society for Africa and the East, 1825–6.

PUGH, Judy F. 'Into the Almanac: Time Meaning and Action in North Indian Society', *Contributions to Indian Sociology*, 17, 1, 1983, 27–50.

PUTHIAKUNEL, T. *Syro-Malabar Clergy*, Vincentian Publishing Bureau, Ernakulam, 1964. *Qurbanakramam*, Oriental Printing House, Thadiyoor, 1981.

RABB, Theodore K. & RUTBERG, Robert I. (eds.), *The New History: The 1980s and Beyond*, Princeton University Press.

REDFIELD, Robert. *The Folk Culture of the Yucatan*, University of Chicago, Chicago, 1941.

RICOUER, Paul. *History and Truth*, North-Western University Press, Evanston, 1966.

——, 'The Model of the Text', *Social Research*, vol. 38, no. 3, 1971, 529–662.

——, *The Conflict of Interpretations*, North-Western University Press, Evanston, 1974.

Royal Court of Final Appeal, Keralodayam Press, Trivandrum, 1890.

SAMUEL, Raphael. 'Local History and Oral History', *History Workshop*, Issue 1, Spring 1976, 1991–9.

——, Editorial, *History Workshop*, Issue 8, Autumn 1976, i–vi.

SCHOLES, Robert & KELLOG, Robert. *The Nature of Narrative*, Oxford University Press, New York, 1978.

SEARLE, J R. (ed.), *The Philosophy of Language*, Oxford University Press, Oxford, 1974.

SHILS, Edward. *The Torment of Secrecy*, Heinemann, London, 1956.

SILVERSTEIN, Michael. 'Shifters, Linguistic Categories and Cultural Description', in K M. Basso and H. A. Selby (eds.), *Meaning in Anthropology*, University of Mexico Press, Albuquerque, 1976.

SILVERMAN, Kaja. *The Subject of Semiotics*, Oxford University Press, Oxford, 1983.

SIMMEL, George. *On Individuality and Social Forms*, University of Chicago Press, Chicago, 1971.

SINGER, Milton. *When A Great Tradition Modernizes*, Praeger Publishers, New York, 1972.

———, 'Personal and Social Identity in Dialogue', in Benjamin Lee (ed.), *Psychosocial Theories of the Self*, Plenum Press, New York, 1982.

SMITH, Jonathan. *Map Is Not Territory*, E J. Brill, Leiden, 1978.

SPIEGEL, Gabrielle. 'Genealogy: Form and Function in Medieval Historical Narrative', *History and Theory*, vol. 22, 1973, 45–53.

SRINIVAS, M N. *Social Change in Modern India*, Orient Longman, Delhi, 1972.

STEIN, Burton. 'The Segmentary State in South Indian History', in Richard Fox (ed.), *Realm and Region in Traditional India*, Vikas, Delhi, 1977.

STOIANOVICH, Traian. *French Historical Method: The Annales Paradigm*, Cornell University Press, Ithaca, 1976.

STRAWSON, P F. 'Intention and Convention in Speech Acts', in J R. Searle (ed.), *The Philosophy of Language*, OUP, Oxford, 1974.

THOMAS, Sunny. *Behold a Saint*, Printaid, New Delhi, 1977.

TROELTSCH, Ernest. *The Social Teaching of the Christian Churches*, vol. I, George Allen & Unwin, London, 1956.

TURNER, Terence. 'Narrative Structure and Mythopoesis: A Critique and Reformulation of Structuralist Concepts of Myth, Narrative and Poetics', *Arethusa*, vol. 10, 1977.

TURNER, Victor. *The Ritual Process: Structure and Anti-structure*, Routledge & Kegan Paul, London, 1969.

———, 'Sacrifice as Quintessential Process: Prophylaxis or Abandonment', *History Of Religions*, 16 (3), 1977, 189–215.

———, *Process, Performance and Pilgrimage*, Concept Publishing House, New Delhi, 1979.

———, 'Liminality and the Performative', in John S. MacAloon (ed.), *Rite, Drama, Festival, Spectacle*, ISHI, Philadelphia, 1984, 19–43.

VAN GENNEP, Arnold. *The Rites of Passage*, Routledge & Kegan Paul, London, 1960.

VATUK, Sylvia. 'Gifts and Affines in North India', *Contributions to Indian Sociology*, n.s., vol. 9, no. 2, 1975.

VINCENT, David. 'The Decline of the Oral Tradition in Popular Culture', in Robert Storch (ed.), *Popular Culture and Custom in Nineteenth Century England*, St Martin's Press, London, 1982.

WARNER, Lloyd W *Family of God*, Greenwood Press, Connecticut, 1975.

WARNER, Maria. *Alone of All Her Sex: The Myth of the Virgin Mary*, Picador, 1985.

WEBER, Max. *Economy and Society*, Guenther Roth & Claus Wittich (eds.), University of California Press, Berkeley, 1978.

———, *The City*, Free Press, Illinois, 1958.

———, *The Protestant Ethic and the Spirit of Capitalism*, Charles Scribner, New York, 1958.

WOLF, Eric. 'The Virgin of Guadalupe', in William A. Lessa & Evon Z. Vogt (eds.) *Reader in Comparative Religion*, Harper & Row, New York.

YALMAN, Nur. 'On the Purity of Women in the Castes of Ceylon and Malabar', *Journal of the Royal Anthropological Institute*, vol. 93, 1967, 25–58.

———, *Under the Bo Tree*, University of California Press, Berkeley, 1971.

ZALESKI, L. *The Apostle St Thomas in India*, Codiarbail Press, Mangalore, 1912.

ZERUBAVEL, Eviator. *Hidden Rhythms*, University of Chicago Press, Chicago, 1981.

Index